LONG ISLAND

LONG ISLAND

People and Places · Past and Present

A NEWSDAY BOOK

Bernie Bookbinder

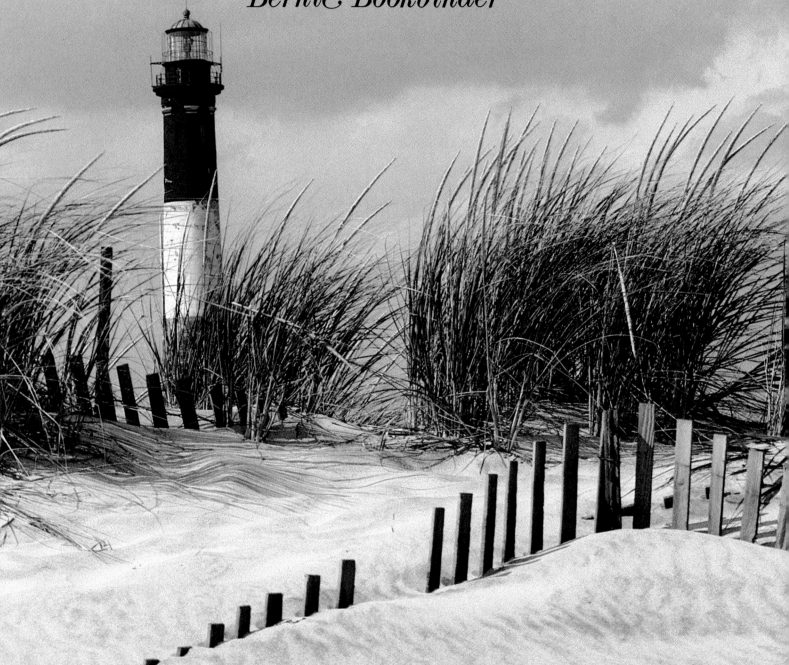

Photography by

HARVEY WEBER

HARRY N. ABRAMS, INC.

Publishers

TO MARILYN

HALF-TITLE:
Summer at Long Beach

TITLE PAGE:
Fire Island Lighthouse

PAGES 4–5:
Parades in Northport and Centerport

COPYRIGHT PAGE:
Old First Church in Huntington

PAGE 8:
*Canada geese; Home Sweet Home
and Pantigo Windmill, East Hampton*

PROJECT DIRECTOR: *Hugh L. Levin*
EDITORS: *Nora Beeson, Rachel Tsutsumi, Nicole Columbus*
DESIGNER: *Judith Michael*
PICTURE EDITOR: *Barbara Lyons*
RESEARCHER: *Gaynell Stone*

LIBRARY OF CONGRESS CATALOGING-IN-PUBLICATION DATA

Bookbinder, Bernie.
Long Island : people and places, past and present / Bernie
Bookbinder ; photography by Harvey Weber.— [Updated ed.]
p.   cm.
"A Newsday book."
Includes bibliographical references (p.   ) and index.
ISBN 0–8109–4255–0 (hardcover)
1. Long Island (N.Y.)—Social life and customs. 2. Long Island
(N.Y.)—History. 3. Long Island (N.Y.)—Description and travel.
F127.L8B66   1998
974.7'21— dc21   98–21839

Harry N. Abrams, Inc.
100 Fifth Avenue
New York, N.Y. 10011
www.abramsbooks.com

CONTENTS

PREFACE

In 1983 the original edition of this book opened a window for Long Islanders. An ambitious volume, it vividly conveyed the richness of Long Island's history in a way no one had ever done.

But more than a decade later, we at *Newsday* felt that one of the nation's richest veins of history was still largely untapped and underappreciated. So we set out to tell the story in a way that would get everyone's attention. The result was "Long Island: Our Story," the largest series and most extensive project in *Newsday*'s history.

More than 100 *Newsday* staff members contributed to the project, which uncovered previously unknown stories about Long Island and corrected some old misconceptions as well. "Long Island: Our Story" was told in many ways: as a newspaper series and special section, a new Internet site (lihistory.com), versions on radio and television, and a major museum exhibition. Long Islanders—here and around the world—responded with an unprecedented outpouring of enthusiasm and pride.

The release of this new edition is a fitting punctuation mark. Bernie Bookbinder's new chapter adds a wealth of recent history, illustrated with the best work of *Newsday* photographers. Spend time with this book and you will gain a new appreciation of Long Island's past and a deeper understanding of where we're going.

RAYMOND JANSEN
Publisher, *Newsday*

INTRODUCTION

Long Island's story has been determined largely by forces it could not control. It has been compelled to deal with the inescapable reality that it is surrounded by water. And, more than most, it has been a victim and beneficiary of natural phenomena, glacial and oceanic, that have shaped its profile, its surface, and its character.

Its story begins before recorded history, when Long Island's endowments— a temperate climate, rich soil, abundant game, and beneficent seas—enabled Indians to develop a culture that provided them with peace, progress, and purpose. Successive societies have seen in Long Island a similar opportunity for fulfillment and have bent it toward their own needs and ends. From the earliest English and Dutch colonists who braved uncertainty and deprivation to the most recent former city residents looking for a good place to raise the kids, newcomers have altered Long Island's appearance and its direction.

Still, its location in the shadow of the greatest city in the world has made Long Island hard-pressed to assert itself. Politically, economically, culturally, it rarely has succeeded in diverting attention from New York City. Yet historically, it enjoys a background and a tradition rivaling that of any place in America, or America itself.

For many of us, Long Island's past is, at best, hazy, disjointed, incomplete: a montage of Indians, clamdiggers, and potato farmers. It was a past without a presence. The purpose of this book is to resurrect that past. To re-create, through words and pictures, the Long Island that *was*, that is responsible for the Long Island that *is*. This is not intended as a definitive history, but as an evocation of time and of place, of how people lived, and even of what they thought. Its goal is to make today's Long Islanders more aware of what preceded them. For if it succeeds, they will be more concerned about what follows them.

The purpose of this second edition is to update, in photographs and text, the Long Island story. The Eighties and Nineties have seen the population age, the economy falter and rebound, the image of the Island remade. We have sought, in this revision, to identify the significant events and the changes they have wrought, as Nassau and Suffolk struggle to solve old problems and meet new challenges.

Taking Shape

Long Island is *new*, a recent addition to the Atlantic coastline, to the silhouette of America. Its familiar fish shape—mouth nibbling at Staten Island, flukes pointing eastward toward Europe—is only about 6,000 years young; just a tick or two of the geologic clock, a blink of God's eye.

Its origins lie in New England, where the stuff from which the Island is made once reposed. Think of Long Island as a three-tiered layer cake: its base, called bedrock, is really a 500-to-600-million-year-old extension of southern Connecticut that slid beneath Long Island Sound; its middle layer of sands, clays, and gravels is thought to be the deposits left by ancient rivers 60 to 70 million years ago, when dinosaurs roamed the earth.

But the top, or surface, layer concerns us most: it is where we live. And it is essentially the product of a vast continental glacier that visited the Island twice—first about 60,000 years ago and again about 21,000 years before the present. This glacier, called the Wisconsinan, is largely responsible for writing the history of Long Island. It determined where and how the Battle of Long Island would be fought, where the Long Island Rail Road would run, where ships would be built, potatoes would be grown, and housing developments would sprout. It gave the Island its contour, size, terrain, and soil. And each of these factors affected the kind and location of vegetation and wildlife, which, in turn, influenced where people lived and what they did.

Like the blade of a monstrous snowplow, the glacier moved imperceptibly but inexorably south across what is now Canada and the northern United States, filing the peaks off mountains, scraping the surfaces of plateaus and valleys, and carrying along with it the natural debris of boulders, rocks, gravel, and soil in a frozen, unending wall of ice hundreds of feet high. Nothing could stand in its way. But it was vulnerable to heat, and when it reached a point roughly between Long Island's North and South Shores, the glacier's leading edge began to melt. As it melted, it deposited the huge mounds of debris it had carried—the way dirt and stones scraped up by a modern snowplow line the roadside after the piled-up snow thaws. These mounds, actually a string of hills stretching from Brooklyn east to Montauk, comprise what geologists call the Ronkonkoma Terminal Moraine.

Besides the moraine, the melting of the Wisconsinan gave birth to great rivers which flowed from the glacier's face to the sea, creating a vast expanse of flatlands. These flatlands, extending from the moraine south to the Atlantic Ocean, are called the Hempstead Outwash Plain.

During this period of the earth's history, the northern hemisphere was undergoing radical temperature changes, fluctuating between warm and cold over intervals that lasted tens of thousands of years. After the first advance of the Wisconsinan Glacier as far south as Long Island, a global warming trend caused it to melt back, or recede. The change of climate also caused the sea level to rise, probably separating what is now Long Island from the mainland.

Some 40,000 years later, the climate began to cool once again, the glacier readvanced almost to the same position, stayed for a while along what is now the North Shore, began melting again, and deposited another terminal moraine. This ridge, which runs from Brooklyn Heights to Orient Point, including Harbor Hill in Roslyn, is named the Harbor Hill Moraine. It, too, has an outwash plain, called the Terryville Outwash Plain after the community south of Port Jefferson.

These four major features, going from north to south—the Harbor Hill Moraine, Terryville Outwash Plain, Ronkonkoma Terminal Moraine, and Hempstead Outwash Plain—make up Long Island's surface. Because of the glacier, the Island is not all hilly like the North Shore, nor pancake-flat like the mid-Island area; there is an elevation to Brooklyn Heights that enables its residents to look down on New York Harbor, while those in Coney Island stare the Atlantic Ocean in the eye.

The glacier left Long Island other mementos of its visits. Geologists believe that claws of ice projecting out of its main wall carved the deep indentations on the North Shore that now bear names such as Oyster Bay and Cold Spring Harbor; and that when these claws melted, their deposits created the bluffs on the peninsulas such as Great Neck and Manhasset Neck.

The Wisconsinan can also be credited with giving lakes, gullies, and boulders to Long Island. The depressions that dot the terrain are called kettle holes, and were created by huge chunks of glacial ice that had torn loose, had been buried, and later melted. Some became dry hollows while others, fed by underground streams, became lakes and ponds (Lake Ronkonkoma, Lake Success, Artist Lake). Except for some exposed bedrock near today's Hell Gate Bridge in Queens, no rocks or boulders are indigenous to the Island's surface. Those found here, such as Shelter Rock in Manhasset, the large graffiti-covered rock on the campus of the State University at Stony Brook, and many others were borne from New England and are called erratics to indicate that they came from elsewhere.

When another warming period sent the glacier on its final retreat, it also raised the worldwide sea level once more and gave Long Island's shoreline, as well as coastal areas around the globe, its present contour.

ABOVE
Originally a salt marsh, Sanctuary Pond was dammed and is now the largest freshwater pond on the Mashomack Preserve, Shelter Island.

LEFT
Stones, typical of North Shore beaches, were carried from New England by the Wisconsinan Glacier that helped shape Long Island; these line the beach at Caumsett State Park, Lloyd Neck.

RIGHT
Not only rocks and stones, but large boulders called "erratics," such as these at Caumsett State Park, were borne by the glacier during its two visits to Long Island. Long Island Sound, in background, probably was formed more than 30,000 years ago, separating Long Island from the mainland.

Scientists think that Long Island was free of ice about 18,000 years ago; that Long Island Sound was reflooded by sea water about 12,000 years ago; and that the Island's fishlike outline emerged some 8,000 to 6,000 years ago.

After the Wisconsinan Glacier disappeared, its influence lived on through a chain of causes and effects that began with the distribution of different types of soil. In and around the moraines, Long Island's generally sandy soil is mixed with a silty sediment that enables it to retain moisture and nutrients and thus sustain such moisture-loving hardwoods as white and red oaks, hickories, chestnut trees, and tulip trees.

By contrast, the sandier, drier soil of the outwash plains primarily supports softwood pitch pine forests. Because the dryness greatly increases the chances of fire, flames swept repeatedly across the outwash plains for thousands of years, shaping—and transforming— its vegetation. Some trees even have become dependent upon fires: in the Dwarf Pine Plains around Westhampton, the pigmy pine trees cannot reproduce unless flames singe their closed cones, melting the resins, and causing the cones to open and disperse their seeds.

These differences in vegetation between the moraines and outwash plains attracted different types of animal life to each. The cool shade and numerous springs and ponds of the morainal hardwood forests appealed to deer and turkey; these, in turn, drew predators such as wolves, bears, and cougars. One exception to the pattern of rich morainal soil and sandy outwash is found on the extreme eastern end of Long Island, where silt, carried by the winds, blanketed the sandy plains that characterized most of the North Fork and some of the South Fork. This windblown silt, called loess, enriched those areas, making them fertile and the eventual site of productive farmland.

The life and history of Long Island also have been influenced significantly by other distinctive landscape features: the Hempstead Plains, the barrier islands, and the tidal marshlands.

The Hempstead Plains, a 60,000-acre portion of the Hempstead Outwash Plain in the heart of what is now Nassau County, is the easternmost prairie in North America and something of an enigma because it cannot be explained from its geological foundation. Some scientists speculate that the vast expanse was burned every year or two, possibly by the Indians as an aid to hunting or farming. Such fires might have killed trees and shrubbery while stimulating the growth of grass which provided forage for generations of Long Island cattle and sheep.

Another important asset that developed after the glacial epoch are the barrier islands, particularly those off the South Shore, such as Fire Island, Jones Beach, and Long Beach, which were—and still are—built and shaped by the powerful Atlantic. Ocean waves acting on the shallow sea bottom have reworked the sandy glacial outwash into offshore islands, which then have been extended westward by the prevailing currents.

After their formation, these islands served as a buffer between the mainland and oceanic storms. They also created quieter bodies of salt water—lagoons that are named Shinnecock, Moriches, Great South, South Oyster, and Jamaica Bays. For thousands of years, the barrier islands and bays have participated in a process that has enriched the bay floors and shoreline. As the tides swept in and out of the bays through breaks in the islands called inlets, they brought nutrients into those sheltered waters to nurture marine life on the bottom. They also fostered the growth of salt marshes, which served as a breeding ground for both vegetation and sea creatures. These marshes proved extremely important during the colonial period, when they provided salt hay that was rich in nourishment and a valuable source of food for livestock.

The shallow waters surrounding both shores of Long Island produced bountiful quantities of shellfish that played a key role in the lives of the area's early human inhabitants. Evidence unearthed from the campsites of prehistoric Indians suggests that they, like the Island's contemporary residents, enjoyed clambakes, savored venison, and kept dogs as pets. (While dogs may have been man's best friend even then, the reverse was not always true: bones found at some sites indicate that dogs occasionally served as food for their masters.)

The presence of these people dates to about 5,000 years before the present time, during what is called the Archaic or Hunting and Gathering Stage. That stage is the second of four prehistoric periods designated by archaeologists to reflect the evolving development of Indians in this region. Based on the way people lived, these periods have been reconstructed from artifacts, such as weapons and tools, and from "garbage," such as shells and bones.

These early Indians also shared today's predilection for waterfront sites, making their camps along bays, streams, and the Island's four rivers: the Peconic, Carmans, Connetquot, and Nissequogue. Such locations provided abundant hard-shell and soft-shell clams, oysters, and scallops, which were gathered and cooked in pits of burning coals or hot stones. Waterfowl, turtles, and fish also were readily available, along with many deer.

The lifestyle of the Archaic people was eased by the use of stone tools, such as adzes, gouges, drills, and scrapers. These primitive versions of today's basic handtools enabled the Archaic Indians to engage in woodworking, hide processing, and food preparation. They also used spear points, blades, and knives, possibly inherited from those believed to be the area's first humans, the so-called Paleo-Indians. (While little is known about them, archaeologists speculate that the Paleo-Indians—or their ancestors—probably originated in Asia and followed the retreating glaciers more than 12,000 years ago in pursuit of huge elephantlike mammoths and mastodons. Consequently, the period of their presumed

ABOVE
Salt marshes, such as these at Bass Creek in the Mashomack Preserve on Shelter Island, provided farmers during colonial times with nutritious salt hay for their cattle. The shadbush is a white blaze from April to June.

BELOW
The innumerable bays, coves, and harbors that delight North Shore sailors, such as Northport Bay seen here at dusk, are, geologists believe, the result of fingers of ice that reached out of the glacial wall as it melted back during a worldwide warming trend.

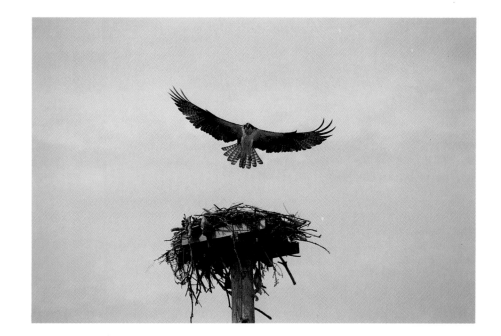

ABOVE
Pollution and other attacks on the natural environment by modern Long Islanders have affected deeply the area's vegetation and wildlife. Ospreys are beginning to reappear after being threatened with extinction.

RIGHT
Long Island was involved with ducks for centuries before farmers began raising them in the 1870s. Its location on the migratory routes accounted for the presence of many species of waterfowl, including these canvasback ducks.

BELOW
Prehistoric Long Island Indians started steaming shellfish in pits, similar to this one constructed for an exhibit at the Garvies Point Museum in Glen Cove.

existence on Long Island is called the Big Game Hunting Stage.)

A major advance during the Hunting and Gathering Stage of the Archaic people was the development of the dugout canoe. Paddling these sturdy craft out of the fine natural harbors of the North Shore, they were able to extend their mobility considerably and even trade with other groups in upstate New York and the Great Lakes. The canoes, made mostly from tulip trees felled and hollowed out with the aid of fire, enabled Long Island's Archaic Indians to exchange rare or strategic materials with nearby groups. These, in turn, were traded for desirable items only available in distant regions to the north and west. Such networks explain the discovery on Long Island of flint implements, when flint came from the region along the Hudson River; copper jewelry, when the nearest source of copper was in the Great Lakes; and jasper beads and pendants, when jasper was located in New England and Pennsylvania.

About 3,000 years ago the Archaic people were supplanted, during what has been labeled the Transitional Stage, by Indians who are thought to have come from New England and the Pennsylvania-New Jersey region. Their lifestyle is referred to as the Orient Culture because their campsites were discovered in the Orient area on the North Fork, where they left extensive evidence of their preoccupation with death and life beyond death. From their elaborate burial rituals, archaeologists have learned that virtually every item used by the living was buried with the dead: spear points for hunting, celts and adzes for woodworking, quartz and iron pyrite for firemaking, stone vessels for cooking, and graphite and hematite paintstones for body painting.

For their burial ceremonies, the Orient Indians selected hilltops in eastern Long Island from which they could simultaneously look out over several bodies of water: the Sound, Plum Gut, and Peconic Bay in one case, and Peconic Bay and the Atlantic Ocean in another. Fire played a significant role in Orient funerals and one can imagine the dramatic sight of a communal burial with its bonfire blazing on a windswept hill.

Sometime during the Transitional Stage, but before the Indians of Long Island came into contact with European explorers about 500 years ago, a new prehistoric lifestyle emerged. It is called the Woodland Stage, although its most significant development was farming. Trees were cleared and, using the prototypes of hoes, these Indians planted fields with corn and possibly beans and squash. Their mortars and pestles imply a more sophisticated diet, probably some type of meal cake, while the utilization of smaller projectile points suggests the evolution of spears into more effective arrows and bows.

Artifacts from the Woodland Stage include pottery pipes of a size and shape that indicate these Indians had acquired the nicotine habit—something, like Long Island itself, they would soon pass along to as yet unimaginable strangers.

Challenge and Conflict

Robert David Lion Gardiner, sixteenth lord of the manor, displays a portrait of King Charles I of England, from whose agents Lion Gardiner, the first lord of the manor, obtained a patent for Gardiner's Island in 1639. In the background is the magnificent manor house.

Portrait of Long Island's discoverer, Giovanni da Verrazzano, an Italian who, while sailing for King Francis I of France, dropped anchor in what is now New York Harbor on April 17, 1524.

From the beginning, Long Island enjoyed what colloquially might be called "a good press." Early explorers sent back glowing reports to Europe extolling the natural beauties and bountiful resources of this portion of the New World.

One of the first visitors, Florentine explorer Giovanni da Verrazzano, sailing in 1524 under the French flag, "found the country . . . well-peopled, the inhabitants . . . being dressed out with the feathers of birds of various colors" until "a violent, contrary wind forced us to return to our ships, greatly regretting to leave this region which seemed so commodious and delightful." Henry Hudson, an Englishman outfitted by the Dutch East India Company, sent some crew members ashore in Brooklyn in 1609 who reported that "the lands were as pleasant with grass, and flowers, and goodly trees as ever they had seen, and very sweet smells came from them." Sir Edmund Plowden, who sought a grant of Long Island from Charles I of England in 1632, found that "there is great variety, and also all deputies [kinds] of fruits that Italy or the gardens of Spain affordeth may be had out of those rich grounds, for it is as hot as Spain or Italy, and as full of pleasure and comfort."

While this was news to the Europeans, Indians had been enjoying the fruits of Long Island, figuratively and literally, for a long time. By the time America was being "discovered" during the so-called Contact Period of the 1500s, Indians were living in Long Island from one end (Brooklyn) to the other (Montauk Point). Loosely divided into between six and twenty groups (many historians have settled on thirteen), Long Island Indians were not, strictly speaking, organized into tribes: they did not wear different costumes, inhabit separate territories with fixed boundaries, and have different customs. Rather, they comprised extended family groups living in geographic areas—along a river, near a beach, beside a pond—from which each group took its name.

These early Long Islanders were among the first American Indians to come into contact with Europeans. For this, they paid heavily, becoming the first to be acculturated through intermarriage and to be decimated through violence, slavery, and diseases such as smallpox and alcoholism. By the early 1700s, their presence was barely felt on Long Island; before

long, their existence was reduced to life on the Poosepatuck and Shinnecock Reservations, and preserved largely through the names of places: Montauk, Shinnecock, Setauket, Massapequa, Matinecock, Rockaway, and Canarsie.

Anthropologists suggest that the Indians of Long Island were peaceful and industrious, far more interested in trading with the Europeans than in fighting with them. One researcher speculated that the Long Island Indians' lack of aggressiveness, compared with the Plains Indians of the West, stemmed from the relatively "soft" life afforded them by the availability of shellfish and other seafood.

Dealings between the Indians and the Europeans were aggravated by a host of misconceptions and deceptions on both sides. The Europeans assumed that Indian society was organized along the same lines as their own—a faulty perception that led them to seek out a chief, or sachem, with whom to negotiate. But the Indians frequently had two leaders, one for war, the other for ordinary affairs. And neither was reluctant to accept whatever designation—and resultant reward—the Europeans seemed so eager to extend in their zeal to make a deal. It is thought that some chiefs sold the same land several times to different Europeans, as well as selling land over which they had no jurisdiction. This somewhat tarnishes the legendary cleverness of Europeans for having obtained vast tracts for trinkets.

The confusion resulting from differences in political organization was compounded by dissimilar concepts of property. The Europeans assumed that the purchase of land gave them ownership and total control; the Indians assumed that they were merely allowing the Europeans to use their land, and that the Indians would be able to hunt and fish on it as always. Such misunderstandings often led to disputes, some of which found their way into the colonial courts. Generally, the Indians lost and were forced, one way or another, to move to successively smaller and less desirable areas, or off Long Island.

Perhaps the most cynical appraisal of the interaction of the Indians and Europeans on Long Island came from an Indian chief in 1788:

The avidity of the white people for land and the thirst of the Indians for spirituous liquors were equally insatiable. The white men had seen and fixed their eyes upon the Indians' good land, and the Indians had seen and fixed their eyes upon the white men's keg of rum; and nothing could divert either of them from their desired object, and therefore there was no remedy; but the white man must have the land and the Indians the keg of rum.

Alcohol addiction almost claimed one of Long Island's most extraordinary Indians, Samson Occom, a convert to Christianity, who was ordained by the Suffolk Presbytery in 1759, taught and preached among the Montauks and Shinnecocks, and even went on a British lecture tour raising funds for the establishment of a college for Indians that became Dartmouth College. Occom, hailed in England as "the first Indian gospel preacher that ever set foot on this island," confessed his alcoholism, from which he subsequently recovered, in a 1764 letter to the Presbytery.

The devastation of most of the Long Island Indians so soon after contact with the Europeans has severely limited our knowledge of their culture and lifestyle. Probably the most comprehensive—if biased—first-hand account of how those early Long Islanders appeared and behaved to seventeenth-century European eyes survives in a report by Daniel Denton, one of Jamaica's first settlers and a prominent representative of that community. Published in 1670 as *A Brief Description of New York*, it offers a fascinating look at those for whom the advance of one civilization meant the termination of another. The son of a minister, Denton wasted no time in finding religious justification for the mistreatment of these people:

To say something of the Indians, there is now but few upon the Island, and those few no ways hurtful, but rather serviceable to the English, and it is to be admired, how strangely they have decreast by the Hand of God, since the English first settling of those parts; for since my time, where there were six towns, they are reduced to two small Villages, and it hath been generally observed, that where the English come to settle, a Divine Hand makes way for them by removing or cutting off the Indians either by Wars, one with the other, or by some raging mortal Disease.

With an observant eye—and the racism and condescension of his European contemporaries—Denton examined many aspects of Indian lifestyle. Tasks were determined by gender, with the males hunting and fishing while females tilled the land and planted corn. "The meat they live most upon is Fish, Fowl and Venison; they eat likewise Polecats, Skunks, Racoon, Possum, Turtles, and the like."

The Indians of that period were mobile, moving seasonally from their cornfields to their hunting grounds and fishing waters by simply packing up their possessions and transporting them to the new site. For recreation, they played "Foot-ball and Cards, at which they will play away all they have, excepting a Flap to cover their nakedness."

Denton seemed particularly interested in the Indians' drinking habits and described them in some detail:

They are great lovers of strong drink, yet do not care for drinking, unless they have enough to make themselves drunk. And if there be so many in their Company, that there is not sufficient to make them all drunk, they usually select so many out of their Company, proportionate to the quantity of drink, and the rest must be spectators. And if any one chance to be drunk before he hath finisht his proportion (which is ordinarily a quart of Brandy, Rum, or Strong-water), the rest will pour the rest of his part down his throat.

ABOVE LEFT
A Montauk Indian village site from the 1700s is inspected by an employee at the Montauk County Park.

ABOVE RIGHT
Council Rock in Oyster Bay was the site of a Quaker meeting in 1672 at which the founder of the Society of Friends, George Fox, preached during a visit to America from his native England.

BELOW
A tree bisects the rock used as a headstone for the last Matinecock Indian in the graveyard at Zion Episcopal Church, Douglaston. The tree growing from the stone replicates a custom of the Matinecocks.

He noted that drinking frequently got out of hand and violence resulted. "They often kill one another at these drunken Matches, which the friends of the murdered person do revenge upon the Murderer, unless he purchase his life with money, which they sometimes do. Their money is made of a Periwinkle shell, of which there is black and white, made much like unto beads, and put upon strings."

The fighting style of the Indians, which contrasted sharply with the open formations of the British troops, was the focus of many early European observers and did not escape Denton's observation. He wrote that when an enemy approached, the Indians would hide their wives and children, "and then with their guns and hatchets they waylay their enemies, some lying behind one, some another, and it is a great fight where seven or more is slain."

When Indians died, it was considered highly disrespectful ever to mention their names, since doing so would renew the grief of their loved ones. Similarly, all those named for the deceased would change their names to spare the feelings of the survivors. "Their names are not proper set names as amongst Christians," Denton explained, "but every one invents a name to himself, which he likes best, some calling themselves Rattlesnake, Skunk, Bucks-horn, or the like. And if a person die, that his name is some word which is used in speech, they likewise change that word, and invent some new one, which makes a great change and alteration in their language."

Denton was fascinated by the sexual and marital practices of the Indians and could not resist passing judgment on their moral code. "Their Marriages are performed without any Ceremony, the Match being first made by money. The sum being agreed upon and given to the woman, it makes a consummation of their Marriage, if I may so call it. After that, he keeps her during his pleasure, and upon the least dislike turns her away and takes another."

Adultery was permissible for wives if they informed their husbands or close relatives; if not, they could be put to death. "An Indian may have two wives or more if he please; but it is not so much in use as it was, since the English came amongst them; they being ready, in some measure, to imitate the English in things both good and bad. Any Maid before she is married doth lie with whom she please for money, without any scandal or the least aspersion to be cast upon her, it being so customary, and their laws tolerating of it."

Their criminal justice system, according to Denton, included capital punishment, although he pointed out that it was used sparingly. The death penalty was carried out by sending the condemned prisoner into the woods with the "King" (chief) and his executioners in hot pursuit. When found, he was shot to death (the "King" taking the first shot) and then scalped.

Finally, Denton described the cosmetology of Long Island's Indians:

While Indians still live on Long Island on two reservations, the Shinnecock near Southampton and the Poosepatuck near Mastic, intermarriage has altered the racial characteristics of many. A Shinnecock from an earlier generation, shown in the photograph taken by W. R. Harrington about 1900, was Mary Ann Cuffee, 81, with a wooden mortar and pestle then in use.

"They grease their bodies and hair very often, and paint their faces with several colours, as black, white, red, yellow, blue, &c., which they take great pride in, every one being painted in a several manner."

The relationship between the Europeans and the Indians on Long Island, as elsewhere in America, was essentially based on exploitation. Yet, for the most part, it was surprisingly peaceful. This pattern was ripped apart in 1643 by a merciless attack on a group of Indians in what is now New Jersey. It was launched from New York by Governor William Kieft of the Dutch West India Company, a harsh authoritarian who earlier had imposed stringent penalties for offenses by Indians against Europeans. David De Vries, who had been with Kieft when the assault was ordered, described the aftermath:

When it was day, the soldiers returned to the fort, having massacred or murdered eighty Indians, and considering they had done a deed of Roman valor, in murdering so many in their sleep, where infants were torn from their mothers' breasts, and hacked to pieces in the presence of the parents, and the pieces thrown into the fire and in the water, and other sucklings, being bound to small boards, were cut, stuck, and pierced, and miserably massacred in a manner to move a heart of stone. Some were thrown into the river, and when the mothers or fathers endeavoured to save them, the soldiers would not let them come on land but made both parents and children drown—children from five to six years of age, and also some old and decrepit persons.

Those who fled from this onslaught, and concealed themselves in neighboring sedge, and when it was morning came out to beg a piece of bread and to be permitted to warm themselves, were murdered in cold blood and tossed into the fire or the water. Some came to our people in the country with their hands, some with their legs, cut off, and some holding their entrails in the arms, and others had such horrible cuts and gashes that worse than they were could never happen. And these poor simple people, as also many of our own people, did not know any better than that they had been attacked by a party of other Indians. After this exploit, the soldiers were rewarded for their services and Director Kieft thanked them by taking them by the hand and congratulating them.

As might be expected, this atrocity provoked retaliation by the Indians against Europeans throughout the area, including Long Island. Yet, within a decade or so, relations had improved to the extent that a number of Indians were invited to what is now Brooklyn to attend their first religious meeting, which was being conducted by Domine Johannes Megapolensis of the Dutch Church of Long Island. Apparently the recent hostilities had not been forgotten entirely. When the Indians asked the minister why he was speaking at such length to the congregation and he replied, "I admonish the Christians that they must not steal, nor drink, nor commit lewdness and murder," they reportedly considered this for a moment and then inquired, "Why do so many Christians do these things?"

Dealings between the Dutch and Indians had been alternately friendly and strained from the outset. When Hudson, under Dutch sponsorship, first visited the Brooklyn area in 1609, one of his crew, John Colman, was shot to death with an arrow and buried at Sandy Hook at a spot the captain named Colman's Point. Hudson and his men admitted having killed three Indians during their exploration of the river that was to bear the adventurer's name.

The Dutch reinforced their early claim to New Netherland with a series of exploratory and trading voyages, including the extraordinary experience, in 1614, of Captain Adriaen Block. When his ship was destroyed by fire on Manhattan Island, Block and his crew, using only the tools they had brought from Holland or could obtain from the Indians, built a 44-foot vessel named *Onrust*, meaning restless (the first constructed by Europeans in North America), sailed it through Long Island Sound, discovered "Adriaen Block's Eylandt" (subsequently shortened to Block Island), determined that Long Island was, in fact, surrounded by water, and drew the first map to show "Lange Eylandt" as an island and to bear the term "Nieuw Nederlandt."

While the Dutch were interested largely in trading with the Indians for furs, particularly beaver pelts, and focused their activities in Manhattan

The monument in Mill Neck commemorates the military exploits of Captain John Underhill, who defeated the Massapequa Indians in the only battle between English colonists and Indians on Long Island. It took place at Fort Neck, near what is now Massapequa in 1653 or 1654. Underhill later fought for the Dutch, as Jan Van der Hyl, against the Canarsie Indians.

(which they called New Amsterdam), up the Hudson, and in western Long Island (Brooklyn, Jamaica, and Flushing), the English were busy colonizing Long Island's eastern end and its northern shore. Although the Dutch settlers came to the Island directly from Europe during the early 1600s, most of the English took a much shorter route, sailing across Long Island Sound from Connecticut and Massachusetts, where the religious fervor and intolerance of the Puritan leaders, or the harshness of the New England climate and soil, or the lack of a sufficient market for their goods and services, had made life in that part of the New World too demanding.

The first substantial English property holder on Long Island was Lion Gardiner, a prominent engineer who lived in Saybrook, Connecticut, where he directed the construction of a fort. Gardiner purchased an island, which he called the "Isle of Wite" (now Gardiner's Island), from his friend, Chief Wyandanch, sachem of the Montauk Indians, for "one large black dog, one gun, some powder and shot, some rum and a pair of blankets." Their long and valued relationship was derived in part, so the story goes, from Gardiner's successful negotiation for the release of

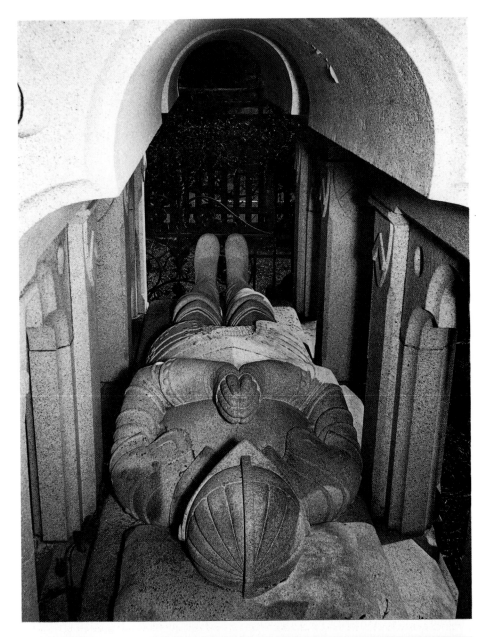

ABOVE
The elaborate granite tomb of Lion Gardiner, one of the earliest Long Island colonists and friend of the Indian sachem Wyandanch, from whom he purchased Gardiner's Island. The tomb is located at the South End Burying Ground in East Hampton.

BELOW
Travel by horse-drawn vehicles could range from the crude to the elegant. This example of the latter was constructed during the nineteenth century by Brewster and Company of New York for the affluent Gardiner family and is on display at The Museums at Stony Brook.

Wyandanch's only daughter after she had been kidnapped by the hostile Narragansetts on her wedding day.

In colonizing North America, the English paid strict attention to the legal niceties associated with British law and custom. Complying with this policy, Gardiner confirmed his title to the island by obtaining a patent from James Farrett, an agent of the Earl of Stirling, to whom Charles I had given Long Island. Gardiner occupied his island, which is still owned by his descendants, in 1639, and two years later his daughter, Elizabeth, became the first English child born in New York State and the first European born in Suffolk.

Shortly after the Gardiners moved in, English settlements were established in Southold and Southampton in 1640, and soon colonists began spreading into East Hampton (1648), Shelter Island (1652), Huntington (1653), Brookhaven (1655), and Smithtown (1665).

Despite a charming myth and a bronze statue on Jericho Turnpike celebrating it, there is no evidence that the boundaries of Smithtown were established by Richard Smith, through a daylong ride astride his bull, Whisper. It is generally believed that Smith, nicknamed Bull because supposedly he rode one, purchased much of what is now Smithtown in about 1665 from Lion Gardiner, who had obtained it from Wyandanch.

The colonists most often established their first settlements where Indians had already cleared the forests. For while they came from a society that was technologically more advanced than that of the Indians, they had arrived in the New World with few European implements and little opportunity to repair or replace those they had brought. In most important respects, the colonists were as affected and controlled by the vagaries of nature as were the Indians, and they sought to exploit the same natural resources: fresh water, trees, and shellfish.

Although the English focused their efforts in Suffolk, they also settled in among the Dutch villages on the western end of the Island, principally at Hempstead, Jamaica, and Oyster Bay. Most of the Dutch were concentrated in nearby Brooklyn and Flushing, and so a confrontation between these two great colonial powers seemed inevitable.

An attempt to resolve the tensions between English and Dutch colonists took place in 1650 at Hartford with the signing of a treaty that divided Long Island between them with an "international line," which corresponds to the present Nassau-Suffolk border. It specified that "a line Run from the westernmost part of Oyster Bay, and soe in a straite and direct line to the sea, shall be the bounds betwixt the English and Duch there, the Easterly parte to belonge to the English, and the Westerly parte to the Duch."

Despite the fact that it gave the British control of about three-quarters of Long Island, the treaty was never ratified in London, perhaps because the British had even bigger plans. When the monarchy was restored in England following the rule of Oliver Cromwell, and exiled King Charles

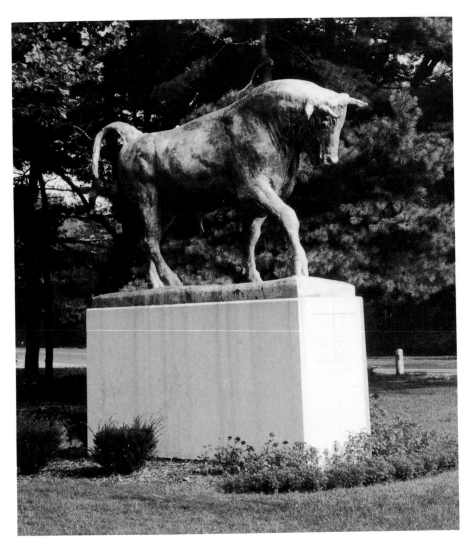

LEFT
This bronze statue of a bull at the intersection of Routes 25 and 25A in Smithtown commemorates the mythical establishment of the community's boundaries by Richard (Bull) Smith. There is no evidence to substantiate the story that the Indians agreed to sell Smith as much land as he could cover during a day's ride on the back of a bull.

OPPOSITE
Windmills, such as this one on Gardiner's Island, played a significant role in grinding grain for both Dutch and British colonists.

II was put on the throne in 1660, he decided to take over New Netherland, including Long Island, and turn it over to his brother, James, the Duke of York. To that end, in 1664 a British expeditionary force of 500 soldiers and four warships under the command of Colonel Richard Nicolls arrived at New Amsterdam and demanded the surrender of New Netherland from the Dutch governor, Peter Stuyvesant. Unable to gain assistance from Holland, Stuyvesant soon capitulated.

New Amsterdam promptly was renamed New York in honor of James, Duke of York, by Nicolls, who changed New Netherland to Yorkshire Province, after Yorkshire in England, and divided that territory, including Long Island, into three sections in the manner of the original Yorkshire: West Riding included Staten Island and the extreme western part of Long Island; North Riding included Westchester and mid-Long Island as far east as the 1650 "international line"; and East Riding included the remainder of Long Island, what is presently Suffolk County. (This arrangement lasted until November 29, 1683, when the General Assem-

bly divided the colony into twelve shires or counties, including Kings, Queens, and Suffolk.)

But Nicolls' most controversial act was the imposition of a rigid code, called The Duke's Laws, dealing with everything from the compulsory establishment of churches to penalties for fornication. In the case of the former, it stated that "in each parish within this Government a church be built in the most Convenient part thereof, Capable to receive and accommodate two Hundred Persons." While in the case of the latter, it established that "if any Person commit Fornication with any Single woman they shall both be punished by enjoyning Marriage, fine or Corporal Punishment, or any of those According to the discretion of the Court."

Long Islanders bridled under the code's restrictive rules, which they were given an opportunity only to ratify, not to formulate. In fact, representatives of Southold and Southampton refused to sign them. This dissatisfaction surfaced significantly in 1673 when the Dutch threatened New York City with a small fleet. The colonists showed little enthusiasm for sacrificing their lives in defense of a government they regarded as harsh and authoritarian and so the English were compelled to surrender. The Dutch immediately changed New York's name to New Orange, but a year later it was New York once again as Holland exchanged New Netherland with England for the South American territory of Surinam. This trade marked the peak of Dutch influence on Long Island—and America—and indelibly stamped English on our nation's culture, laws, and, of course, language. One Dutch custom we may be thankful never prevailed was their system of giving names, which were systematically changed with each generation, so that no son ever bore the family name of his father.

In what the Dutch did pass along, their legacy is mixed: an architectural style (Dutch Colonial), a religion (Dutch Reformed Church), a myth (Santa Claus), and an abomination (slavery). For two hundred years, slaves, brought in chains from Africa or impressed from the local Indian population, greased the wheels of Long Island's economy. And it was the Dutch, in 1626, who were responsible for introducing that institution, although the English proved readily receptive.

It did not take the early settlers long to realize that the rigors of life in the New World would require additional manpower. The most available source to perform the boring and laborious tasks necessary for survival was the Indians. But by nature and experience they resented and resisted domesticity. The Dutch then asked the East India Company in Holland for indentured servants, but the request was rejected as too costly. Instead, the company directors suggested that the Long Island colonists imitate those in Virginia and import slaves from Africa. The idea gained ready acceptance, and soon slave ships, slave auctions, slave quarters, and all the paraphernalia and trappings associated with the antebellum South were in evidence throughout the Island.

The Dutch introduced slavery to Long Island in 1626 as an alternative to providing indentured servants for their colonists. The English soon took up the practice and scenes such as this became commonplace.

By 1700, there was a greater proportion of slaves in New York—15 percent of the population—than in Virginia. By 1732, the census showed 7,232 black slaves on Long Island among a white population of 40,048. Male slaves, being stronger and more versatile, were in greater demand than females, although both, and even children, were highly valued. For example, an estate inventory in 1719 appraised a black woman and child at sixty pounds, while five milk cows, five calves, three young bulls, and two heifers were collectively priced at twenty pounds.

Although slavery was more common in western Long Island, where the Dutch and a farming economy predominated, it was widespread both geographically and demographically; that is, it was practiced by virtually all economic and social classes. Merchants, farmers, even ministers and Quakers, owned slaves. Slaveholding was to colonial status on Long Island what car-owning is to contemporary status: prosperous families owned fourteen or more slaves, while poorer residents could afford only one or two.

The Quakers, however, began to agitate against slavery and soon were in the forefront of those calling for its abolition. It was not a quick battle. Slavery reached its peak on Long Island between 1750 and 1790; much of the impetus for its abolition came immediately after the Revolutionary War when, ideologically, freedom was in the air, and, economically, there was a labor surplus. Consequently, it was not unusual for owners whose slaves were no longer productive, being aged or infirm, to welcome the opportunity to get rid of them—to the accompaniment of moral platitudes.

As late as 1779, according to local records, slavery was still very much in style: "$5 reward. Ran away from John Lefferts, Hempstead, Charles, a very black negro. He speaks good English, had an old homespun bearskin short-coat, tow shirt and trowsers, and small old felt hat."

Slavery finally was ended legally in New York State in 1827, although it was carried on surreptitiously by seamen in the Fire Island area until the Civil War.

Besides having slaves to perform drudgery, the colonists used indentured servants, generally English, who contracted their labor for many years or hundreds of dollars in return for passage to America and maintenance. For them, living and working conditions were at least as bad as those experienced by slaves, for in the case of the latter, slaveholders had a lifetime investment in maintaining their health and well-being. Few indentured servants outlived the terms of their contracts; many died from illness or, in despair, took their own lives.

The resort to slavery and the tenacity to maintain it stemmed, among other reasons, from the difficulty of living in Long Island in those harsh times. Even the most well-to-do endured living standards far below those they had enjoyed in Europe. Since there was no industry during the early days of colonization, and because the cost of obtaining manufactured articles from England or Holland was prohibitive, the settlers were compelled to live without many of the tools, utensils, and other amenities they had taken for granted before emigrating. If it became necessary to replace worn clothing or bedding, they had first to weave cloth. To weave cloth, they had to spin woolen yarn or flaxen thread. And to get the yarn or thread, they had to raise sheep or cultivate flax.

Life was consumed with providing food, clothing, and shelter, and everyone, from children to grandparents, participated. Everything was scarce, nothing was wasted. When, for example, a cow was slaughtered, some use was found for every bit. Anything that could be eaten was consumed including the head, which was boiled until the meat fell off and was mixed with spices to make a pickled dish called souse. Organs, too, were boiled and eaten with spices, while intestines were stuffed with chopped meat to make sausages. The fleshy parts were either smoked or cured with salt and spices. The fat was melted for candles and soap; the hide was scraped, dried, and tanned for leather breeches, jackets, and shoes, or book covers, or drumheads. Even the horns and bones were utilized: after being heated, the horns were shaped into cups, combs, and powder horns, while bones were converted into buttons and knife handles.

But for the early colonists, domestic animal meat was a treat. Aside from shellfish, which were eagerly gathered and devoured by those living close to the bays and beaches, and the finfish they were able to catch by line or seine, their diet essentially was unchanged from medieval times: its mainstay was grain and corn, the latter being ground Indian-style into a meal called samp and eaten as samp porridge. Even so prosaic a dish as this required monumental effort to prepare, particularly by today's frozen-food standards.

The corn first was parboiled for at least twelve hours and then placed

This salt swamp at Caumsett State Park, Lloyd Neck, is typical of Long Island marshes.

in a hollowed-out tree stump. A short log, tied at one end to the top of a nearby sapling, was used to pound the kernels into cornmeal. The process was so noisy and so commonplace that seamen would joke that even in a fog they knew they were off the Long Island shore by the pounding of the samp mortars. It was a slow, tedious job, taking an entire day to convert a half-bushel of corn into meal, and so the work generally was assigned to slaves.

Farming was carried on with the most primitive implements made almost entirely from wood. In addition to corn, the colonists raised wheat, oats, rye, and barley, and, when they could obtain seed, peas, beans, parsnips, turnips, carrots, and pumpkins. Wild fruit was abundant: strawberries, raspberries, huckleberries, mulberries, cranberries, persimmons, plums, and grapes. The strawberries grew in such profusion that eating them became a form of recreation, as this account by Denton suggests:

Such abundance of strawberries is in June that the fields and woods are dyed red; which the country people perceiving, instantly arm themselves with bottles of wine, cream, and sugar, and instead of a coat of Mail, every one takes a Female upon his Horse behind him, and so rushing violently into the fields, never leave till they have disrobed them of their red colors and turned them into the old habit.

In the early years, the colonists were more concerned with building their herds of cattle, sheep, and hogs, than consuming them. But in time, cattle became plentiful: by the Revolutionary War, there were an estimated 100,000 head of cattle on Long Island and each was identified by a special ear notch that designated its owner. Cattle were so common that they became a unit of exchange in Hempstead: taxes were paid "in fatt cattle delivered alive."

The grassy Hempstead Plains comprised a vast communal pasture of 60,000 acres, and thousands of acres of South Shore salt marshes provided an almost unlimited source of nutritious salt hay. The salt hay grew in the high marsh, closest to solid land. Cattle were grazed there as recently as 1956 in what is now Caumsett State Park in Lloyd Neck. The marshlands were cut each year, and it was a community event that lasted into the twentieth century in parts of the South Shore. The adjacent low marshes, which yielded thatch for colonial roofs, were flooded twice daily by the tides and consequently were treacherous since cattle could become mired in them. The marshes' value was such that they generally were held in common trust, like the village greens.

Clothing was designed, using the term loosely, for wear not style. The farmer's everyday suit was made from homespun. Later in the seventeenth century, it is likely that he also owned a suit of broadcloth, which he wore on Sundays and holidays throughout his life. On his death, it

was inherited by a son. Laborers wore buckskin, leather breeches, checked shirts, flannel jackets, felt hats, heavy shoes with huge brass buckles, and leather aprons.

In the latter stages of the colonial period, as people of wealth and substance began to emerge, they dressed in a manner that clearly set them apart from others. A gentleman powdered his hair, braided it in a queue, and placed a three-cornered hat over it. He wore knee breeches, striped stockings, and pointed shoes with large buckles. A vest was put on under a light-colored coat, which was decorated with silver buttons and worn beneath a small cape. And he carried a cane. His lady was likely to wear a gown of brocade or taffeta over hoops, which extended about two feet in every direction. A high hat or bonnet covered her hair.

For Long Island's earliest colonists, shelter was little more than a glorified cellar. They dug square pits six or seven feet deep, lined them with timber and bark, used rough planking for floors and ceilings, and raised a roof of spars, covered with bark or sod. Nevertheless, these underground homes enabled the settlers to survive the first few years until they could erect more substantial structures.

ABOVE
The earliest Long Island housing development was composed of glorified cellars similar to these in Salem, Massachusetts. Most of the living space was below ground.

OPPOSITE ABOVE
What has been described as one of the oldest houses in New York State and "finest example of English domestic architecture to be found in this country" is called, appropriately, Old House. Built in 1649 in Southold by John Budd, it was moved in 1660 to Cutchogue.

OPPOSITE BELOW
Although it was built by Captain Josiah Hobart sometime after 1676, this venerable structure on James Lane, East Hampton, is called the Mulford House after the family that lived here from 1712 until World War II.

The second generation of housing utilized stone foundations, timbers, and beams that were attached by a mortise and tenon joint using wooden pegs (nails did not come into general use until the eighteenth century), chimneys, and thatched or shingled roofs. Many of these houses were two rooms wide, one room deep, and one-and-a-half stories high. Bedrooms were located on the upper floor loft, although with family members invariably outnumbering bedrooms, beds were placed in virtually every room. The ground floor was dominated by the chimney-fireplace, which provided the only source of heat both for warmth and cooking.

The kitchen was the main room. Heavy three-legged pots hung from iron hooks and chains in the fireplace. An alcove off the kitchen contained a pantry for storing food and utensils, and often doubled as a bedroom at night. Because the lumber was roughly hewn with broadaxes, drafts swept through the walls and, in the dead of winter, would freeze any water left standing. The floors were bare, except in the Dutch communities where they were sprinkled with sand.

This desk of cherry, pine, and poplar at the Mulford House in East Hampton dates from 1749 and is an example of colonial workmanship.

Featherbeds, filled with duck and goose down, were comfortable but bone-chilling until a covered metal pan filled with hot coals was rustled between the sheets. The only light other than that provided by the fire came from candles, which were made by dipping flaxen wicks repeatedly into melted fat. Whenever possible, the colonists saved labor by adapting natural objects to their own uses. Turkey wings became brooms and brushes, clam shells became spoons, and gourds became cups and ladles.

If material life was hard, so was the life of the spirit. Perhaps total religious commitment was essential to the colonists' survival; surely, it was present in all aspects of colonial existence. Paradoxically, since they had fled Europe to seek freedom from religious oppression, both English and Dutch settlers were unremitting in their efforts to impose puritanism upon all who lived within their communities. Religion and government were inseparable and implacably hostile toward nonconformity.

Because the ecclesiastical and political leaders were the same people, settlers who disobeyed or questioned the prevailing narrow beliefs and practices of church and state were without recourse. Religious officials made the laws and the laws supported religious orthodoxy. For example, in many communities only church members in good standing were permitted to vote. The construction of churches and parsonages, and the salaries of ministers, were paid through taxes levied by the towns against all residents. Further, attendance at services was compulsory. In Hempstead, failure to go to church twice (morning and afternoon) on Sundays and holidays was punishable by fines initially, and by corporal punishment and even banishment for repeated occurrences. It was also against the law to travel on Sundays, except, of course, to attend church.

Among those most severely affected by this church-state collaboration were newcomers, Quakers, and "witches." To maintain the moral standards of their communities, townspeople throughout Long Island were very cautious about accepting new residents. Town committees were established to probe the character of those seeking admission and a three- to six-month probationary period was required so that their behavior could be observed. Those who failed to pass scrutiny were forced to move on; it was illegal to sell property or rent quarters to them.

Few groups in America have suffered such persecution as that felt by the Quakers under the Dutch and English during the colonial period. In New England, they were fined, imprisoned, whipped, shorn of their ears, had their tongues bored with hot irons, and were put to death. On Long Island, under Peter Stuyvesant, it was against the law to shelter them even for a single night, to "hold converse" with them, or to bring them to New Netherland by ship.

Yet dramatic support for freedom of conscience emerged when thirty freeholders reacted to this discrimination in 1657 by issuing the *Flushing Remonstrance*:

Ye have been pleased to send up unto us a certain prohibition, or command, that we should not retaine or entertaine any of those people called Quakers. . . .

We cannot condemn them, . . . neither can we stretch out our hands against them, to punish, banish or persecute them. . . . Wee desire . . . not to judge lest we be judged, neither to condemn lest we be condemned, but rather let every man stand and fall to his own Master.

Therefore if any of these said persons come in love unto us, we cannot in conscience lay violent hands upon them, but give them free egresse or regresse into our town and houses.

Stuyvesant promptly jailed the principals, forced apologies from them, and outlawed town meetings for Flushing in favor of a seven-member "advisory" board. A few years later, when Stuyvesant banished Quaker John Bowne to Holland, he got his comeuppance from the directors of the West India Company, who voided the banishment with the rebuke: "The conscience of men ought to remain free and unshackled. Let every one remain free, as long as he is modest, moderate, his political conduct irreproachable, and as long as he does not offend others or oppose the government."

When the English took control of Long Island during the following decade, the Quakers received somewhat better treatment, and in 1672 their founder, Englishman George Fox, visited America and conducted meetings at Oyster Bay, Flushing, Gravesend, and Shelter Island. His stay at Shelter Island was particularly noteworthy because that area had served as a haven for persecuted Quakers.

What made the Quakers the targets of such hatred and abuse? For one thing, their principles, such as the refusal to take oaths, were regarded as a defiance of civil authority, contempt of court, and subversive. Further, their conduct was not always gentle and orderly. For example, they sometimes would "bear testimony" by running naked through the streets, cursing all who differed with them.

Even if justification could be found occasionally for the treatment of nonconformists, there is little doubt that Puritanical paranoia hit a peak of frenzy in 1692 in Salem, Massachusetts, when twenty people were executed within six months for allegedly being in league with Satan and practicing witchcraft. On Long Island, however, there was no corresponding panic, although belief in witchcraft and laws forbidding it existed.

Two cases did take place: one in 1657 against Elizabeth Garlick of East Hampton for causing the death of Elizabeth Howell, the daughter of Lion Gardiner; and the second in 1665 against Ralph and Mary Hall of Setauket for killing both George Wood and an infant child of widow Ann Rogers. When Elizabeth Garlick's husband, Joshua, retaliated by suing one of his wife's accusers for defamation, the town, uncertain of how to deal with the situation, put itself under the jurisdiction of Connecticut, thus passing the case to that colony. As a result, Goody (for Goodwife; only wives of distinguished men were called Mrs.) Garlick was tried in Hartford, where a jury found insufficient grounds to convict her but enough for suspicion. Both Garlicks were placed on a loose form of probation and eventually returned to East Hampton with a letter urging the town to "carry on neighborly and peaceably without just offense to Joshua Garlick and his wife and they should do like to you."

The principal basis of the charge against Goody Garlick was the ailing Elizabeth Howell's fevered cry, "Oh, Mother! I am bewitched!" and her vision of two figures at the foot of her bed, "Goody Garlick in the far corner and a black thing in the near corner. . . ."

The case against the Halls was tried in New York City, where they pleaded not guilty and "threw themselves to bee Tryed by God and the Country." In fact, they were tried by a jury which found that "there are some suspitions by the Evidence, of what the woman is Charged with, but nothing considerable of value to take away her life. But in reference to the man wee finde nothing considerable to charge him with." Considering that the charge carried the death penalty, Mary Hall may well have considered her sentence a triumph. The Halls were required to check in with the court periodically for about three years before being "released & acquitted from any & all Recognizances, bonds of appearance or othr obligations. . . ."

A third case involving a Long Islander, Mary Wright of Oyster Bay, illustrates both the unreasoning zeal of the witch-hunters and the dangers of unorthodoxy in those times. One of twenty-eight Quakers jailed in Boston in 1661 for telling the court to lay aside "carnal weapons" and stop slaughtering the Indians, she was tried for witchcraft but convicted of Quakerism. Her penalty was banishment.

By the eighteenth century the clamor over witches had begun to ebb throughout the colonies, to some extent through the excesses of Salem

ABOVE
Sheltering Quaker refugees, the Sylvester Manor on Shelter Island, rebuilt in 1733 since its original construction in the mid-seventeenth century, is said to have housed George Fox during the founding Quaker's 1672 trip to America.

LEFT
Clinton Academy, New York's first secondary school, was opened in 1784 in East Hampton and soon became recognized as a preparatory school for Yale. One of the academy's early teachers was William Payne, father of songwriter, actor, and playwright John Howard Payne, author of "Home Sweet Home."

RIGHT
A robust and enthusiastic man despite his forbidding demeanor, the Reverend Samuel Buell, a founder of Clinton Academy, had three wives and rode fourteen miles on horseback to preach on his eightieth birthday.

which resulted in greater demands for evidence; demands that of course could not be met. Time brought increasing skepticism about the supernatural, a possible consequence of the spread of public education.

The Dutch had been very educationally oriented in Europe and were quick to institute schools in their communities on the western end of the Island. This was true, too, of the English towns. In fact, the English community of East Hampton was the site of the first secondary school in New York State. Named Clinton Academy, after then-Governor George Clinton, it opened in 1784 largely through the efforts of the Reverend Samuel Buell, a dynamic Presbyterian preacher; installed by the famed evangelist Jonathan Edwards, Buell played an important role himself in the early eighteenth-century revivalist movement known as the Great Awakening.

Before Clinton Academy, public education was limited to the elementary level, although it was given a high priority in many settlements. In Huntington, for example, a schoolmaster, Jonas Houldsworth, was hired in 1657, just four years after the town's founding. He was appointed for four years, given a house, his "diet," firewood for the schoolhouse (to be supplied by the parents of attending children), and an initial salary of twenty-five pounds to be paid in butter, corn, wheat, cattle, cloth, and wampum.

The earliest reading materials in schools were hornbooks, so called because a transparent piece of animal horn was placed protectingly over the precious paper on which the lesson (usually the alphabet, phonic sounds, and the Lord's Prayer) had been written. The bone and paper were attached to a thin board, which, with a handle at its bottom, resembled a rectangular hand mirror. Sometimes the hornbook was hung around a pupil's neck on a string.

While there is no record of what transpired in Houldsworth's classroom, descriptions of early schools probably convey the general atmosphere. Discipline was very strict: a hickory stick was displayed prominently and used without hesitation across the back or shoulders of any disobedient boy. Some schoolmasters also wielded a long, broad ruler, called a "ferule," across the palm, pulled hair, or pinched ears. It would be some years before more "civilized" punishments came into vogue, such as standing on one leg, holding out a stick of firewood at arm's length, wearing a fool's cap, committing some lines to memory, or detention after school.

Learning was confined almost exclusively to reading, writing, and arithmetic. There were no steel pens, no ruled paper, no readymade writing books. The schoolmaster kept a sharp knife to make, mend, and nib the pens made from goose quills, as well as a leaden plummet and ruler to line the writing books. Each writer contributed a penny to buy a packet of Walkden's famous ink powder, which, when mixed with a gill of vinegar and three gills of rain or river water, made a pint of ink.

There is no doubt that education was less than universal in colonial

Elias Pelletreau, Sr., was born in 1726 and spent a seven-year indenture before perfecting his craftsmanship and becoming Long Island's most notable eighteenth-century silversmith, as this initialed porringer attests. A resident of Southampton and Patriot sympathizer, Pelletreau fled to Connecticut to escape the British occupation of Long Island during the American Revolution.

This gateleg table of maple and pine is one of the earliest (1700–30) examples of colonial woodworking on Long Island. It is said to have been used at the Sammis Tavern in Hempstead.

Long Island. Attendance was not compulsory; older boys (some of them nineteen or twenty years old) attended during the winter, while older girls often went during the summer with the younger boys. For the most part, education still was regarded as a luxury compared with the compelling necessity around the farm for helping hands.

This need began to ease somewhat toward the end of the seventeenth century, as farmers, while hardly prospering, at least found they could produce more than enough food to satisfy their own requirements and thus trade surplus crops for items they desired but lacked. This, combined with the growth of communities and the resulting availability of more diverse skills, led to the specialization of labor taken for granted today.

While farmers continued to predominate, many communities were able to boast a blacksmith, mason, carpenter, wheelwright, cooper, shoemaker, butcher, tanner, potter, weaver, ropemaker, glazier, sailmaker, chandler, and miller. There were also itinerant workers, frequently shoemakers and weavers, who visited those hamlets too small to support their own craftsmen. And there was, as well, a thriving wampum industry.

Long before the arrival of the Europeans, Long Island had been the Indian equivalent of a gold mine because of the abundance of shells from which wampum was made. So plentiful were quahogs (hard-shell clams) and whelks that the Island was called Seawanhacky, meaning Land of Shells. And the Indians were so adept at turning this raw material into wampum that Long Island became known as a colonial mint.

Black wampum was made from the purple part of the quahog shell and was worth twice as much as the white wampum of the whelk. The shells were worked into polished cylinders about one-quarter inch in diameter and one-eighth inch long, and strung on hempen or skin cords. Wampum was computed in terms of a "fathom," a string measured from the end of the little finger to the elbow, and was worth five English shillings or four Dutch guilders. The Dutch reportedly complained that the Indian agents either had very long or very short forearms, depending on whether they were buying or selling.

With colonization, parts of Long Island were transformed from a mint to a sweatshop, and some European traders, notably John Jacob Astor, hired Indians to grind out wampum day and night to trade for beaver and other valuable pelts. By 1641, the colonial economy had become so dependent on wampum that counterfeit had to be controlled. The Dutch passed an ordinance contending that "bad wampum is at present circulated here, and payment is made in nothing but rough, unpolished stuff . . . and the good, polished wampum is wholly put out of sight or exported." Consequently, the ordinance said, inferior wampum would have only three-fourths the value of good wampum.

Along with wampum, barter was the colonial medium of exchange, as farmers and craftsmen traded their produce and skills. The first industries that developed were mills, run by wind, water, and tides, to grind grain,

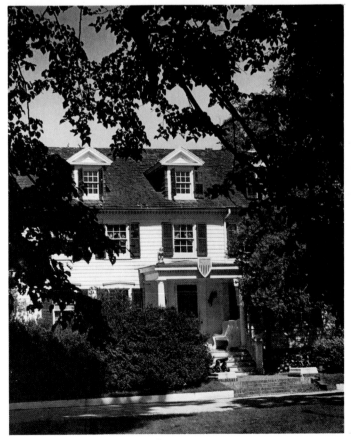

OPPOSITE ABOVE
The Thompson House on North Country Road, Setauket, was an unusually large timber-frame building for its time of construction, which was about 1700. It contains high ceilings and decorative detail on its exposed beams. There is a colonial herb garden on its grounds.

OPPOSITE BELOW
Sagtikos Manor in West Bay Shore was one of Long Island's earliest manorial estates when it was built in 1692. Used as a British headquarter during the Revolutionary War occupation, it later became one place where George Washington did sleep when he toured Long Island in 1790.

ABOVE
Wampum-making was one of the mainstays of the Indian economy during the colonial period since wampum was used by European settlers as a medium of exchange. White wampum was made from the columella—the central spiral—of whelk shells.

BELOW
Samples of black and white wampum are on display at the Garvies Point Museum in Glen Cove. Black wampum had double the value of the white.

saw logs, and make woolen cloth and paper. The importance of grain was reflected in the controls exercised over grist mill operators, who could be made to forfeit their businesses if they cheated, performed unsatisfactorily, or unreasonably refused service. The usual method of payment was for the miller to retain a portion of the wheat or other grain he ground, trading this for other items or services.

As the colonists developed systems of journeymen and apprentices, improved the quality of their skills and products, and increased their output through mechanization, England became aware that it was not gaining its anticipated benefits from the exploitation of its New World holdings. The Crown had seen the American colonies as a market for British goods, which often were marked up from 100 to 300 percent, but the colonists were not buying.

Recognition of the incipient economic failure of the colonial system was expressed by New York Governor Lord Cornbury, when he noted: "I myself have seen serge made on Long Island that any man may wear. Now if they make serge, they will in time make coarse cloth and then fine. I hope I may be pardoned if I declare my opinion to be that all these colonies, which are but twigs belonging to the main tree, ought to be kept entirely dependent upon and subservient to England."

Attempts by subsequent colonial administrators to bring about such policies would not be accepted unquestioningly. The colonists, with their self-confidence fed by the knowledge that they had not only survived the wilderness but had tamed it and had begun to shape it to their own tastes, resented British attempts to impose British merchandise—at British prices—upon them. In time, that resentment would combine with others to become an ideology and to force a confrontation that would alter the future of the world.

CHAPTER THREE

Defeat and Survival

F or Long Island, the American Revolution meant seven disastrous days of battle and seven devastating years of occupation.

The battle was the least of it, although the losses were heavy and the implications dire. The brief Battle of Long Island, a clear defeat, came early in the war, in 1776, threatening the strength and spirit of the American cause. But the occupation was grindingly long, cruel, and destructive. It left deeper scars, claimed a heavier toll, produced more heroes and villains than the battle that preceded it.

"The history of that seven years' suffering will never be told," an East Hampton orator later said of the British military occupation of Long Island. "Left to the tender mercies of the foe; plundered by countryman and stranger of their property and ripened harvest; robbed of the stores which they reaped and garnered; slandered by suspicious brethren; taunted and scoffed at by the mercenary victors, they never wavered." Even discounting oratorical hyperbole, those were the harshest of times for Long Islanders. Surely, the war and occupation would have been painful enough under any circumstances. But their impact was heightened, coming, as they did, after the colonists finally had wrested a secure and decent life from the wilderness.

In the decades before the Revolution, the relationship between the Crown and the colonies was ambivalent. In part, there was a feeling of mutual interest and cooperation. Colonial militiamen had joined British troops to win the French and Indian War (1754–63), adding Canada to England's possessions and ejecting France from North America. Throughout the colonies, mere subsistence had given way to stability, even comfort. Many of the villages on Long Island had been in existence for a century by then and boasted attractive homes embellished with the works of American craftsmen. A tradition of higher education had been sown with the establishment of most of today's Ivy League institutions. Government and its foundation, law, were in place and functioning; there were doctors and ministers, artisans and artists, shopkeepers and innkeepers. In short, a society modeled closely on that of England and Holland had taken shape and was seeking to meet material and spiritual needs in much the same way that they were being fulfilled in Europe.

It was precisely this growth, this relative prosperity, that triggered the

When Patriots, such as William Floyd, fled to Connecticut following the British occupation of Long Island during the Revolutionary War, their homes were often turned into barracks and stables. Floyd Mansion in Mastic suffered such a fate and was severely damaged.

crisis with England. After all, the purpose of colonization was exploitation: a colony was supposed to be a source of raw materials and a market for imported products; its function was to serve the mother country, not rival it. But the Americans refused to accept such a definition, and while they were willing, in fact, eager to have the British represent them in foreign affairs, at home they wanted to run their own business.

And so tensions grew between England and its colonies as the British tried to make the Americans dependent, and the Americans sought to assert their newfound identity. An act by the colonists imposing a duty on European goods was repealed by the Crown (1724); the colonies were prohibited from exporting hats to the West Indies (1732); Parliament banned the establishment in America of slitting mills (1750); Parliament imposed a duty on molasses and sugar (1764) and passed the Stamp Act, compelling the use of stamps on all documents (1765); the Mutiny Act required the colonies to quarter and supply British troops stationed in America (1765); the Townshend Acts levied new duties on paper, glass, painters' colors, and, significantly, tea (1767); the Restraining Act threatened to suspend the New York Assembly if the colonists failed to comply with these impositions (1767).

Lacking any representation in Parliament, the colonists could rely only upon persuasion and recalcitrance. This they did with some effect. The Sons of Liberty was formed to oppose the odious Stamp Act, and succeeded in rallying the public against compliance, led demonstrations, and won support for a boycott of British goods. As a result, the Stamp Act was repealed in 1766 and the Townshend Acts, with the exception of the duty on tea, were rescinded in 1770. But these concessions by the British did not resolve the problem, which, while economic in origin, had escalated into a political and philosophic deadlock because Parliament and the Crown miscalculated the American will.

Still, there was far from unanimity among the colonists. Loyalists or Tories, those who supported King George III, comprised a substantial portion of the Long Island population, compared with the Patriots or Whigs, those who opposed the British position. These divisions were based on socioeconomic and geographic, as well as political alignments. Wealthier, higher-status Long Islanders, particularly merchants, tended to identify with the Crown, and since they were more likely to be concentrated in western Long Island, Queens was a stronghold of Loyalist sympathizers. Farmers, fishermen, and Suffolk residents, who tended generally to identify more with New England, the core of anti-British feeling, lent their backing to the Patriot cause. Differences were so intense within Hempstead between the Patriots in the northern portion and the Loyalists in the southern, that in 1775 the Patriots seceded, and in 1784 the area was split officially into the Towns of South Hempstead and North Hempstead, with the former becoming simply Hempstead later on.

Thus, it is not surprising that in 1774, fully two years before the

ABOVE
William Floyd, a fervent Patriot, soldier, politician, and one of the Long Island signers of the Declaration of Independence, made notable contributions to the founding of the nation.

LEFT
This portrait of Anna Floyd, William's sister, was painted by Ralph Earl, a prominent colonial artist, who also portrayed Floyd's son-in-law, Ezra L'Hommedieu.

RIGHT
Francis Lewis, who lived in Whitestone and achieved prominence as a signer of the Declaration of Independence, has been characterized by some as a shady businessman and war profiteer.

BELOW
Long Island craftsmen of the colonial period made furniture such as this writing table owned by William Floyd.

writing of the Declaration of Independence, a resolution foreshadowing that historic document was adopted at a town meeting in Huntington. Later called Huntington's Declaration of Rights, it stated in part:

That every freeman's property is absolutely his own, and no man has a right to take it from him without his consent, expressed either by himself or his representatives.

That therefore all taxes and duties imposed on His Majesty's subjects in the American colonies by the authority of Parliament are wholly unconstitutional and a plain violation of the most essential rights of British subjects.

The resolution went on to call for a boycott of British goods to pressure Parliament into repealing taxes imposed on the colonists, and to reopen the Port of Boston, which had been punitively shut down. It concluded by appointing a committee to work with other towns and New York City to achieve those goals.

As the Patriots organized, the Loyalists consolidated too, and it became increasingly difficult for colonists to remain neutral. Feelings intensified and positions hardened. There were conflicts within families rivaling those that would afflict the nation a century later during the Civil War. In Queens the following year, after Loyalists had soundly defeated a slate of Patriot delegates to the Provincial Congress, the Congress held the Loyalist voters in contempt, published their names in the newspapers (there was no secret ballot in those days), sent soldiers to disarm them, and arrested their leaders.

Colonel Nathaniel Heard of New Jersey, who headed the Patriot troops sent into Queens, won some measure of prominence when protesting Loyalists composed the following lyrics to the melody of "Yankee Doodle":

Colonel Heard has come to town,
In all his pride and glory;
And when he dies he'll go to Hell
For robbing of the Tory.

Colonel Heard has come to town
A'thinking for to plunder;
Before he'd done, he had to run—
He heard the cannon thunder.

And when he came to Hempstead Town
He heard the cannon rattle—
Poor Colonel Heard he ran away
And dared not face the battle.

And now he's gone to Oyster Bay
Quick for to cross the water;
He dare no more in Hempstead stay
For fear of meeting with a slaughter.

By the spring of 1775, the battles of Lexington and Concord already had been fought between the British and the colonists in Massachusetts, and while some leaders on both sides still hoped for an accommodation, it was becoming increasingly evident that this was unlikely. On July 4, 1776, Congress passed the Declaration of Independence, asserting the "right of the people to alter or to abolish it [any government that deprives them of the right to 'life, liberty and the pursuit of happiness'], and to institute new government," thus sealing the inevitability of all-out war.

Three of the signers of the Declaration—William Floyd, Francis Lewis, and Philip Livingston—had ties to Long Island, although Livingston's was somewhat tenuous, consisting of a summer house in Brooklyn Heights. Floyd, born in 1734 on the Mastic Beach estate now maintained by the National Park Service as an historic site open to the public, was one of the Island's most prominent native sons. A wealthy landowner and politician, he fought as a colonel in the First Suffolk Regiment during the Revolution and was commissioned a major general at its conclusion. More distinguished in his political than military career, he represented New York at the First and Second Continental Congresses, and served in the State Senate and first U.S. House of Representatives.

Despite his affluence, social position, and the fact that his first cousin, Richard Floyd, was a leading Loyalist, William Floyd steadfastly espoused the Patriot cause, a decision that compelled his family to flee to Connecticut during the war and, no doubt, encouraged the looting and damaging of his estate by the British or Loyalists. After the war, he rebuilt and expanded the manor house before moving to upstate New York to what is now Westernville, where he died at the age of eighty-six. Floyd is remembered both through the preservation of his home and the parkway bearing his name that traverses Brookhaven from Route 25A, near Wading River, to Smith Point on Fire Island.

Like Floyd, Francis Lewis has achieved immortality through Long Island's transportation network: Francis Lewis Boulevard runs through Queens from Whitestone to Elmont. Unlike Floyd, Lewis' reputation is somewhat questionable.

Born in Wales in 1713, Lewis emigrated to New York when he was twenty-five and formed a partnership with a former Englishman named Richard Annesley, whose sister he later married. During the French and Indian War, Lewis had a contract to clothe the British Army and, while handling this business at upstate Oswego, he was captured by the French. Upon his release, according to one version, the British rewarded him with a tract of land and he built a farm in what is now Whitestone.

In 1775, he was chosen to represent New York in the Continental Congress, where his business experience and executive talent were highly regarded. The following year, Lewis and fifty-five colleagues signed the Declaration of Independence; shortly thereafter, while he was in Philadelphia, British troops retaliated by ransacking his house and taking his elderly wife prisoner. Mrs. Lewis was held for months in a filthy room until finally freed in a prisoner exchange arranged by George Washington, the American commander-in-chief. But her health had been severely impaired and she soon died. Lewis moved to New York City in 1796, died in relative obscurity on December 31, 1802, and was buried in an unmarked grave in Trinity churchyard.

The controversy surrounding Lewis concerns his business activities. One account lauds him for spending "the bulk of his large fortune, for which he was never repaid," to obtain military stores for the colonial cause. However, a legal document in the New-York Historical Society's library accuses Lewis of having defrauded the estate of his late partner, Richard Annesley, a charge denied by Lewis, who portrayed himself as the victim.

A more scathing indictment came from Judge Thomas Jones, who, in a book entitled *History of New York During the Revolutionary War*, contended that before being captured at Oswego, Lewis, "by selling his tobacco, his pipes, his sugar, and his salt, at a most exorbitant price, extorted a great deal of money from the poor soldiery." Jones further charged that Lewis later made considerable money from privateering in collaboration with a corrupt judge of the Admiralty, and, during the Revolution, had speculated with his sons in soldiers' certificates, with which they bought confiscated lands. If, in fact, Jones' accusations were true, they were not extraordinary. Profiteering was widespread throughout the Revolutionary War and was imputed to many in high places.

Whatever the credentials of those who signed the Declaration, the effect of their efforts was galvanizing. In the days and weeks following July 4, 1776, the stirring document was read to gatherings of excited listeners throughout the thirteen colonies. In Huntington, for example,

An artist's recreation of a crucial phase of the Battle of Long Island, when Americans under General William Stirling retreated across Gowanus Creek. Stirling was one of two American generals captured during that disastrous encounter.

on July 22, the reading was accompanied by a flourish of drumbeats and an enthusiastic response. The British Union Jack, which had hung on the Liberty Pole, was replaced with one bearing the word Liberty in white on a red field. This became known as the Long Island Flag and was carried by Patriot troops in the Battle of Long Island.

Powder horns, such as this one made and ornamented by Gilbert Vail in 1762, were used in times of war and peace.

OVERLEAF
Taking their history seriously, Long Islanders frequently don replicas of Revolutionary War uniforms to relive skirmishes by troops of both sides. During the 1976 Bicentennial celebration, military buffs reenacted activities of Continental Army regulars (ABOVE LEFT), Huntington Minutemen (BELOW LEFT), and British troops opposing the Americans (ABOVE RIGHT).

OVERLEAF BELOW RIGHT
Built in 1740, this arsenal was used by the Huntington Militia to store arms and gunpowder until 1776, when the British took it over. It is located on Park Avenue, just south of Route 25A, in Huntington Village.

An effigy of King George III was made, wrapped in the discarded British flag, labeled King George III, filled with powder, hung from a gallows, and exploded. There was a parade of some three hundred members of the Huntington militia and volleys of musket fire. Later, thirteen toasts were drunk, one for each of the self-proclaimed independent colonies. Then Dr. Gilbert Potter, a lieutenant colonel in the militia, with Major Jesse Brush, one of Huntington's most noted Patriots, concluded the celebration by reading the following poem from the *Constitutional Gazette*:

> Rudely forced to drink Tea, Massachusetts in anger,
> Spills the Tea on John Bull; John falls on to bang her.
> Massachusetts, enraged, calls her neighbors to aid,
> And gives Master John a severe bastinade.
> Now good men of the law! Pray, who is in fault,
> The one who began, or resents the assault?

With their spirits high, Huntington Patriots, and thousands of like-thinking Long Island neighbors, made ready to take on John Bull. They did not have long to wait. A month later, in August 1776, the British fleet landed troops between Old Man's (now Mt. Sinai) and Wading River, where they shot cattle and carried off the beef. Potter, on learning of the foray, wrote to General Nathaniel Woodhull that, although he felt under-manned, he was preparing his militiamen for a possible attack in Huntington Bay, needed help, and thought that "General Washington should be acquainted."

Potter did not know it, but the Battle of Long Island already was under way, not in Huntington Bay, but in Brooklyn, and not with a few hundred or thousand British soldiers, but with one of the largest expeditionary forces ever launched against an enemy in the history of Great Britain: 32,000 troops. The immensity of that military effort was a tribute both to

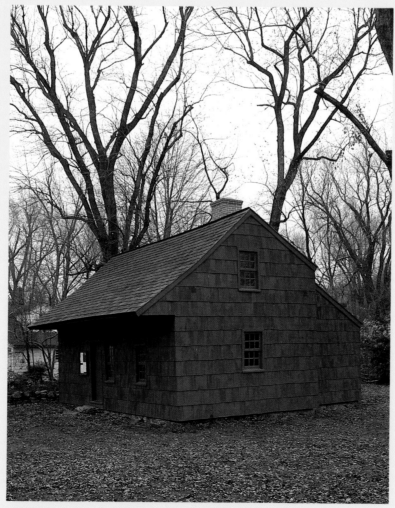

the fighting skills of the Americans and the grand strategy of the British high command. A few months earlier, 7,000 British troops had been besieged in Boston by the Continental Army and compelled to evacuate. Clearly, the British generals learned, it would require far greater strength than had been assumed to put down the colonial rebellion.

The British also had determined from that experience the necessity of crushing the rebels throughout the thirteen colonies not merely by capturing a few key cities and towns. To this end, they decided to divide the colonies into three segments, isolating New England, the middle colonies, and those in the south. The first step was to cut off New England by sending one column down from Canada to meet another coming up from New York. That required the capture of New York City, which consequently made Long Island of vital strategic importance. The expeditionary force was being built up on Staten Island. There, British regulars, augmented by Hessian mercenaries, were under the command of General Sir William Howe, whose brother, Admiral Lord Richard Howe, had recently brought the bulk of the troops fresh from England aboard a fleet of 150 ships.

George Washington, anticipating an attack on New York, moved his 19,000 raw and poorly equipped soldiers into the area, noting that "it is the Place that we must use every Endeavor to keep from them. For should they get that Town, and the Command of the North River, they can stop the Intercourse between the northern and southern Colonies, upon which depends the Safety of America." He set his soldiers to work building fortifications on the southern tip of Manhattan and in Brooklyn Heights.

On the morning of August 22, 1776, Americans stationed at Gravesend (near the present Bensonhurst section of Brooklyn) awoke to see an armada approaching from Staten Island, ships loaded to the gunwales with British troops. The invasion was on. The Americans fled and soon joined the bulk of Patriot soldiers who were aligned either behind the Brooklyn Heights fortifications or along a ridge that ran from near Gowanus Bay eastward toward Jamaica. The ridge, called the Heights of Guan, was thickly wooded and formed a natural barrier, penetrable only through four openings, the easternmost of which was called Jamaica Pass.

After several days of skirmishing, the British took up positions in front of the three other passages, engaging the attention of about 2,500 American militiamen defending the ridge. While Washington waited for the attack, General Howe led his main force of 10,000 on an all-night march to Jamaica Pass, where only five Patriot officers had been posted. Capturing the five before they could warn their cohorts, the British learned that the pass had been left undefended and quickly poured through. Howe's strategy worked to perfection. He had positioned overwhelming forces both in front of and behind the American lines; the final blow was to be coordinated with a naval bombardment of Brooklyn Heights from the East River.

Had nature not intervened, it is possible that the Revolution would have ended then, with the capture or destruction of the entire American army, including Washington and three generals under his command. But a stiff north wind and an ebbing tide prevented Admiral Howe from moving his fleet northward, and so only the battle, not the war, was lost.

Yet, the situation was still desperate. Patriot troops, caught in the British pincers, suffered severely and were barely able to retreat behind the fortified Brooklyn Heights positions. There, they faced a force, superior in every regard, that was prepared to win victory by siege or assault. Confronted by this terrible dilemma, the American commander conceived and executed a brilliant stratagem, of which the noted English historian George O. Trevelyan said: "It may be doubted whether any great national deliverance since the passage of the Red Sea has ever been more loudly acclaimed or more adequately celebrated than the masterstroke of energy, dexterity, and caution, by which Washington saved his army and his country."

A witness to the operation, Major Benjamin Tallmadge of Setauket, who entered Yale at the age of twelve, served in the Connecticut militia, and later performed heroically during the British occupation, gave the following description:

General Washington was so fully aware of the perilous situation of this division of his army, that he immediately convened a council of war, at which the propriety of retiring to New York was decided on. After sustaining incessant fatigue and constant watchfulness for two days and nights, attended by heavy rain, exposed every moment to an attack by a vastly superior force in front, and to be cut off from the possibility of retreat to New York by the fleet which might enter the East River, on the night of the twenty-ninth [of August] . . . Washington commenced recrossing his troops from Brooklyn to New York.

To move so large a body of troops with all their necessary appendages across a river full a mile wide, with a rapid current, in face of a victorious, well-disciplined army nearly three times as numerous as his own and a fleet capable of stopping the navigation so that not one boat could have passed over, seemed to present most formidable obstacles.

But in face of these difficulties, the Commander in Chief so arranged his business that on the evening of the twenty-ninth by ten o'clock, the troops began to retire from the lines in such a manner that no chasm was made in the lines, but as one regiment left their station on guard, the remaining troops moved to the right and left and filled up the vacancies, while General Washington took his station at the ferry and superintended the embarkation of the troops.

The evacuation resulted in the extrication of some 9,500 American soldiers, with their equipment and supplies, from positions only 600 yards from the British lines to safety in Manhattan. Moments before its completion, with Washington still on the Long Island side, British scouts, suspicious of the silence, infiltrated the Patriot lines and discovered what was happening. But before they could act, a fog rolled in and concealed the departure of the remaining boats, one of which bore Washington. Of the 10,000 Americans actively engaged in the Battle of Long Island, an estimated 300 were killed and at least 1,100 were wounded, captured, or missing. These losses, which were appreciably worse than those suffered by the British, included two generals, Stirling and Sullivan, who were taken prisoner.

One of the most poignant (although possibly embroidered) incidents to emerge from the battle involved General Woodhull, the officer to whom Potter had addressed his belated warning about a British invasion. Woodhull had been given the vital, but hardly glamorous, task of rounding

Ranking high among the cruel and harrowing episodes of the Revolution were the rotting ships used by the British to hold American prisoners of war. The most notorious ship was the Jersey, *pictured above in Wallabout Bay, New York Harbor, which accounted for a significant share of the estimated 11,500 deaths attributed to these vessels.*

up the Patriots' cattle in Queens and driving them east of the vast Hempstead Plains to keep them out of enemy hands. Despite wholesale desertions, he accomplished his assignment and sought permission to join the fight in Brooklyn. He waited anxiously in Jamaica, within the sound of cannon fire, for orders that never came. Instead, a detachment of British dragoons arrived and took him prisoner. The general surrendered his sword, but when his captors demanded that he say "God save the King!" he replied instead, "God save us all!" This infuriated the dragoon leader, who slashed at Woodhull with his saber and would have killed him had not other officers intervened.

General Woodhull was treated by a doctor and then placed aboard one of the notorious prison ships that the British kept at Wallabout Bay in

Brooklyn. The wounds he had suffered required the amputation of an arm, and he died less than a month after his capture. From his deathbed, Woodhull wrote his wife, urging her to bring a wagon filled with provisions for his fellow prisoners.

The prison ships were among the most atrocious aspects of the Revolution and resulted in the death of an estimated 11,500 American seamen and soldiers from starvation, disease, and neglect. The following account by the Reverend Thomas Andros of Berkeley, Massachusetts, a prisoner who survived confinement on the former battleship *Jersey*, depicts the horrors of imprisonment.

When I first became an inmate of this abode of suffering, despair and death, there were about four hundred prisoners on board; but in a short time they amounted to twelve hundred, and in proportion to our numbers, the mortality increased.

All the most deadly diseases were pressed into the service of the king of terrors, but his prime ministers were dysentery, smallpox and yellow fever. There were two hospital ships near to the old "Jersey," but these were soon so crowded with the sick that they could receive no more. The consequence was that the diseased and the healthy were mingled together in the main ship. In a short time we had two hundred or more sick and dying lodged in the fore part of the lower gun deck, where all the prisoners were confined at night.

Utter derangement was a common symptom of yellow fever; and, to increase the horror of the darkness that shrouded us (for we were allowed no light betwixt decks), the voice of warning would be heard, "Take heed to yourselves! There is a madman stalking through the ship with a knife in his hand!" I sometimes found the man a corpse in the morning by whose side I laid myself down at night. . .

Washington's evacuation to Manhattan left Long Island to the British, and they wasted no time in taking control. Fearing the worst, Patriots and their families and slaves fled across the Long Island Sound to Connecticut. Refugees jammed the docks of North Shore communities, as about one in six Long Islanders—5,000 out of a population of less than 30,000— left their homes, farms, businesses, and most of their possessions for the next seven years.

Painful as it may have been to leave, the ordeal of those who remained made the decision to flee appear sound. Loyalists, particularly those who had suffered under Patriot rule, now emerged to welcome their conquering British heroes. To symbolize their support for the Crown, they wore red cockades or ribbons, a practice quickly adopted by boys, slaves, the elderly, and all who wished to avoid British persecution. The use of red rags for this purpose became so widespread that women had to tear up their red petticoats to meet the demand. The more ardent Patriots sneeringly derided these wearers of red as members of the Petticoat Brigade.

Not only the Loyalists regained stature and power. New York Governor

William Tryon, the Crown's appointee who had been forced out by the Patriots, now returned with the Howe brothers to reinstitute the Crown's authority. Martial law was declared and, with the assistance of Loyalists, Patriot leaders were identified, rounded up, and either imprisoned or kept under surveillance. The British also were interested in raising an army of Long Islanders to take part in their continuing effort to suppress the Revolution. But despite inducements and threats, recruitment of both Loyalists and former Patriots proved disappointing.

Aside from providing some manpower, Long Island served the British cause in two principal respects following the Battle of Long Island: it helped protect the British occupation of vital New York City, which Washington had been forced to abandon a few months later, and it supplied the British troops with food and shelter until the end of the war.

In exploiting the land and people to fulfill this latter function, the British exhibited the callousness, greed, and cruelty that bred hatred for them among generations of Long Islanders. Compelling the losers to sustain a victorious army was hardly a new concept; while the official British policy was to pay for goods and services, practice was something else. Long Islanders soon found themselves giving provisions, labor, and quarters to about 8,500 occupying soldiers, often with only the promise of eventual compensation.

When it came to the property and possessions of self-exiled Patriots, the British simply took what they wanted "for the King's use." Oliver De Lancey, whose family was prominent in New York affairs, commanded the Loyalists recruited into the regular British army and played an active role in subjugating Long Islanders throughout the seven years of occupation. His subordinates ordered their troops to "take into your custody all the grain, forage, and creatures you can find on L.I., being the property of persons actually in rebellion, or who have deserted their habitations."

Cattle, grain, and wood were given top priority by the army of occupation—the first two for food, the third for fuel and construction. Since one of four people living on Long Island at that time was a British soldier, the demand for meat, bread, cereal, and fresh fruit and vegetables was tremendous and immediate. In addition, Long Island was seen as a key source of food for the entire British expeditionary force, roughly equivalent in number to the Island's civilian population.

Keeping their cattle out of British hands (and bellies) required considerable ingenuity on the part of Patriot farmers who were continually on the lookout for places where herds could graze undetected. Among the best hideaways were the kettle holes, broad, deep cavities created by huge chunks of glacial ice. On one occasion, when British soldiers demanded to know the location of some Patriots' cattle in the Smithtown area, the Americans replied: "Oh, we sent them to Yorke"—the name of a nearby kettle hole. The British, assuming that New York City was

The mechanism of the Lefferts Mill is illustrated in this drawing; most of the fine gear is still intact.

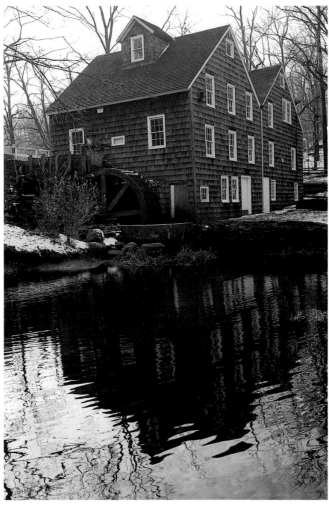

meant, ended their search.

One devastating consequence of the war, although unintentional, involved the destruction of substantial wheat fields by an insect brought to America from Germany together with German wheat and Hessian troops. It soon ravaged the native wheat, beginning in western Queens where Tory farmers planted some of the infected imported grain, and became known as the Hessian Fly.

The effect would have been much worse had it not been for a farmer and miller from Flushing who, having heard of a type of wheat that resisted the Hessian Fly, acquired some and planted it. According to a 1786 newspaper account:

> The insect that has destroyed the wheat many years past continues to spread, but it has no effect on the white-bearded wheat raised on Long Island. This wheat was brought here from the southwest during the war, and a few bushels sown by a Flushing farmer grew well, and afforded a fine crop. He kept on, and has supplied his neighbors. It grew twenty bushels to the acre, and weighs over sixty pounds. It is of a bright yellow color, and makes fine flour. The straw is harder, and resists the poison of the fly, and supports the grain, while bearded and bald wheat were cut off.

Another indirect result of the war was the wasting of Long Island's vast hardwood forests, particularly on the North Shore. These woodlands held a special attraction for the occupation forces, but the appeal was hardly aesthetic. The British needed wood to construct fortifications and to burn as fuel, and they chopped down those forests indiscriminately, altering the look and the ecology of large portions of that area. After the war, logging operations continued for more than a century on Long Island and played an important role in the economy.

Generally, both during the occupation and later, the trees were cut and carted or dragged by horse to villages on Long Island Sound for shipment to New York. The method of loading the cordwood on the ships involved what was called "laying on." The sailboats would come as close to the beach as possible during high tide and stand by. As the tide receded and exposed more beach, the logs would be hauled across the sand and loaded aboard. When the tide rose again, the boats were ready to sail. This meant that men had to be available for loading whenever the tide made it possible, whatever the hour of day or night, and the British troops made certain Long Islanders responded.

But by far the most odious experience suffered during the occupation was the billeting, or quartering, of British and Hessian troops during the winter. This was done in an arbitrary manner, with concern only for the accommodations, not for the family's circumstances. British officers would tour the Long Island countryside, frequently with a Loyalist as guide, and inspect farmhouses to determine their capacities. Houses with only one fireplace were rejected, since soldiers were not supposed to become

OPPOSITE ABOVE

OPPOSITE ABOVE

Among the forts used by British troops during their seven-year occupation of Long Island was Fort Franklin in Lloyd Neck, overlooking Cold Spring Harbor. Its earthworks are still visible.

OPPOSITE BELOW

Raynham Hall in Oyster Bay, the home of Samuel Townsend, played a critical role during the Revolution when it served as British headquarters for a regiment of the Queen's Rangers. Townsend's son, Robert, was a member of George Washington's spy ring.

RIGHT

Although most of the British forts on Long Island were built on the North Shore to defend against assaults by Patriot troops stationed across the Sound in Connecticut, Fort St. George was located on the South Shore at Mastic Beach. As the plaque indicates, American Major Benjamin Tallmadge led a successful amphibious attack on the fort in 1780.

Woolen pocketbook belonging to Samuel Townsend of Oyster Bay, the master of Raynham Hall and bearing his name, was made in 1755, possibly by his wife or one of his daughters.

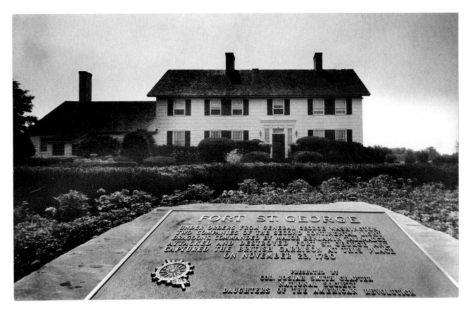

closely involved with the families, and fireplaces provided the only heat for warmth and cooking.

After some rooms were set aside for the family, and at least one fireplace was allotted for heating and cooking, the remaining rooms with fireplaces were assigned to soldiers. The touring officer decided how many soldiers a home could contain and marked the number on the front door with chalk. The owner was then informed: "Madam, we have come to take a billet on your house." And that was it. A door was nailed shut to keep the soldiers and family apart, but the number of intermarriages suggests that the separation was less than total.

To maintain their occupation of Long Island and to defend against anticipated Patriot forays from Connecticut, the British built a series of forts, principally on the North Shore: the Oyster Bay Encampment, Fort Franklin on Lloyd Neck, Forts Slongo and Golgotha in Huntington, and Fort St. George in Mastic.

The Oyster Bay Encampment served as headquarters for the Queen's Rangers, Americans who had volunteered to fight for the Crown, and its fortress was located at what presently is the intersection of Orchard and Prospect Streets in the village. Always ready to meet an attack, the fortification never was called upon to do so.

Fort Franklin, named for the Loyalist son of Benjamin Franklin, was designed by Colonel Benjamin Thompson, a figure of prominence and controversy who achieved a reputation in the military, scientific, and philanthropic fields, both in America and England. Thompson, later named Count Rumford, was born in Massachusetts and would have become a leader in the Continental Army but for internal wrangling and jealousy. Frustrated, he went to England, returning near the end of the Revolutionary War in 1781 to command the King's American Dragoons, a Loyalist regiment, and supervise construction of Fort Franklin and Fort Golgotha.

The earthworks of Fort Franklin, which dominated a bluff overlooking the entrance to Cold Spring Harbor, are still visible on the former estate of Mrs. Willis Delano Wood. It was Fort Golgotha, which ominously was given the Hebrew name for Calvary, the site of Christ's crucifixion, that earned Thompson notoriety as one of the most reprehensible figures of the occupation. Built in late 1782, when hostilities had ended and a peace treaty was being concluded, the fort—located at the present intersection of Nassau Road and Main Street in Huntington Village—was constructed by tearing down the Old First Presbyterian Church for lumber and uprooting a burial ground for tombstones.

The desecration was unbelievable: the tombstones were used for ovens, so that bread bore the reverse imprint of the epitaphs it was baked upon. Thompson reportedly pitched his tent over the grave of the Presbyterian minister, the Reverend Ebenezer Prime, so that when he entered or left he could "step on the damned old rebel's head." The Reverend Prime, before his death a few years earlier, had seen British officers take over his house, wreck his furniture, and destroy the most valuable books in his library. Thompson rounded out his unusual career in France, acquiring considerable wealth through various inventions, and bequeathed a portion of his estate to Harvard College.

Fort Slongo, named for its builder, Philadelphia contractor George Slongo, was located at Treadwell's Neck and commanded a magnificent view of Long Island Sound. The outline of its blockhouse still is visible on the ground behind the house at what is now 46 Brookfield Road, Fort Salonga. ("Salonga" is a corruption of "Slongo.")

Fort Slongo, along with Forts Franklin and St. George, became the target of raids by Major Benjamin Tallmadge, an heroic Patriot officer who launched hit-and-run guerrilla attacks against the British throughout the occupation. From the safety of Connecticut, which was held by Washington's forces, Tallmadge and other American soldiers waged "whaleboat warfare" across the Sound.

ABOVE
Major Benjamin Tallmadge, born in Setauket, escaped to Connecticut after the Battle of Long Island and launched whaleboat forays against British occupation forces.

LEFT
Portraitist Ralph Earl's painting of Major Benjamin Tallmadge's wife and child.

OPPOSITE ABOVE
Robert Feke's Self-Portrait *dates from about 1750. Born in Oyster Bay some forty years earlier, he became a prominent portrait painter.*

OPPOSITE BELOW
Feke's portrait of Josiah Martin, from 1746, shows the wealthy, successful merchant and landowner wearing a powdered wig and an elegant white brocade waistcoat. Martin is typical of the eighteenth-century aristocracy. His fine house, Rock Hall in Lawrence, was probably built in the early 1770s and included numerous outbuildings such as the kitchen building, smoke house, carriage house, and ice house.

In the assault on Fort Slongo, 150 Continental troops crossed to Long Island in the whaleboats, which were about thirty feet long, pointed at both ends, swift, light enough to be easily portable, and superbly maneuverable. After a brief engagement, the 140-man garrison was subdued, the fort destroyed, the blockhouse burned, and twenty-one prisoners, one field piece, and seventy muskets captured. Not a single Patriot was lost in the encounter, a tribute in large measure to the espionage activities of Henry Scudder, a refugee from Great Cow Harbor (now Northport), who visited the fort and made detailed sketches of it. Scudder, a lieutenant captured during the Battle of Long Island and released, took part in many of the raids against the British.

On one occasion, while Scudder hid in the chimney of his home in Crab Meadow, a British cavalry officer named Captain Coffin pointed a pistol at his wife's head and said, "If I don't find your rebel husband in a week, I'll be in my coffin." Less than a week later, Scudder and a Patriot raiding party surrounded a house where British soldiers were relaxing, took sixteen prisoners, and shot Coffin dead as he played cards.

While the Patriots used the whaleboats to great advantage in Long Island Sound, they by no means dominated that body of water. The British struck across the Sound on several occasions, destroying Danbury, Connecticut, and damaging New Haven, Fairfield, Green's Farms, and Norwalk for aiding the whaleboaters. However, the Patriots were not cowed by these assaults. In retaliation for the Danbury raid, Lieutenant Colonel Return Jonathan Meigs took 170 men across the Sound and, without a single casualty, returned to Connecticut within twenty-four hours of his departure after having attacked a British outpost at Sag Harbor with devastating effectiveness.

But perhaps the most spectacular of the amphibious assaults in and around Long Island was commanded by Major Tallmadge in November, 1780. The objective was Fort St. George, from which 200 Loyalists reportedly were plundering the countryside. It was located near Smith's Point on the South Shore, which meant the Patriots had to cross not only the Sound but the Island as well. Further, the base, consisting of three strongholds (the Manor of St. George, another fortified house, and a small fort), was protected by a triangular, twelve-foot-high stockade.

Tallmadge first visited the fort in disguise to familiarize himself with its defenses and plan his attack. Later, accompanied by eighty soldiers in eight whaleboats, he sailed across Long Island Sound to Mt. Sinai, was delayed a full day by a storm, and made an all-night march to strike at dawn with three columns. Shouting, "Washington and Glory!" his dragoons crashed through one stockade wall and scaled the other two to capture the fortification and fifty-four prisoners without loss.

The effectiveness of the whaleboaters tempted some to allow personal greed to overcome patriotic zeal. They eagerly sought "letters of marque," entitling private vessels to prey on enemy vessels—and retain part of the spoils. These "privateers" sometimes found it difficult to distinguish foe from friend and were accused of plundering their fellow Patriots as well. On Long Island, the line between privateering and piracy was anyhow a thin one historically. Captain William Kidd, a Scotch minister's son, was sent out in 1695 under the aegis of British King William III to curb piracy and, incidentally, capture enemy ships. Six years later, he was hanged in London for committing piracy, after part of his loot was unearthed on Gardiner's Island at a spot now marked by a bronze plaque.

At the time of the Revolution, the phenomenal success of the whaleboat expeditions stemmed to a large degree from the first-hand information gathered by Patriot soldiers and agents. During the course of the war, the Patriots developed an excellent espionage system—with the glaring exception of perhaps the most famous American spy, Nathan Hale.

Hale's career as a Patriot secret agent, which ended almost as it began, proved calamitous for him and useless for his sponsors. That he is remembered at all, much less in laudatory terms, seems less a tribute to anything he did or said than to the determination of many historians to perpetuate questionable anecdotes. Handsome, graceful, and refined, Hale, a native of Connecticut, graduated from Yale with honors, became a schoolmaster, enlisted in the Continental Army in 1775, and, at the age of twenty-one, bored with inactivity and fervent with patriotism, responded to a desperate request from General Washington and volunteered to spy. For about two weeks in the fall of 1776, Hale visited enemy forts on Long Island under the guise of being a job-seeking Dutch teacher. When captured, probably in Huntington Bay, possibly on a tip from a Tory cousin, Hale was carrying his own Yale diploma, and diagrams and descriptions of British fortifications. He readily admitted who and what he was.

Hale was hanged the next day in New York City. It was not until seventy-two years later, in a book published by the daughter of a friend and classmate, William Hull, that the famous phrase "I only regret that I have but one life to lose for my country" emerged. Those words were attributed to Hale by a British captain who witnessed the execution and described it to Hull.

Although Hale's information never reached Washington, his death inspired Tallmadge, also a friend and classmate, to accept an appointment from Washington in 1778 as head of the Secret Service, and thus chief of intelligence. Tallmadge recruited three Setauket neighbors—Austin Roe, a tavernkeeper, Abraham Woodhull, a farmer, and Caleb Brewster, a whaler—and an Oyster Bay merchant, Robert Townsend, to form what became known as the Setauket or Culper Spy Ring. (Samuel Culper Sr. was Woodhull's code name and Samuel Culper Jr. was Townsend's.)

Woodhull and, later, Townsend gathered information in New York City about British troop movements and transmitted it either on paper using invisible ink or orally to Roe, the courier. Roe took it to Setauket, where it was passed to Brewster, who carried it by whaleboat across the Sound to Tallmadge, who usually was stationed in Fairfield, Connecticut. Tallmadge would then send the intelligence to Washington, wherever he happened to be at the time.

The espionage ring also included two women: one, known only by her code number "355," became Townsend's sweetheart and bore his illegitimate child; the other was Anna Smith Strong, who lived alone on Strong's Neck since her husband, Selah, a judge, had been imprisoned by the British for aiding the Patriot cause.

Agent "355" circulated among the New York elite, where she was able to overhear the conversations of ranking British officers. She died aboard the *Jersey*, after being arrested in the wake of the execution of Major John André, the British soldier to whom Patriot traitor Benedict Arnold turned over plans for the capture of West Point.

Mrs. Strong's role was to designate in which of six hidden coves Brewster had moored his whaleboat so that Roe could deliver secret messages to him. She would signal Brewster's arrival on Long Island by hanging a black petticoat on her laundry line, and indicate the appropriate cove by adding from one to six handkerchiefs. The ring played a vital as well as romantic part in the Revolution and won the praise of Washington, who said succinctly of Townsend: "I rely upon his intelligence."

Although the war did not end formally until the Treaty of Paris was signed in 1783, its outcome had been evident since the surrender of Lord Cornwallis at Yorktown in 1781. For Long Islanders, more than most Americans, war's end was a momentous event. For Patriots, it meant freedom at last from the oppressive British occupation. For Loyalists, it meant the removal of British protection and the fear of Patriot retribution. And so, for many supporters of the Crown, it was a time to consider fleeing, as the Patriots had done after the Battle of Long Island. But their destination was not Connecticut but far-off Nova Scotia and New Brunswick, where the British provided land.

By the end of 1783, British troops had gone and Long Islanders were either celebrating or leaving. In Jamaica, according to a newspaper report, music, parades, and the display of the Stars and Stripes marked the afternoon festivities. At night, "every house in the village, and several miles around, was most brilliantly illuminated, and a ball given to the ladies concluded the whole. It was pleasing to view the different expressions of joy and gratitude apparent in every countenance upon the occasion. In short, the whole was conducted with the greatest harmony, and gave universal satisfaction."

But for Long Island, the satisfaction was short-lived. And this time humiliation came at the hands of their countrymen. In 1784, despite the degradation, deprivation, and suffering Long Islanders had experienced during the Revolution, the New York Legislature levied a tax against them to compensate the rest of the state for Long Island's failure to take an active part in the war against England.

CHAPTER FOUR

Moving Ahead

The end of the Revolutionary War freed Long Islanders to wrest their farms and fields and forests from the ruin wrought by the enemy and the deterioration brought by abandonment. The ruin had come at the hands of British occupation troops; the deterioration had come while absent Patriots fled to Connecticut or fought under General George Washington.

Although some Americans may have been heady over the prospects of their newly gained political freedom, most were overwhelmed by the task of rebuilding their lives. It is not surprising that Washington, on a journey through Long Island just a year after his election as the struggling nation's first President, seemed more concerned with crop-yields-per-acre than with the spirits of his constituents. But, like many another prospective visitor, Washington had to contend with the weather. His diary entry for April 19, 1790, states: "Prevented from beginning my tour upon Long Island today from the wet of yesterday and the unfavourableness of the morning."

Once on his way, however, the President recorded daily comments and gave his overall impressions about the five-day coach visit that took him from New York City as far east as Patchogue, Coram, and Setauket. A wealthy Virginia landowner who has been described as "the first farmer of his day," he expressed interest in all the aspects of farming that he encountered, including the "living fences" that Long Islanders made by splitting live saplings and forcing their trunks to grow horizontally.

"Their fences, where there is no stone, are very indifferent," he wrote. "Frequently of plashed (entwined) trees of any and every kind which have grown by chance; but it exhibits an evidence that very good fences may be made in this manner either of White Oak or Dogwood, which from this mode of treatment grows thickest, and most stubborn. This, however, would be no defense against Hogs."

The President also took note of where he ate and slept, often commenting baldly on the quality of his hosts and their offerings. Thus, in Jamaica, a "Tavern kept by one Warne" was "a pretty good and decent house," while a meal taken with a Mr. Barre of New Utrecht, he dismissed as, "the Man was obliging but little else to recommend it."

Washington's focus, however, was upon agriculture. And he pursued it by questioning the farmers he met and analyzing their responses. "From

a comparative view of their crops," he concluded, "they may be averaged as follows: Indian Corn 25 bushels—Wheat 15—Rye 12—Oats 15 bushels to the acre. According to their accts. from Lands highly manured they sometimes get 50 of the first, 25 of the 2d and 3d, and more of the latter . . ."

Such concern reflected the times: Long Island and most of America were deeply involved in farming by the end of the Revolution; even as late as 1820, two-thirds of Long Islanders—and four-fifths of those outside Brooklyn—were engaged in it. Mostly they raised cattle, sheep, and the staples Washington had noted. But their methods were primitive, virtually unchanged from the Middle Ages, and the Long Island soil had become thin and unproductive from more than a century of exploitation.

Although, as Washington had noted, the value of manure was known, it was not in general use, nor was such a simple technique of soil enrichment as crop rotation. However, there were stirrings: Ezra L'Hommedieu, a Southold resident of broad interests ranging from public affairs and education to law and farming, pioneered in fertilizing with the inedible, herringlike fish called menhaden or "mossbunkers."

The fish were so plentiful in local waters, and the results proved so remarkable that a new profitable industry arose to revive and stimulate one that was languishing. The menhaden were readily netted in vast numbers and spread over the fields to decay at the rate of eight thousand to the acre. Caught by the hundreds of thousands in the early years of the nineteenth century, the once-useless fish were in such demand by 1850 that they were being harvested by the hundreds of millions, providing jobs and profits to Long Island fishermen and farmers alike.

Menhaden were not the only bounty the sea provided. Long before the arrival of Europeans, Indians on Long Island had found a use for the whales that frequently ran aground on South Shore sandbars during migratory journeys. They boiled the blubber and mixed the resultant oil with their corn and peas, rubbed blubber into their leather moccasins and leggings to waterproof and preserve them, and offered the huge tails and fins as sacrifices to their gods. In time, they learned to pursue stragglers by canoe and drive them into shallow water where the enormous mammals became helplessly beached. The Indians then let the whales die naturally or shot them to death with arrows.

The early colonists found the blubber useful for lubricating and protecting their metal tools, and its oil effective for illumination. Further, they discovered that the waxy spermaceti in the sperm whale's head cavity could be used to make candles, and, when mixed with bayberry oil, provided a pleasant scent. Initially, the colonists depended largely on the whales that were washed ashore during storms, although this random harvest led to many disputes. To resolve them, Southampton in 1644 divided its beachfront into wards, with the residents of each entitled to whatever whales were washed up within its boundaries. This, apparently, was the first involvement of government in whaling, but hardly the last.

Before long, the colonists were going out, Indian-fashion, to force whales onto the beach or to kill them just offshore. They augmented this with the construction of watchtowers along the South Shore beaches from the Rockaways east, where, from fall until spring, observers would scan the seas and signal or shout at the sight of a "spout."

With that, the boats would push off through the breakers and pull for the whale. When they reached their target, wrote Charles Wooley in his 1678 diary, "About the Fin is the surest part for the Harpiner to strike . . . as soon as the whale is wounded he makes all foam with his rapid violent course, so that if they be not very quick in clearing their main ways to let him run upon the tow, which is a line fastened to the Harping-iron (harpoon), about fifty fathoms long, it is a hundred to one he oversets the boat."

Once the dead whale had been floated ashore, the men would begin the week-long task of converting it to their purposes. Most common were the right whales, large mammals with huge but harmless mouths lined with a sievelike substance rather than teeth like a sperm whale. Using long, razor-sharp cutting tools, the whalers would strip off the lips to extract the valuable baleen, or whalebone, from the jaws and remove the oil-rich tongue. Baleen was the bonus offered by right whales; from the sperm whales, there were ivory teeth and valuable spermaceti, which was dipped out of the cranial "case." The resilient baleen was used to make corset stays and umbrellas, while the bone and teeth were con-

Whaling was a major Long Island industry for decades and the inspiration for stories, poems, songs, and paintings. Three whaling scenes captured by artists include Captain Selah Young Striking a Sperm Whale on a Voyage Aboard the "Odd Fellow" Out of Sag Harbor (ABOVE); Whale Fishery "Laying On," *a print by Nathaniel Currier of Currier & Ives fame* (MIDDLE); *and* Sperm Whale "In a Flurry," *another Currier print* (BELOW).

OVERLEAF
The majesty of a ship under full sail was captured by Nathaniel Currier in a print entitled Homeward Bound.

verted into piano keys, fans, buttons, or scrimshawed into delicately carved cane handles, chessmen, and other art objects.

Then the whale would be decapitated, and the foot-thick blubber, actually a layer of fat separating the skin and flesh, peeled from the entire body. Finally, the blubber would be cut into smaller strips and rendered into "oyle" by being boiled in big iron try-pots. After cooling, the whale oil would be ladled into barrels for shipment.

Since the whales weighed considerably more than the try-pots, the pots would be hauled to the point where the whale was beached and the tryworks, consisting of the pots, a brick fireplace, and plenty of driftwood, was assembled on the spot. The stench of the boiling oil was so offensive, however, that in 1669 Southampton banned the operation of a tryworks within a certain distance of the community because "the trying of oyle so near the street and houses is soe extreme noysome to all passers by, especially to those not accustomed to the sent thereof, and is considered hurtful to the health of the people."

The cost of producing whale oil was relatively expensive, and soon whaling companies were formed as partnerships: one partner would contribute the boat, another the harpoons, and a third the try-pots. The boats were manned, as Wooley explained, by "four oarsmen or rowers; a Harpiner and a Steersman."

But it did not take long for the colonial governors, British appointees, to recognize the taxation potential of this shore-whaling trade. By the early seventeenth century, they were seeking to license the whalers, levy tariffs as high as 20 percent on their profits, and even claim for the Crown as "Royal Fishes" all "drifft" whales stranded on shore or found floating in coastal waters.

The profits from shore whaling were often considerable but usually uncertain. In 1708, Lord Cornbury, one of the governors, pointed out that Long Island's production of whale oil varied greatly from year to year and from whale to whale. "Last year," he wrote, "they made 4,000 Barrils of Oil, and this season only about 600. A yearling will make about forty barrils of Oyl, a Stunt or Whale two years old will make 50 or 60 barrils, and the largest I ever heard of yielded 110 barrils and 1,200 weight of bone."

Long Islanders resisted this governmental interference, frequently evading the tax collectors by illegally shipping their oil directly to New England instead of going through New York City. But the governors retaliated and the dispute raged for years. The tax finally was reduced in 1720 after Samuel Mulford, a leading citizen of East Hampton, took the whalers' case to London, where he petitioned King George I. Mulford not only endeared himself to Long Islanders because of his success, but to the British public as well when it became known that he had sewn fishhooks into his coat and trouser pockets to forestall London thieves.

ABOVE
One of the nation's first two ports of entry designated by President George Washington was Sag Harbor; the other, New York City. To carry out those responsibilities, this Custom House was built in Sag Harbor.

BELOW LEFT
Sag Harbor's importance as a port was represented by its authority over trading, fishing, and whaling. This coasting license was issued in 1790 to Captain Nathan Fordham of the sloop Polly.

BELOW RIGHT
Henry Packer Dering, member of a prominent Suffolk family, was appointed the first inspector of revenue for the Sag Harbor Port of Entry by President George Washington in 1791.

COASTING LICENCE.

DISTRICT OF SAGG-HARBOUR.

Nathan Fordham, Master of the Sloop Polly

of the burthen of *Twenty Seven* Tons, having entered into Bond with sufficient Security for the Payment of one Thousand Dollars to the United States, with Condition that the said Vessel shall not be employed in any illicit Trade during the Continuance of this Licence, and having paid the Tonnage Duty thereon, the said *Sloop*

Polly is hereby licenced to trade between the different Districts of the United States, or to carry on the Bank or Whale Fishery for one Year from the Date hereof.

GIVEN under my Hand, and Seal of Office, at the Custom-House in Sagg-Harbour, this *Twentieth* Day of *October* one Thousand seven Hundred and *ninety*

Henry P. Dering
Collector

GEORGE WASHINGTON, President of the United States of America.

TO ALL WHO SHALL SEE THESE PRESENTS, *GREETING.*

KNOW YE, That reposing special Trust and Confidence in the Integrity, Diligence and Discretion of *Henry P. Dering of New York* I DO APPOINT him *Inspector of the Revenue for the Port of Sagg-Harbour in New York* and do authorize and empower him to execute and fulfil the Duties of that Office according to Law; AND TO HAVE AND TO HOLD the said Office, with all the Rights and Emoluments thereunto legally appertaining, unto him the said *Henry P. Dering* during the Pleasure of the President of the United States for the Time being, and until the End of the next Session of the Senate of the United States, and no longer.

IN TESTIMONY whereof I have caused these Letters to be made patent, and the Seal of the United States to be hereunto affixed. GIVEN under my Hand, at the City of Philadelphia, the *Twenty first* Day of *March* in the Year of our Lord one thousand seven hundred and ninety *One* and of the Independence of the United States of America the *Fifteenth*

G Washington
By the President
Th Jefferson

Even before the Revolutionary War, the pods of whales that appeared close to shore in earlier days had all but disappeared, forcing whaling to enter a new phase: those seeking whale oil would have to pursue it on the open seas. To do so meant building or outfitting ships especially to track, kill, and process whales. Some whalers did go out, principally from Nantucket rather than Long Island, but the timing was poor. War brought the British Navy to the Island's coastal waters and prevented any attempts to take up the new business called "offshore whaling."

Nor did the American victory improve the situation. The defeated British, who had moved into whaling during the Revolution, remained highly competitive, placing duties on American oil to discourage its purchase in England. Disputes with Great Britain continued to forestall the growth of the whaling industry on Long Island at the turn of the century. In 1807, President Thomas Jefferson imposed his embargo on trade with both the warring French and British, thus virtually limiting the market for American whale oil to the United States.

Whalers suffered a further setback when a divided Congress declared war on Great Britain in 1812 over the harassment of American seamen and confiscation of goods. For the most part, the war was characterized far more by preparations for and fear of conflict than by conflict itself. On Long Island, the preparations primarily involved the construction of fortifications at Sag Harbor and in Brooklyn. But the anticipated invasion never came, possibly for the very reason that Long Island was prepared. A British fleet under the command of Commodore T. M. Hardy spent a good deal of the war in Gardiner's Bay, while its single attempt to land troops, a brief foray at Sag Harbor, was repulsed.

The War of 1812 ended in 1815, enabling Sag Harbor to resume its profitable activities as a port of entry, a designation it had received, together with New York City, from President Washington in 1789. In those pre-income tax days, the revenue from duties, which were collected through Sag Harbor's Custom House, was a principal source of governmental funds. More significantly, the end of the war brought a tremendous demand, both foreign and domestic, for whale products. The long-delayed advent of offshore whaling established Sag Harbor as one of the world's preeminent whaling ports and, with Cold Spring Harbor, earned Long Island whalers a global reputation.

Fired by dreams of romance and riches, young Long Islanders left their farms by the thousands during the ensuing decades to remain at sea for as long as five years on a single voyage and brave injury, illness, and death from winds, waves, whales, disease, and authoritarian masters. The crews, recruited and occasionally "shanghaied," represented virtually every racial and ethnic strain, with Long Island blacks and Indians playing important roles that until recently remained buried in time. Contemporary researchers have discovered black shipbuilders, owners, and

ABOVE
The Whalers' Church in Sag Harbor was designed and constructed in 1844 by Minard Lafever of New York under a commission from the port's whaling men. Its unusual Chinese-style steeple was blown down by the 1938 hurricane, leaving the remainder of the church as it appears today.

BELOW
Long Island boasts not one but two museums dedicated to the lore of whaling: one in Cold Spring Harbor and this one in Sag Harbor, in a building that originally was the home of whaling ship owner Benjamin Huntting and later became a Masonic Lodge. Both museums house memorabilia from the glorious days of whaling in the mid-nineteenth century.

captains, as well as crews, who, despite the restrictions imposed by racial prejudice, contributed significantly to the whaling and maritime history of Long Island.

The material rewards of whaling, especially for owners and captains, could be considerable. A successful voyage could yield as much as $100,000, with a captain receiving perhaps $5,000. Whaling captains were generally well-to-do, comparable to today's lawyers, enjoyed high social status, and often lived in substantial homes whose roofs were crowned with "widow's walks," permitting a view of the ship's return to the harbor.

Whaling exploits, while perhaps exaggerated (a contemporary writer contended that "no whaleman author has ever told the exact truth since Herman Melville set the standard of whaling mendacity"), lent an aura of mystery and danger to Eastern American life in the nineteenth century that paralleled the deeds of Western cowboys and cavalrymen. And, with the likes of Sag Harbor Captain Mercator Cooper, who sailed to Japan in 1845 and aided the State Department in opening the Orient to Western overtures, contributed considerably to the extension of American trade and influence abroad.

"I remember when black, bull-bowed whale ships lay three abreast along yonder dock, and eight hundred coopers, riggers, sailmakers, and stevedores went to and from the wharves to their work morning and evening," recalled blacksmith John Fordham about Sag Harbor's nineteenth-century days of glory.

In cellars along shore thousands of barrels of oil lay piled tier on tier and covered with sea weed. Yonder were great warehouses, three stories high, their upper stories filled with spermaceti and whalebone, the lower used as sail lofts and rigging lofts, and cheek by jowl with them were long cooper shops and here and there a candle factory.

The bosom of the bay was covered with lighters, piled high with products of the whale coming from ships at anchor and returning with provisions and outfits. An army of carts were moving oil and bone from the docks, the cooper's adse and the blacksmith's hammer made merry music all day long, and the streets were filled with crews of incoming and outgoing vessels, attended by their wives, daughters, sisters or sweethearts, making a strange jumble of welcome and farewell, smiles and tears, weeping and laughter.

Most of the sixty-four whalers that sailed out of Sag Harbor in 1845, Fordham said, were converted packet ships.

Sometimes it was an old craft that had become unsafe for passenger service. The vessels were of course overhauled, put in ship shape, refitted, and sent out on voyages of from one to four years' duration. At first the whalers cruised near home, in the North and South Atlantic mostly, but as the whales, hunted so remorselessly, foresook their favorite cruising grounds and withdrew to South

Black seamen were a common sight on nineteenth-century ships sailing out of Sag Harbor, but it was only recently that their contributions to whaling and maritime history gained recognition.

Pacific and the icebound fastnesses of the Arctic, their voyages were extended until they embraced the circle of the globe.

It was no light job to fit out a whale ship in the forties. First the sails, rigging, and boats were inspected with the greatest care, for on those depended the safety of the vessel and crew, and of course her success. This done, the captain picked out his crew of twenty-two men, aiming to get the most expert at this command, and ranging the country from Montauk to Shinnecock for them. The crew was a motley lot when gathered—whites, Indians, half-breeds, ne- groes—but they were picked men. To complete the outfit there was to be pro- vided three boats, with tubs, harpoons, lances, lines, hatchets, spades, etc., with from two to three thousand barrels well-seasoned and a great variety of provisions and miscellaneous stores.

As Fordham indicated, whaling had a sizable economic impact on Long Island, particularly during its most prosperous era between 1820 and 1850. It triggered an expansion of the shipbuilding industry in North Shore villages such as Port Jefferson, Northport, Stony Brook, and Setauket, prompted the growth of subsidiary businesses such as sailmaking, ropemaking, and barrelmaking, and gave an important boost to the production and sale of the food and provisions required for long voyages.

The decline of whaling usually has been attributed to the discovery of gold in California in 1848, which, with its similar appeals of excitement and quick riches, supposedly siphoned off the whalers, and to the discov- ery of petroleum in Pennsylvania in 1859, which undercut the price of whale oil. However, recent research suggests that whaling had reached its peak in 1847 and that its end was brought about by overkill. Whales still could be found, but the time and distance consumed in finding them priced whaling out of the market. Further, a devastating fire ravaged the Sag Harbor waterfront in 1845, destroying almost one hundred structures.

At any rate, except for sporadic demands such as during the Civil War, the whaling industry on Long Island entered a depression in the mid-nineteenth century from which it never recovered. The last whaler to sail from once-proud Sag Harbor left port in 1871 and was condemned as unfit three years later at Barbados.

While the industry of whaling had a considerable effect on many aspects of local life, it did little to improve transportation, which always had constituted a challenge for Long Islanders. The surrounding seas were restricting, and the Island's long, thin shape limited the direction of road networks.

From Long Island's earliest days, its inhabitants showed a preference for traveling by water. The Indians used dugouts whenever possible to transport themselves and their goods in and across Long Island Sound, a practice followed by the colonists and their descendants using, progressively, oars, sails, steam, and gasoline. Trade between eastern

Suffolk and New York City was carried on almost totally by water. Packet sloops, carrying passengers, mail, and cargo, plied the Sound in a steadily increasing number. To New York, they brought wood and farm produce; to the Island, merchandise, ashes, and manure.

By 1824, one hundred vessels of all types were running between New York and the town of Brookhaven alone. Excursions were a popular form of diversion, although they occasionally proved disastrous. The most

ABOVE
Shipbuilding became a substantial industry on Long Island during the nineteenth century, particularly on the North Shore. This drawing by Edward Lange pictures the shipyards and residence of Jesse Carll in Northport Harbor.

BELOW
The silent splendor of two three-masted schooners off Orient has been preserved in this 1915 photograph.

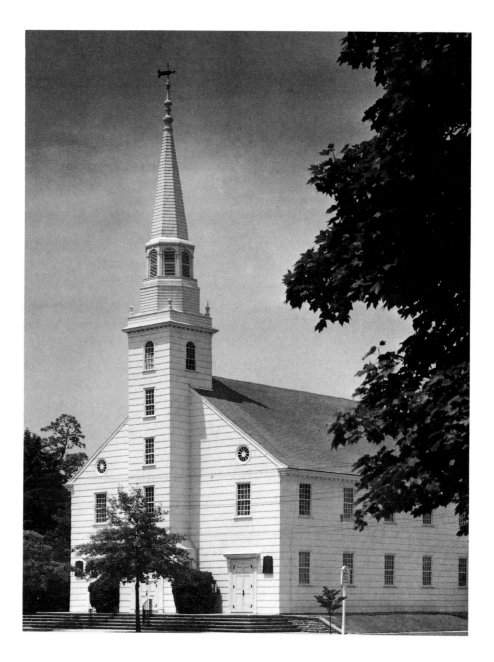

The influence of the sea on Long Island life during the eighteenth and nineteenth centuries appeared in many unlikely places. Old First Church on Main Street, Huntington, was constructed by ships' carpenters in 1784.

terrible marine tragedy during this era occurred on January 13, 1840, when the steamboat *Lexington*, owned by Cornelius Vanderbilt among others, burst into flames on Long Island Sound off Eaton's Neck during a trip from New York to Stonington, Connecticut. Of eighty-seven passengers and forty crew members, all but four either were burned to death or drowned. The voyage was the ship's first after having been equipped to use coal, rather than wood, as fuel.

But the accident did not dim the demand for ships. They were needed and Long Island shipbuilders responded. In 1840, shipyards could be found in almost every coastal community. And by 1860, at shipbuilding's height, there were at least twenty-five yards in Suffolk, turning out catboats, fishing smacks, sloops, schooners, brigs, and barks. The Island's configuration and the accessibility of navigable waters made travel by land a reluctant choice even centuries before completion of the Long Island Expressway.

The earliest roads followed Indian trails, invariably accepting rather than challenging nature's design—skirting hills, forests, ponds, and other obstacles without regard to distance or time. These "cow paths," deeply rutted and often filled with sand or mud, were neither designed, repaired, nor maintained. The first real attempt at roadbuilding came in 1704 when the Legislature mandated a route from Brooklyn Ferry to East Hampton that still exists in part as King's Highway. In time, other east-west roads were constructed, however primitively, and served mainly to move produce and farming supplies.

The turnpike system—the introduction of toll roads—made its appearance in the country in 1801, and Long Islanders soon were driving their wagons and coaches from Brooklyn to Jamaica, Hempstead, Jericho, and Smithtown, for a price. With Jamaica as a hub, toll payers were able within a few years to travel to Oyster Bay on the North Shore and Babylon on the South Shore, while on the East End, a turnpike was operated between Sag Harbor and Bridgehampton. The roads were built by private enterprise and the tolls retained by the builders. There was a brief but frantic demand for wood-surfaced highways, called plank roads, to overcome mud, but the high costs of maintenance outweighed their relative comfort and they were abandoned after a short time.

Most developments arise out of need, and the need for good roads on Long Island during the colonial and Revolutionary periods was limited because of the self-sufficiency of most of the communities. Not even an interest in mail was sufficient to create the necessary demand for a decent highway network in those days. In fact, about the time of the Revolutionary War, mail was delivered not by the government but by "a respectable old Scotchman named Dunbar," according to a contemporary report, who made a weekly circuit from New York City to Babylon and Brookhaven.

Before the end of the eighteenth century, stagecoaches were running on a weekly schedule between Brooklyn and Sag Harbor, "but the service was miserable, the patronage poor, and . . . promptness in starting and arriving were neglected, while none of the schemes to promote the comfort of passengers . . . were ever dreamed of."

However, by 1835, a coach trip through Long Island could be a positive delight, as Gabriel Furman, author of *Antiquities of Long Island*, makes evident in the following first-hand account:

The practice was to leave Brooklyn about nine o'clock in the morning—they were not, however, particular to half an hour—travel on to Hempstead, where

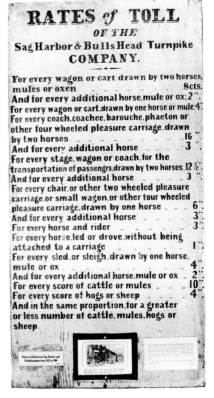

ABOVE

Turnpikes or toll roads were built for profit by private companies during the nineteenth century. These rates were charged for travel between Sag Harbor and Bridgehampton from 1852 to 1900.

BELOW

This whimsical weathervane was fashioned in 1870 in the shape of the sidewheeler Index. *It is a fine example of nineteenth-century Long Island folk art.*

ABOVE
Travel by stagecoach was not exclusively a Western custom, as illustrated by this 1852 painting by Henry Boese of The Stage Sewanhackey. *The building in the background is Brooklyn's City Hall.*

RIGHT
Sometimes travel by horsedrawn coach was less than elegant.

BELOW
A later mode of transportation was by trolley car. Here is opening day in 1911 of the trolley service in Patchogue.

they dined, and after that, jog on to Babylon, where they put up for the night. A most delightful way this was to take a jaunt: there was no hurry, no fuss and bustle about it. . . . No mode of traveling ever suited our taste better; it was the very acme of enjoyment.

The next morning you left Babylon just after daylight, which in the summer was itself worth living for, journeyed on to Patchogue, where you got your breakfast between nine and ten o'clock, with a good appetite for it, we warrant you. You would get no dinner this day, nor would you feel the want of it after your late and hearty breakfast, but travel along slowly and pleasantly until you reached the rural postoffice at Fire Place, standing on the edge of a wood. Here, if you have a taste for the beautiful in nature, you would walk down the garden to look at the trout stream filled with the speckled beauties. . . .

Shortly after sunset, you would stop for the night, the second one of your journey, at a place called Quagg or Quogue. Here you might, after supper on a moonlight night in the beginning of August, if you were so fortunate as to be there at such a time, as we were, cross the meadows with a guide, and walk down to the sea-beach, where, with no sound but the beating of the waves upon the shore, swelling in from a waste of waters of three thousand miles, and making the earth tremble under your feet, with scarcely a breath of air to move the hair upon your forehead, and nothing in sight for miles upon miles but the white sand hills glistening in the moonbeams on one side, and this world of waters on the other, you would more than at any other time realize the immensity of creation, and your own comparative insignificance.

The following morning you would breakfast at Southampton, after passing through a pine forest, in a portion of which, from the early hour and blindness of the road, you would probably require a guide to go ahead of the horses with a lighted lantern. . . . Sag Harbor would be reached in time for dinner, after which the mail stage would travel on to its final destination at East Hampton, arriving there just before sunset on Saturday afternoon, thus occupying nearly three days to traverse a distance of one hundred and ten miles. But most pleasant days they were, and no one has ever tried this mode of journeying through Long Island who had pleasure in view, who did not wish to try it again.

It is difficult to reconcile Furman's romantic description of travel through a pastoral Long Island of 1835 with the fact that the gritty Long Island Rail Road already had been in existence for a year and, within a decade, would be running smoky, clangorous trains through the length of the same island.

The history of that railroad is a story of vision and grubbiness, of public service and venality, of unfettered imagination and unbelievable stupidity. It is replete with contradictions and ironies. The most striking: while the LIRR was conceived—without regard for Long Islanders—as simply the best way to get from New York to Boston, it became the most heavily traveled local railroad in the world.

The LIRR was born out of the desire for a rail link between New York and Boston that would eliminate the need to lay track across the hills,

ABOVE
Despite contentions by some commuters, some Long Island Rail Road trains, such as this one from the nineteenth century, have been retired from service.

BELOW
Long Island Rail Road locomotive #92 at the Cross Islands Cycle Path, Medford, 1897.

This Long Island Rail Road train presents a dramatic silhouette against the horizon.

The Long Island Rail Road constructed most of its own stations, but this one at Shinnecock was a former post office.

valleys, and rivers of Connecticut. As an alternative to such a direct but expensive route, planners and promoters decided to build a 95-mile line from Brooklyn to Greenport, at the end of Long Island's North Fork, where passengers and goods would be ferried across Long Island Sound to Stonington, Connecticut, a few miles west of the Rhode Island border. There, they would continue the journey to Boston on the existing Norwich & Worcester Railroad.

The principal engineer of the Brooklyn & Jamaica Railroad Company, which was formed in 1832 and later would be leased by the Long Island for the venture, assured prospective investors of the scheme's feasibility. He reported in 1834:

The public mind is quite familiar with speeds of twenty to thirty miles per hour, and numerous locomotives in various parts of the country are wheeling daily over their respective tracks, at these rates, without a murmur of alarm or disapprobation. I think it not unreasonable, therefore, to assume five hours as a fair average trip from Brooklyn to Greenport. . . . The ferry will then occupy two hours, but by making the ferry boat a convenient hotel, with proper arrangements for rest and refreshments, this will prove only an agreeable and profitable relaxation. The remainder of the trip to Boston will be performed easily in four hours and a half, so that only eleven hours and a half will be required for the entire journey from New York or Brooklyn to Boston.

There were several factors that would burst this bubble of optimism. But first, the railroad had to be put into operation. And this required a route from Brooklyn to Greenport. Three choices were considered: along the North Shore, approximating the present Route 25A; a few miles further south, approximating the present Route 25; and still further south, through the flattest and most barren areas. The last was selected because its topography made it the cheapest and easiest for laying track. It now constitutes the LIRR's Main Line.

Through a combination of construction and the leasing and purchasing of other lines, the road was completed by 1844. There were to be only two stops en route—at Hardscrabble (Farmingdale) and Punk's Hole (Manorville)—to take on fuel (wood) and water. When a delay in the shipment of rails from England threatened to delay the highly publicized opening, the track crew at Punk's Hole, mostly Irish immigrants, successfully substituted heavy timbers topped with iron strips.

The inaugural run took place on July 27, 1844, and featured a special three-section train filled with railroad and civic officials, stockholders, celebrities, and newsmen. Spurred by the occasion, the train covered the ninety-five miles in three and one-half hours instead of the scheduled five. Horses and wagons crowded the site of the celebration, and boats of all description crammed Greenport harbor. According to one description, it clearly was a day to remember:

A large tent was spread north of the tracks. . . . Four tables one hundred feet long were spread under the tent, and dinner was served to the parties who had come on the train and a few villagers. The provisions were brought from New York, and included forty baskets of champagne and half a case of brandy. As a natural consequence, many of the excursionists were so stupidly inebriated that it was necessary to put them on board the cars. . . . The whole affair was discreditable in the extreme.

That inaugural celebration seems to have marked a high point in relations between the railroad and Long Island. In the months and years that followed, the main feeling apparently shared by the line and the community was tension. The woodburning locomotives sent sparks showering into the air to fall on fields, woodlands, and barns, setting them ablaze and causing considerable damage to farmers' property, produce, and livestock. The farmers fought back in court and outside of it. They tore up sections of track and set fire to depots. They fired at armed guards hired to ride "shotgun" on the locomotives. They even sawed through the timbers on the Peconic River bridge, sending an escort engine crashing into the water.

There were other concerns, too. In the Deer Park area, named for the herds that roamed wild, when locomotives accidentally ran down the animals, the engineers placed their antlers on the cowcatcher and joined the villagers in a venison feast at which the engineer with the most "trophies" was crowned. Near Yaphank, an old woman, angry because the railroad refused to recompense her for running over her cow, poured a bucket of soap over the rails at a grade before the arrival of each train. After numerous trains failed to negotiate the hill, railroad officials agreed to pay the woman twenty dollars. And there was moral indignation, too, at the LIRR's violation of the Sabbath by scheduling Sunday "Milk Train" excursions; they finally were withdrawn.

But the railroad's most egregious miscalculations surfaced in 1848, when competitors laid tracks through Connecticut on the "impassable" route LIRR officials had eschewed. The new line offered an "all-rail" connection between New York and Boston, putting the Long Island into bankruptcy in two years. At that point the folly of having placed its own rails "through the most sterile and desolate parts of the Island" became apparent. Forced to rely on Long Islanders alone for its revenues, the railroad found that it had placed its tracks miles from most of the villages it would have to serve.

Through acquisitions of local lines and extensions of its own, the Long Island Rail Road finally established a transportation network that provided service to virtually all who might wish to use it. The quality and cost of that service have been something else, however, and for much of its life, the LIRR, fairly or not, has been characterized more with ridicule than appreciation.

But toward the end of the nineteenth century, under the direction of Austin Corbin, one of America's most imaginative and successful entrepreneurs, the Long Island Rail Road provided a glimpse of what might have been. Corbin, a Harvard Law School graduate who made a reputation and a fortune in banking, real estate, shipping, and transportation, was appointed receiver during one of the LIRR's bouts with bankruptcy in 1880, lifted it out of its distress within a year, and became its most productive president. Through far-sighted and prudent management, Corbin was largely responsible for extending lines, improving service, pruning liabilities, and carrying out needed rehabilitation projects.

However remarkable Corbin's accomplishments were, they represented only a prelude to what he envisioned for the railroad and Long Island. For it was Corbin's dream to refashion transatlantic steamship travel by creating new terminals in each continent: Fort Pond Bay at Montauk would replace New York Harbor, and Milford Haven in Wales would replace Southampton or London. The proposal would have embarked and debarked passengers sooner than under the system then (and now) in use, and transported them by train, rather than ship, to their destinations in New York and London.

Corbin was no idle dreamer, and, although he had wealthy and influential friends, he clearly had taken on an incredible task. It would require the approval of two nations over all the entrenched business and political interests that had a stake in the existing route. But for one who had

Throughout the nineteenth century, agriculture was the most important business on Long Island. Glimpses of farm life during that era have been recaptured at the Old Bethpage Village Restoration and are seen in these photographs taken during different seasons, both indoors and out. They show a general view of the community (ABOVE); a farm kitchen (BELOW); (OVERLEAF ABOVE LEFT) hogs being butchered; (BELOW LEFT) a sled; (ABOVE RIGHT) Noon Inn from Layton Store; (BELOW RIGHT) plowing a field.

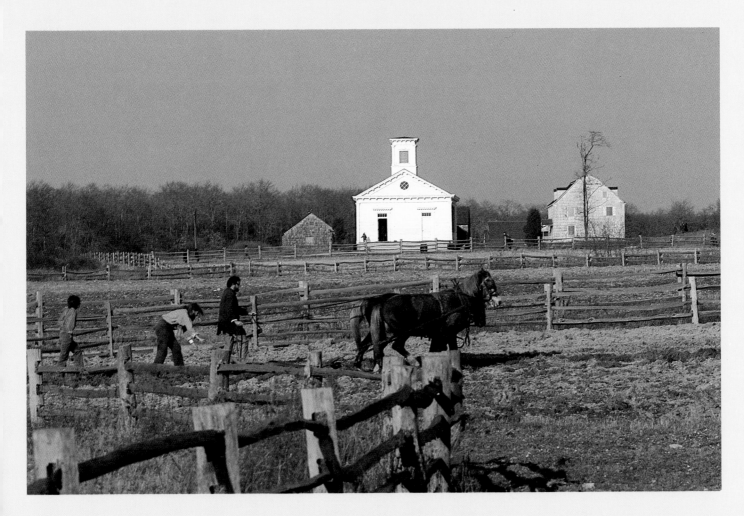

resurrected the Long Island Rail Road, nothing was too awesome or intimidating.

From scores of engineers, accountants, lawyers, surveyors, maritime authorities, financiers, and political operatives, Corbin and his associates devised a plan that would cut about eight and one-half hours off travel time between London and New York in good weather, and possibly days in foul. If that seems relatively incidental in terms of a weeklong journey, Corbin had many other rationales. The most important benefit, he argued, was the elimination of the dangerous and time-consuming approach to New York Harbor past Sandy Hook, which was crowded with ships and in need of dredging.

The project did get off the ground, although it was not destined to fly. Legislation was introduced in Congress and the government ordered a survey. But Army engineers twice turned down the plan and legislative attempts were rebuffed. Still, Corbin went ahead. He extended the existing line from Bridgehampton to Montauk in 1895, and this commitment revived Washington's interest. The next year, with a new bill in the hopper, Corbin pressed his case in the halls and committee rooms of Congress. Just when passage seemed possible, Corbin was killed in an accident, and his associates, while sharing his hopes, lacked his charisma and zeal. The project died with its creator.

Long Island Rail Road President Austin Corbin's dream of a time-saving transatlantic rail-ship route would have given passengers from Europe a look at the Montauk Lighthouse rather than the Statue of Liberty.

Ironically, Corbin's faith in Fort Pond Bay and the new trackage were justified just two years later when they were utilized in the emergency assembly of port facilities and an Army camp necessitated by the Spanish-American War. Rapid transportation between Brooklyn and the tip of the South Fork aided quick construction of Camp Wikoff at Montauk, where yellow fever victims were hospitalized and quarantined.

If it was Corbin's fate to live in a time and among people not yet ready to share his vision, so it was with Josiah Warren. An inventor, reformer, and philosopher, Warren founded the utopian community of Modern Times in what is now Brentwood. For a decade, around the Civil War era, it provided a sanctuary for what Warren and some one hundred followers described as "individual sovereignty" and what headline writers of the day called "free love." Based on the following account by a sympathetic visitor, the Reverend Moncure Daniel Conway, the headline writers seem to have been on the right track:

The arrangements of marriage were, of course, left entirely to the men and women themselves. They could be married formally or otherwise, live in the same or separate houses, and have their relations known or unknown to the rest of the village. The relation could be dissolved at pleasure without any formulae. Certain customs had grown out of this absence of marriage laws. Secrecy was very general, and it was not considered polite to inquire who might be the father of a newborn child, or who the husband or wife of any individual might be. Those who stood in the relation of husband or wife wore upon the finger a

red thread; and so long as that badge was visible the person was understood to be married. If it disappeared, the marriage was at an end.

But Warren's philosophy transcended interpersonal and social relationships. A disciple of Welsh reformer Robert Dale Owen, who established the New Harmony commune in Indiana, Warren put his radical economic theories into practice in his Long Island community through a system in which labor was compensated with labor, not cash. For example, at the Modern Times "Time Store," the price of an item was based on its cost to the merchant, an amount which residents paid with money, plus the salesperson's time spent in serving them, an amount which they could pay with their own labor. The labor cost was calculated by turning on a large clock when service was begun and shutting it off when the transaction was completed.

For a while, everything went like clockwork and so idyllic was Modern Times, said Conway, that it could be found "either by railway or by rainbow." It was described as the most ideal and utopian of all communities in the United States, if not the world, because there was no dishonesty, disorder, or crime, and thus no policemen, prisoners, judges, or jail.

But there was no industry, either, and without a real economic base, together with the depression of 1857, the community began to come apart. Too many residents left to seek work outside, and by the end of the Civil War even Warren had to admit the failure of his experiment to reshape society.

This was a time when America began to look to itself for inspiration: to find it in ordinary people and commonplace activities. In art, nobody better exemplified this search than a homegrown Long Islander named William Sidney Mount, who was born in Setauket in 1807 and spent most of his life in Stony Brook. Roaming the roads of Suffolk, he produced a significant number of paintings depicting colorful scenes of rural life, most of which are displayed at The Museums at Stony Brook. Proudly unconventional, in his later years Mount created a studio in an enclosed, glass-roofed, horse-drawn wagon and traveled the countryside behind it, playing his violin.

In literature, a poet from Long Island became America's voice, describing its beauty, its strength, and its possibilities. Walt Whitman was born in 1819 in a West Hills house (now 246 Walt Whitman Road, Huntington Station) built by his father, moved to Brooklyn as a child, then back to Long Island as a young man to teach, report, publish (*The Long-Islander*, at age nineteen), edit (*Brooklyn Daily Eagle*, at age twenty-six), and write poetry that gained him worldwide recognition.

The most famous and universal American poet, Whitman drew heavily on his Long Island experience. In his reminiscences, *Specimen Days*, he recalled how "the successive growth stages of my infancy, childhood, youth and manhood were all pass'd on Long Island, which I sometimes

Among Long Island's most famous sons was artist William Sidney Mount (ABOVE), *who popularized the rural life of the Setauket-Stony Brook area in paintings such as the typical buildings of* Long Island Farmhouses (OPPOSITE ABOVE), *and* The Sportsman's Last Visit (OPPOSITE BELOW).

While Walt Whitman is regarded as a universal poet, Long Islanders still claim him as their own. Born in this house in West Hills, Huntington Station, he won worldwide acclaim but never forgot the "isle of the salty shore and breeze and brine."

feel as if I had incorporated. I roam'd, as boy and man, and have lived in nearly all parts, from Brooklyn to Montauk point."

He described his Paumanok (its aboriginal name) from the ocean to the Sound, through all the seasons: "The shores of this bay, winter and summer, and my doings there in early life, are woven all through L. of G." (*Leaves of Grass*, his most celebrated work).

And his recollections might have been written yesterday, not a century ago:

Sail'd more than once around Shelter island, and down to Montauk—spent many an hour on Turtle hill by the old light-house, on the extreme point, looking out over the ceaseless roll of the Atlantic. I used to like to go down there and fraternize with the blue-fishers, or the annual squads of sea-bass takers. . . . The soothing rustle of the waves, and the saline smell—boyhood's times, the clam-digging, barefoot, and with trousers roll'd up—hauling down the creek—the perfume of the sedge-meadows—the hay-boat, and the chowder and fishing excursions. . . .

He remained connected to his roots through his poetry many years after moving away, and wrote two poems about Long Island in 1888, as he approached his seventies, that are part of *Leaves of Grass*:

Paumanok

Sea-beauty! stretch'd and basking!
One side thy inland ocean laving, broad, with copious commerce,
    steamers, sails,
And one the Atlantic's wind caressing, fierce or gentle—mighty hulls
    dark-gliding in the distance.
Isle of sweet brooks of drinking-water—healthy air and soil!
Isle of the salty shore and breeze and brine!

From Montauk Point

I stand as on some mighty eagle's beak,
Eastward the sea absorbing, viewing, (nothing but sea and sky,)
The tossing waves, the foam, the ships in the distance,
The wild unrest, the snowy, curling caps—that inbound urge
    and urge of waves,
Seeking the shores forever.

One of the earliest creative Long Islanders, Whitman probably remains one of its most prominent offspring. For him, Long Island provided inspiration; for many of those who followed to his "fish-shape Paumanok"—painters and poets, writers and dancers, architects and musicians—it was Whitman, too, who inspired.

CHAPTER FIVE

City and Suburb

Pumpkins, which abounded on Long Island before the arrival of European settlers, still constitute one of the area's major crops. This field of glowing orange beauties is in Calverton.

The birth of the modern suburban phenomenon that has transformed the look and life of America can be pinpointed. It happened in 1823. In that year, in the *Long Island Star*, Hezekiah B. Pierpont, after having bought up Brooklyn Heights properties for two decades, advertised lots for sale "as a place of residence [providing] all the advantages of the country with most of the conveniences of the city." Anticipating the possibilities of commutation, he pointed out that "gentlemen whose business or profession require their daily attendance in the city, cannot better, or with less expense, secure the health and comfort of their families."

What Pierpont counted on was the safety and predictability of ferry service between Brooklyn and Manhattan following the success of Robert Fulton's *Clermont*, which had steamed up the Hudson River in 1807. Before the invention of the steamboat, winds, currents, and weather had rendered sailboats both dangerous and unreliable as ferries, making the East River a temporarily effective moat separating the populations on both its banks.

With the introduction of steam ferry service in 1814 and the growth of New York City, Brooklyn's future became irreversible: it would develop as an adjunct to Manhattan, but would itself be a city. By 1810, New York State, with a population approaching one million, and New York City, with a tenth of that, supplanted Pennsylvania and Philadelphia as the nation's most populous state and city. Long Island, with fewer than fifty thousand people, had about half the population of New York City, most of it concentrated in Suffolk County (21,000) and Queens County (19,000). Kings County (8,300), with the exception of its riverside communities of Brooklyn and Bushwick, remained largely rural as the towns of New Utrecht, Gravesend, Flatbush, and Flatlands grew imperceptibly.

The completion of the Erie Canal in 1825, which created a water route from the Atlantic to the Great Lakes, made New York's port a magnet for foreign and coastal trade, and, in turn, stimulated the development in Brooklyn of such shipping-related businesses as ropemaking and warehousing. This, together with an influx of European immigrants and freed black slaves, was reflected in an explosive population growth that saw the community doubling in size with each decade between 1800 and 1860. In 1834, over the opposition of New Yorkers who feared competition, Brooklyn officially became a city.

By the middle of the nineteenth century, about half of Brooklyn's expanding population was foreign-born: Irish, escaping the potato famine; Germans, fleeing political persecution following the vain Revolution of 1848; and English, drawn by the lure of economic opportunity. Later, they would be joined by vast numbers of southern and eastern Europeans, particularly Italians and Jews, to form one of the country's most diverse populations—a catalog of the nationalities that comprised America's fabled melting pot.

With each wave of newcomers, ethnic institutions were formed to ease the transition by retaining elements of the past. Brooklyn became the City of Churches, providing houses of worship for Dutch Reformed, Episcopalians, Presbyterians, Roman Catholics, and Baptists. Occasionally institutions, including the churches, became caught up in the changing times: when the interracial congregation of the Sands Street Methodist Church became anxious over the proslavery attitudes of its pastor, black parishioners withdrew and formed the High Street African Wesleyan Methodist Episcopal Church.

By mid-century, growing concern over slavery began to intrude on the national drive toward material progress. Divisions over the issue began to appear between North and South, between Democrats and Whigs, between industrialists and farmers. Long Island did not escape the controversy.

Kings County, in particular, had a tradition of involvement with slavery, stemming from its settlement by the Dutch and its agricultural character. (In New York State, the Dutch were the most likely ethnic group to own slaves, and slavery was more compatible with farming than with other pursuits.) By 1790, black slaves constituted about one-third of the Kings' population, and the county's slaveholders were slow to release their charges voluntarily, although they complied with the state's mandated emancipation in 1827.

Among the most committed abolitionists was the Reverend Henry Ward Beecher, who used his pulpit at Brooklyn's Plymouth Church to condemn slavery as immoral and anti-Christian. "As a Christian nation, we have a right to interfere in this matter," he said in 1850. "We are not to cease our exertions until the victory is accomplished. I will not, as one man, cease my endeavors or hold my peace unless the vile monster is driven from the land."

Arrayed against the abolitionists was the area's Democratic Party apparatus, especially its newspapers, which courted the foreign-born vote by appeals to racial prejudice, and by stirring up unjustified fears that if freed, Southern slaves would travel North to take away their jobs. The election of 1860 marked not only the presidential candidacy of Abraham Lincoln, the first Republican, but a referendum in New York State to give equal voting rights to "people of color" by eliminating the requirement that they own property, a qualification not demanded of whites.

It was a bitter campaign in which a Democratic assemblyman from Brooklyn railed that "the proposition to put negroes on a footing of political equality with the white men is repugnant to the sense of the American people." The fact that the suffrage amendment could have added a maximum of only 1,250 black voters in Brooklyn did not deter the Democratic press from publishing white-supremacist, rabble-rousing editorials and articles. And they apparently carried some weight. Although Lincoln won the state, including Suffolk, he was soundly defeated in Brooklyn. The amendment lost statewide and was rejected by overwhelming margins on Long Island.

Lincoln was not a popular president; even within Republican ranks he was attacked as moving too slowly to end slavery. But the secession of the South and the firing on Fort Sumter in 1861 united Northerners, regardless of party. After the fighting broke out, the defense of the Union became paramount and there was strong support for its position in Brooklyn, as well as throughout Long Island.

RIGHT

Long Islanders who fought in the Civil War, such as young Henry W. Prince of Southold, found themselves in New York's 127th Monitors Regiment. And many, such as Prince and these eight Oysterponds (now Orient) volunteers photographed in Alexandria, Virginia, in 1863, were in Company H. Three of these eight were killed during the next two years.

BELOW

One of the few monuments to Civil War veterans on Long Island is in Roslyn Cemetery, Roslyn.

At the beginning of the Civil War, there was no military draft; communities were expected to recruit through appeals to patriotism, aided by bonuses of fifty or one hundred dollars. In 1862, the President issued a call for 300,000 volunteers for three years, and the 127th New York Monitors Regiment was organized. The press leaped at the opportunity to participate, from the sidelines, as the following editorial in the *Suffolk Times* makes apparent:

The patriotism of our township has finally been aroused. Her sons are flocking to the recruiting offices, leaving the plowshare buried in the furrow, and the stately corn fields to some other harvester. . . . The good old town of Southold desires her sons to be volunteers for the army, and many of our best men have already rallied around the standard, "The Stars and Stripes." A company is now being formed. All who can carry a musket should now come forward. Let no man skulk from his duty!

Like tens of thousands of farmboys, Henry W. Prince of Southold buried his plowshare at the age of twenty-two to sign up with the 127th. His fears and hopes and frustrations, as expressed in his letters home, no doubt convey many of the feelings of fellow Yanks:

A soldier's life is very uncertain. If not wasted away with disease he may die in an instant by the bullet. I have been wonderfully blest since I became a soldier. Have enjoyed good health, have been able to march through cold &

heat & never failed to keep with the Regt. I feel that I have much to be thankful for, & I rejoice that I am able to defend our country. I trust I may see the day when Rebels will be reconciled to the Union & the best of Governments. I am sorry that we have so many Traitors at the North & even on L.I. They are a curse to the country. Talk about the negro being a curse to the country, I think it is the rebellious white man. I am glad the black man can fight for the downfall of Slavery.

In time, young Prince lost some of his earlier partisanship and ruminated about more universal concerns:

I want once more to get in good society. It will seem more like living. Soldiering is a rough coarse life, calculated to corrupt good morals & harden a man's heart. We have no female society to influence us for the better, but are surrounded by coarse vulgar companions. I could not feel contented if I were not a soldier trying to aid the government. As it is I strive to be a man & a son you will not be ashamed to own. Should I live to return probably I shall be coarse & unrefined but I trust I will be as good at Heart as when I left you & I hope better. I think I will never be ashamed of coarse clothes or plain food. We as a nation have been living too fast. Too much pride & care too much for dress. Methinks I have learned a lesson since I became a soldier.

Appeals to patriotism are invariably invoked by the old and answered by the young. Winslow Homer portrayed this youthful Union volunteer in 1864.

Sensitivity to the opinions on the home front is characteristic of soldiers, as Prince made clear:

The "Suffolk Times" has a good deal to say about the Southold Boys & our drunken officers. I wish he would say less, for the officers are mad, & a good many I think dislike Co. H on acct. of that piece in "Times." I believe it true that a number of our officers take too much whiskey, but to say all do is saying too much & to say they are beastly intoxicated is saying too much. Whiskey is a curse & it ought not to be allowed in the Army except for medicinal purposes. As the law now is, officers can get it but enlisted men cannot.

As the war began to wind down, Prince began to consider the future. Farming, particularly on Long Island, seemed to have lost much of its appeal:

I would be pleased to live on or near the homestead, as long as I live where it is convenient & for my interest, but you know Mother, Father has worked hard to make a living on a farm that he bought cheap. Now what chance is there for a poor man at present prices for land & manure on L.I.? I believe I have a little ambition. I desire to do a little good in this world & do something more than make just enough to eat & to clothe me. A hermit can do that. I don't desire riches, for happiness is not found in them.

Prince rose to the rank of sergeant during his three years' service, survived, and returned to Southold, where he farmed, clerked, became a salesman, a merchant, and a banker. He married, had three children, prospered, and served his church and his town as well as having served his country. He was eighty-five years old when he died in 1925.

The Civil War had a mixed impact on Long Island. While siphoning off manpower, it triggered a demand for industrial and agricultural productivity. Orders for armaments, uniforms, ships, equipment, and foodstuffs stimulated the economy, particularly in areas close to New York City. At war's end, the western Island was ready to embark on the period of industrialization and urbanization that would soon embrace the reunified nation.

The most striking change took place in Brooklyn, where the spillover of commerce from Manhattan created a burst of business activity. But differences in size and in land costs between the two adjacent cities gave each its own character. Companies began establishing their executive and sales offices in Manhattan, but put their factories in Brooklyn. Passenger ships tied up at Manhattan piers, but cargo ships docked on the Brooklyn waterfront. Manhattan put on a white collar; Brooklyn's was blue.

The growth of industry in Brooklyn following the Civil War created a new and faster tempo. However, public transportation was slow, crawling along not quite at a snail's, but at a horse's pace. Conveyances called horsecars, drawn by two-horse teams over tracks on scheduled runs, transported as many as forty passengers to destinations as remote as Flatbush and Gravesend. While a major improvement over walking, the horsecars were, like the ferry system, inadequate to the fast-growing demands for speed and mobility.

This dissatisfaction set the stage for what was to become the most significant and dramatic transportation advance of the period, and one that would have far-reaching effects not only on the development and interdependence of Manhattan and Brooklyn, but on the relationship of New York and Long Island, of city and suburb. It was the construction of the Brooklyn Bridge and elevated railways.

A bridge across the East River had been discussed for many years before the State Legislature, responding to proposals from builder John A. Roebling, approved the project in 1867 and put him in charge. The concept was staggering: it was to be the world's longest suspension bridge, requiring the embedding of immense pillars in the bottom of a swift-flowing tidal waterway. Nothing like this had ever before been attempted on such a scale. It called for originality of design, of materials, of construction techniques; it represented the culmination of human efforts to conquer nature for the betterment of society.

It was completed in 1883 by Roebling's son, Washington, who took over upon his father's death from tetanus, and who himself suffered the bends while at work and was crippled for life. The achievement stirred the imagination of America—of poets, as well as engineers, merchants, and public officials.

In dedication ceremonies a century ago, the bridge was hailed as:

without a rival among the wonders of human skill. It is not the work of any one man or of any one age. It is the result of the study of the experience and of the knowledge of many men in many ages. It is not merely a creation; it is a growth. It stands before us today as the sum and epitome of human knowledge; as the very heir of the ages; as the latest glory of centuries of patient observation, profound study, and accumulated skill, gained, step by step, in the never-ending struggle of man to subdue the forces of Nature to his control and use.

From a practical standpoint, the bridge vastly increased the speed and volume of traffic between Brooklyn and Manhattan, created new commercial districts at both ends, and, most important to the development of Long Island, made commuting, and thus suburban living, feasible. The utility of the Brooklyn Bridge was enhanced considerably within a few years by the erection in 1885 of elevated railways—Els—that enabled steam, and soon electric, engines to transport passengers above the crowded streets at many times former speeds. The network of elevated railways, with connections to the cable cars that crossed the bridge, opened vast portions of Brooklyn to residential development and established a precedent for the eventual suburbanization of most of Long Island.

The Brooklyn Bridge, completed in 1883, changed the future of both Long Island and New York. It was regarded as the embodiment of man's ability to control nature.

Swelled both by immigration from Europe and migration from the surrounding area, Long Island's population passed the million mark in the 1890 census, with the overwhelming bulk of it—more than 80 percent —concentrated in Kings County, and virtually all of that in Brooklyn. If further proof were needed that Brooklyn had achieved urban status, it came in 1895 with the Great Trolley Strike. As the trolley owners employed strikebreakers to keep the cars rolling, and more than 6,000 transit workers fought to shut them down, violence erupted and the state militia had to bring it to an end.

One remnant of that bitter dispute, in which at least two workers were shot to death by militia troops, was the rallying song of the embattled strikers:

> Remember we are working men
>   and honestly we toil,
> And gentlemen, remember we
>   were born on Brooklyn soil,
> Nor can the pampered millionaires
>   the spirit in us break,
> The fame of our fair city
>   is clearly now at stake.

GLEN COVE STARCH WORKS,
GLEN COVE, L.I.

Although much of Long Island retained its rural character well after the Civil War, industries, such as this starch works in Glen Cove, began to appear.

The "fair city" was not to exist much longer in that form. Pressure to create Greater New York by consolidating adjacent areas with Manhattan had been building for several decades. So far as Brooklyn was concerned, the need for consolidation became compelling by the 1890s when it could no longer borrow money because it had reached the debt limit imposed by the State Constitution. But political considerations delayed what was a highly complicated process in itself. Of particular concern to Brooklyn's Democratic machine was the effect that the change might have on its power. However, legislative approval was finally obtained, and on January 1, 1898, Brooklyn, the Bronx, Richmond, and Manhattan, together with the western third of Queens, all became boroughs of New York City.

The remainder of Queens—the towns of Hempstead, North Hempstead, and Oyster Bay—was still part of Queens, but not part of New York City. This absurdity was remedied with their embodiment as Nassau County on January 1, 1899.

The tremendous growth of western Long Island following the Civil War had only a limited counterpart in the eastern portion. While some communities flourished by filling a particular need, such as shipbuilding in the case of Port Jefferson, or the huge Duryea Starch Company in Glen Cove, most of Suffolk and the part of Queens that would become Nassau retained a largely rural, agricultural flavor.

The Long Island Rail Road, frustrated in its plan to link New York with Boston, had on its hands hundreds of miles of track, locomotives, and freight and passenger cars. What it did not have was enough business; so it set about to create a demand for its services, and in the process, played a major role in the development of the Island.

There was, for example, milk. In the latter half of the nineteenth century, Long Island dairy farmers, benefiting from inadequate methods of refrigeration that kept upstate producers out of the picture, did a booming business by supplying milk quickly to the vast New York City market. Herds in the mid-Island area around Hicksville and Syosset made Westbury the most important milk-shipping station on the LIRR.

Further east, farmers clamored for the latest labor-saving equipment to increase production and get their vegetables on Brooklyn and Manhattan dinner tables. Potatoes, strawberries, cauliflower, cabbages, asparagus, cucumbers, and brussels sprouts were introduced, accepted, and cultivated with great success. To expedite service, the railroad introduced "piggybacking" decades before most major lines. This involved transporting farmers' wagons on flatbed cars, which then were ferried across the East River from the Long Island City terminal to markets in Manhattan.

While some Long Islanders were farming the land, others were reaping a harvest from the sea. The quiet bays along the Island's North and South Shores and between the flukes of its fishtail had been rich with oysters, scallops, and clams before the arrival of Europeans. The settlers had learned from the Indians to gather and prepare shellfish, and

While technology has altered considerably the look of farming on Long Island, produce has changed little during the past century. Still seen in Suffolk are potato pickers

passed along their techniques and appetites to succeeding generations. Consequently, after a few centuries of exploitation, the oyster beds were becoming depleted. By 1824, Blue Point, near Patchogue on Great South Bay, a community so renowned for oysters it had given them its name, was described as a "former" source of shellfish in an official report.

Local baymen, using rowboats and toothed tongs, were eking out only a meager living until the introduction of the dredge enabled them to scoop up huge quantities of oysters and to move on to other and deeper areas. But by 1870, the public beds in Great South Bay had become so exhausted that a law was passed barring the use of dredges there. It was only then that the baymen realized the threat of well-financed "planters," who for more than a decade had been systematically "seeding" embryo oysters on privately leased beds, property that was not affected by the anti-dredging ordinance. Unable to compete effectively, the baymen unsuccessfully sought legislation to restrict the planters. This led to feuding over territorial rights, pirating, and even some gunplay before the century ran out. The baymen lost, but the oyster industry grew, and the LIRR was used extensively, along with boats and wagons, to transport the shellfish to New York.

Another prime Long Island industry that developed during the nineteenth century and relied heavily on the railroad was duck farming. The familiar white fowl that wind up on menus almost everywhere as Long

Island duckling got their start in 1873 from a clipper ship that had visited the Orient. Called Pekin ducks after their origin in China, they were brought to New York and made their first Long Island appearance on farms in the Speonk-Eastport area. The industry grew rapidly around Moriches Bay, and at its height was providing about 60 percent of the ducks raised in the United States. The ducks, which could look forward to a life span of about three months, were hatched in incubators, moved to brooders and then outdoors until reaching a weight of five or six pounds. Many of the Suffolk farms added railroad sidings to expedite shipping to markets in the city and further west.

The railroad also made a concerted bid for passenger business by promoting Long Island, initially as a summer playground and eventually as a place to live year-round. For the wealthy, the miles of beaches for bathing, woods for hunting, and fields for horseback riding had long made the Island an accessible recreational paradise. Those with money always had been able to leave the city easily to take advantage of the ocean off Brooklyn, at Coney Island and Manhattan Beach, and off Queens, at the Rockaways. Great hotels there and out in Suffolk at such places as Shelter Island and Babylon catered to ever-larger numbers of the affluent who were eager to flee the increasing waves of immigrants crowding the city.

In time, middle-class New Yorkers followed that route eastward, finding accommodations in private homes, which became "guest," "tourist," or "boarding" houses during the summer. After taking the train to Bridgehampton or Bellport, vacationers were met at the station by coaches, which conveyed them to a place of green lawns, shady trees, comfortable verandas and hammocks, and bountiful meals, all for well under ten dollars a week.

ABOVE
The S. S. Sagamore of the Montauk Steamboat Company carried visitors from New York to vacation spots on Long Island.

SEASON 1905
MANHANSET HOUSE
MANHANSET MANOR
SHELTER ISLAND   NEW YORK

LEFT
The Manhanset House on Shelter Island attracted thousands of vacationers at the turn of the century with advertisements such as this one.

BELOW
Before refrigeration, grand hotels such as the Manhanset House depended on ice cutters at work on a Shelter Island pond. Cakes of ice would be stored in icehouses throughout the summer.

OPPOSITE
Many of Long Island's grandest hotels were vulnerable to fire, such as the blaze that is destroying Shelter Island's Manhanset House in this 1910 photograph.

While the fascination that Long Island seemed to hold for many New York City residents was being exploited piecemeal by hotel and boarding-house operators, an immigrant boy, who had pooled energy, imagination, and a small inheritance into one of the nation's greatest fortunes, decided to do it wholesale. He was Alexander Turney Stewart and he had amassed his wealth as a Manhattan merchant. On the advice of architect John Kellum, in 1869 he bought more than 7,000 acres of the vast Hempstead Plains at fifty-five dollars an acre with the intention of building his own community. It was to be his, literally: he would build roads, homes, shops, a hotel, even a branch railroad line and station. And he would keep them all; everything, including the houses, would be for rental only. It was to be called Garden City.

Some of the initial reaction was ebullient. "Hempstead Plain, hitherto a desert, will be made to bloom as a rose," trilled *Harper's Weekly*. "It will be the most beautiful suburb in the vicinity of New York. God speed the undertaking." The project began to pall when Kellum, who had designed the community and was directing its construction, died. Work went on, but interest in renting Garden City's houses was limited; prospective residents wanted to own their own homes. When Stewart died in 1876 and failed to provide in his will for further development of the village, the entire project almost collapsed. However, it managed to stay alive until changes in concept and operation, including the establishment of individual ownership brought about by the Garden City Company, stimulated new interest.

Along with Stewart Avenue, the most enduring tribute to Garden City's creator is the magnificent Gothic Cathedral of the Incarnation, seat of the Episcopal Diocese of Long Island, which was built in 1885 as a memorial to him by his widow. Its 220-foot spire towers over the pink sandstone structure on Cathedral Avenue and has served as a landmark to generations of Long Islanders.

To an elite group of New Yorkers, no public inducement to live on Long Island was necessary. Summer visits had confirmed the area's appeal for them, and they began purchasing vast wooded tracts on the near North Shore and even as far distant as Babylon for what would become some of the most palatial estates in America. Soon manor houses, modeled after those belonging to English royalty, began to rise behind high stone walls. Grand residences set back along miles of landscaped approaches were augmented by guest cottages, carriage houses, barns, stables, greenhouses, pools, ponds, and fountains.

The names of the owners comprised a list of corporate, financial, and social leaders equivalent to, if not indistinguishable from, the "Four

Hundred" of New York's high society: Vanderbilt, Grace, Mackay, Morgan, Hitchcock, Clark, Belmont, Whitney, Phipps, Guggenheim, Bostwick, Swope, Guest, Pratt, Harriman, Roosevelt, Kahn, Tiffany, and more.

Descriptions of their lifestyles seemed to outrival fiction. George C. Taylor, an eccentric millionaire who chose a bayside site in the Town of Islip for his country house, stocked his 1,500-acre estate with deer and game birds for sport, and maintained a herd of elk and peacocks for show. Clarence Mackay bought 650 acres on Harbor Hill, near Roslyn, to house his summer residence—the reproduction of a French chateau that reportedly cost five million dollars to build and landscape.

Along with their great wealth and stature, many of these men developed special interests in art, music, and sports. One of the most prominent was August Belmont, an ardent horseman, who indulged his avocation on 1,100 acres of what is now known as Belmont Lake State Park near Babylon. About half the property was cultivated to feed the horses and other livestock, another sizable portion was used for grazing and paddocks, and there were accommodations for fifty stable boys, as well as a building large enough for winter workouts. A 24-room mansion served as the country home; there was a 40-acre lake with a boathouse, and some thirty other buildings that housed squash courts, game rooms, carriages, ice, and dogs.

This early movement to the suburbs and beyond coincided with a new mood that had captured the American imagination during the close of the nineteenth century. It was a recognition of adult fun, of the value of play, of the importance of recreation in stimulating the spirit and revitalizing the body. It was the first time that the nation had permitted itself to discard the Puritan ethic sufficiently to enjoy leisure without guilt. And it was to lead to a new appreciation of Long Island.

CHAPTER SIX

Fun and Games

By the time America began learning how to play after the Civil War, Long Island was already one of its most popular playgrounds. Horse racing, the national pastime before baseball, had been a part of Long Island life for two centuries, appearing almost as early as the first colonists. Long Island's climate and geography lent itself to hunting, fishing, sailing, ice skating, and bathing. Its affluent sportsmen were quick to adopt imports, such as polo, golf, tennis, and later, motorcar and airplane racing. Its masses learned to cycle, took their bikes on Long Island Rail Road excursions, and marveled at the exploits of "Mile-A-Minute" Murphy.

It was as early as 1665 when the royal governor of New York, Richard Nicolls, became the figurative sire of today's two-dollar bettors by ordering the creation of a racetrack called New Market on the Hempstead Plains "for encouraging the bettering of the breed of horses, which, through great neglect, has been impaired." The sport proved an immediate success, and the approximate location of the track has been maintained through modern times with Aqueduct, Belmont, Jamaica, and Roosevelt Raceway.

By 1670, when Daniel Denton's *A Brief Description of New York* was published, racing and Long Island were as inseparable as stablemates. "Toward the middle of Long Island," he wrote, "lyeth a plain 16 miles long and 4 broad, where you will find neither stick nor stone to hinder the horses' heels, or endanger them in their races. Once a year the best horses in the island are brought hither to try their swiftness, and the swiftest rewarded with a silver cup, two being annually procured for that purpose."

In those days, and until after the Civil War, races involved only two horses. These match races usually consisted of 4-mile-long heats, the winner being the first horse to win twice. Since the heats were run consecutively on the same day, they represented an enormous test of endurance. They also created intense competition and, for the time, vast wagering. The competition and the wagering were increased further by regional rivalries, principally pitting horses from the North against those from the South.

The first of these North-South confrontations took place in 1823 at the Union Course, near Jamaica, between American Eclipse, an unde-

As long as there is bright sunshine to mellow the bite of a winter's day, there will be ice skaters on Long Island. The popularity of the sport has not been diminished by time, and skaters still whirl and spin on St. John's Pond by St. John's Episcopal Church in Cold Spring Harbor (ABOVE), Coindre Hall Park in Huntington (LEFT), and Centerport Mill Pond in Centerport (RIGHT).

feated 9-year-old New York stallion, and 3-year-old Sir Henry, owned by a southern syndicate. Interest was so high that a newspaper compared it to the presidential "balloting in the House of Representatives for Jefferson and Burr." The gate was estimated at 60,000 persons—extraordinary, considering that the combined population of New York City and Long Island was less than 220,000—and more than $200,000 changed hands when American Eclipse won the third and decisive heat by a length.

In 1845, when what proved to be the last regional rivalry was held on Long Island, a crowd of 70,000, "a larger collection of people than we have ever before seen at the Union Course," according to the *New York Tribune*, saw the South's Peytona beat the North's Fashion in "one of the most exciting races the North has ever known. . . ."

At the turn of the century, tracks were operating all over the metropolitan New York area. In Brooklyn alone, there was racing at Gravesend, Coney Island, and Sheepshead Bay, where Futurity Day was a celebrated event. Long Island's place in American racing was fixed in 1905 with the opening of Belmont Park on a 650-acre site in Elmont that included a railroad station, two thousand stalls, and a grandstand for nine thousand fans. Built by the Westchester Racing Association, under the leadership of August Belmont Jr. and William C. Whitney, it took two years to construct and featured clockwise, English-style racing at fall and spring meetings. Despite a disastrous fire that destroyed the grandstand and other buildings in 1917, racing continued, and a rebuilt facility, worthy of the appellation "Beautiful Belmont," was unveiled in time for legendary Man o' War to win the Belmont Stakes in 1920. That race, the final third of the Triple Crown, is regarded by many experts as

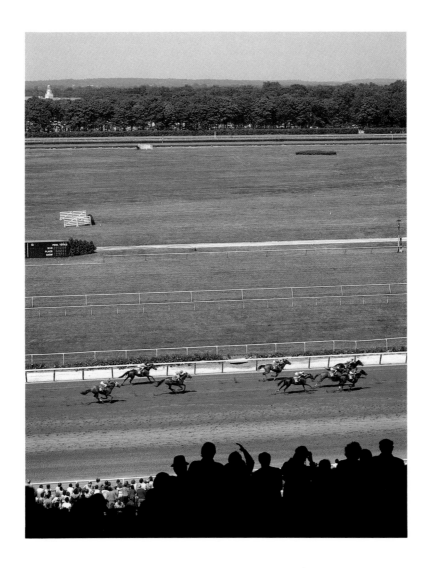

the most important test of 3-year-olds because of its mile and one-half distance.

Harness racing, in which horses pulled drivers in carts called sulkies, was popular, too, and a track was laid out in 1825 near the Union Course in what was then called Centreville and is now Rego Park. It was there, in 1847, that Albany Girl tried to run one hundred miles in ten hours, only to collapse after nine and one-half, just two and one-half miles short of her heartbreaking goal. Harness racing was the feature of the county fairs held annually at alternate sites in Hempstead, Jamaica, or Flushing until 1866, when a permanent location was fixed at Mineola. But the top trotters, such as Lady Suffolk, who broke the two-and-one-half-minute mile in 1845, disdained the fairs for more profitable circuits. It was almost a century later, during World War II, that Freeport attorney George Morton Levy put trotting into the big time and big money by presenting it under the lights at Roosevelt Raceway.

LEFT
Harness racing got an early start on Long Island at a track in what is now Rego Park. Later, it became a popular feature at the annual Mineola Fair, where this photograph was taken in 1936. The area now houses the State Supreme Court complex.

BELOW
Time has not altered the expressions of winning, losing, and anxious bettors, as confirmed by this early twentieth-century Colliers *magazine cover called "Opening of the Racing Season." It was done in 1905 by Charles Dana Gibson, famous for his "Gibson Girl" paintings.*

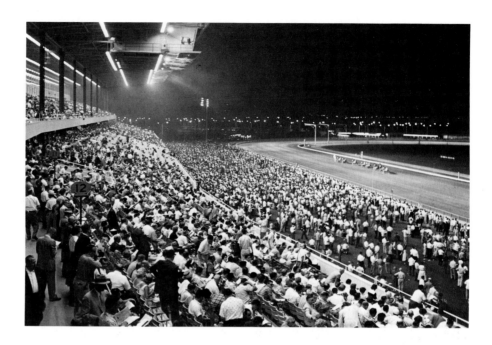

Freeport attorney George Morton Levy envisioned the possibilities of harness racing during the World War II era, and by 1957, as this picture at Roosevelt Raceway, Westbury, indicates, it had become a major sport.

These were the sports that drew the crowds in those times, but admission was rarely charged, and so the costs were borne by a few men of wealth. They were borne easily, it should be added, in those pre-income-tax days when people of means seemed to despair of ways to reduce their fortunes. Another way they found was yachting, and Long Island, with its sheltered coves, deep harbors, and broad Sound, provided all the opportunity they needed.

Estates were built along the Sound, where its ample but protected waters could not only be viewed but used. Docks and boathouses were as *de rigueur* as carriage houses and parlor maids. "Any man who has to ask about the annual upkeep of a yacht," John Pierpont Morgan reportedly asserted, "can't afford one." Morgan, clearly, never had to ask. And his superyacht *Corsair* was the figurative flagship of the sleek armada that luxuriated in Long Island Sound. The yachting crowd required watering holes as well as water, and so yacht clubs were created: the Seawanhaka Corinthian in Oyster Bay, and the New York Yacht Club's Station 10 in Glen Cove.

In the decades that followed the onset of the twentieth century, yachting became boating, and the size of the vessels, along with the net worth of their owners, shrank drastically. As the sport was democratized, sailboat racing became more widespread, power boating more popular, and yacht clubs catering to both preferences proliferated until membership in more than one hundred became available to Long Island's boat people.

Another sport that began with the rich—but stayed with them—was polo. It reached Long Island just before the turn of the century, having been introduced to Newport's high society a few years earlier. But Long Island's horsey set adopted polo—and vice versa—so that the game

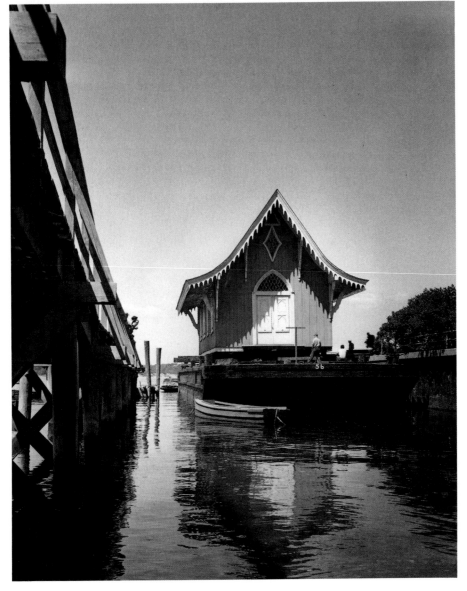

One of the oldest and most unusual looking yacht clubs in America was the New York Yacht Club's Station 10 in Glen Cove. In 1950 it was loaded on a barge for towing across the Sound to Mystic Seaport, Connecticut.

soon became inextricably associated with the place. The Meadow Brook Club in Westbury, and the Rockaway Hunting Club in Cedarhurst were the places in which to play and to watch, as young men from exclusive families traded goals and good sportsmanship in a world of their own making.

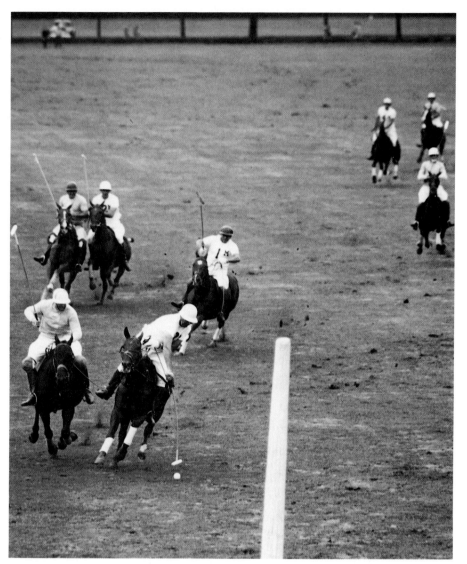

Polo got its American start at Newport around the turn of the twentieth century, but it soon became a fixture on Long Island. This match was at the Meadow Brook Club in Westbury.

OVERLEAF
*The waters off both shores of Long Island were a natural for yachting and boating of all kinds. Sail and power pleasure boats followed in the wake of the millionaires' superyachts and made Long Island Sound and the South Shore Bays a sailor's haven. A summer's day will find sailboats racing (*ABOVE*), sailboats at the Centerport Yacht Club on Northport Harbor (*BELOW LEFT*), pleasure boats under an early morning sun in Northport Harbor (*ABOVE RIGHT*), and power boats passing through the Shinnecock Canal (*BELOW RIGHT*).*

Polo reached its zenith in the 1920s, and names such as Hitchcock, Guest, Bostwick, Iglehart, and Whitney dominated the sport and the headlines when the United States and Great Britain vied for the Westchester Cup, an event that brought the Prince of Wales to Long Island in 1924. The difference between performances, even the players agreed, was not so much athletic as equine. Good polo ponies were eagerly sought, although sometimes, as reportedly was the case with Winston Guest, they came as wedding gifts.

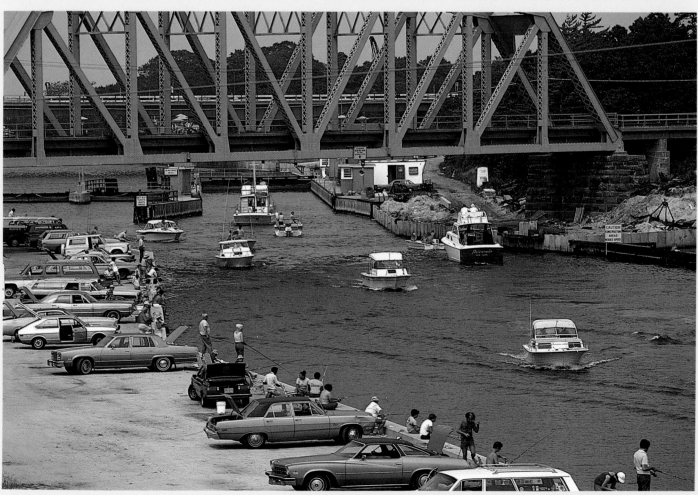

A similar sport, in the sense that its reputation far exceeded the number of its participants, was fox hunting. Scathingly described by Oscar Wilde as "the unspeakable in full pursuit of the uneatable," fox hunting achieved prominence on Long Island among those who prized everything English. Beginning in 1877, pink-coated hunters galloped behind the hounds on North Shore estates, or, later, at the Meadow Brook, Rockaway Hunting, and Queens County Clubs. But progress ended fox hunting in its traditional style (with live foxes) when the construction of divided highways permitted routes to the foxes that were denied to their pursuers. Some hunts are still conducted, but the hounds chase the trail of an anise-scented bag, a change that might meet with Wilde's approval.

For the well-to-do who preferred hunting from less precarious perches, Long Island's location on the Atlantic migratory flyway provided ducks and geese in sky-darkening numbers. Like birds of a feather, wealthy hunters flocked together in exclusive organizations such as the Long Island Shooting Club, which traced its origins to the antebellum days as "an association of gentlemen who had enjoyed trapshooting in England." A decade or two later, in 1858, August Belmont formed the Suffolk Club at Carmans River in South Haven, and in 1865 the Southside Sportsmen's Club was organized on the Connetquot River at West Sayville by a group that included William K. Vanderbilt, W. Bayard Cutting, Pierre Lorillard, Charles Tiffany, and John G. Heckscher.

On the North Shore, the Brooklyn Gun Club, which in 1893 changed its name to the Wyandanch Club in honor of the Indian sachem, provided happy hunting grounds along the Nissequogue River in Smithtown for New Yorkers who could "skip off the evening train, have the morning shoot of the following day and return for business the day after." Other New Yorkers traveled out to Captree Island in the Great South Bay, where members at the Wa-Wa-Yanda Club, mostly politicians, pursued not only game but "the cultivation of friendly feeling, social enjoyment and rational amusement."

Further east, a socially correct group created the Flanders Club at the turn of the century to shoot ducks in Peconic Bay. Their cherished isolation was interrupted in 1920 by the protests of the Long Island Fish and Game Protective Association, which contended that a new state law benefited "clubs of wealthy sportsmen rather than the residents of Long Island and those who are unable to join exclusive organizations." The concern of local hunters was a statute banning from Peconic Bay battery shooting, an extremely effective method of hunting amid decoys from a heavily weighted boat floating very low in the water. They charged discrimination on the grounds that the Flanders and Southside members used improper techniques on their private ponds, such as baiting with corn, while the public was prevented from utilizing equivalent gambits, such as shooting from batteries.

Eventually, protective game laws were enacted prohibiting these and other tricks, although the clubs generally maintained that they had practiced conservationist policies. In time, too, most of the clubs' holdings were taken over by the county or state to become public recreational

OPPOSITE ABOVE
One of Long Island's early appeals to wealthy New Yorkers was its abundance of wild waterfowl. These ducks are enjoying life on a Smithtown pond.

The exclusive hunting clubs of bygone days have become public parks. Connetquot River State Park in West Sayville was once the Southside Sportsmen's Club (OPPOSITE LEFT), and the Canada geese feeding on the lawn of the Nissequogue River State Park in Smithtown could not have done so without risking their lives when it was the Wyandanch Club (OPPOSITE RIGHT).

Duck hunters setting decoys at Patchogue in 1900 (ABOVE). Decoy-making requires skill, patience, and artistry, as these examples from the nineteenth-century collection at The Museums at Stony Brook demonstrate. William Bowman executed Yellowlegs and a Hudsonian Curlew (BELOW LEFT), while the Black-bellied Plovers were the work of Obediah Verity (BELOW RIGHT).

areas. Flanders is in Sears Bellows County Park, Suffolk is in Southaven County Park, Southside is in the Connetquot River State Park, and Wyandanch is in the Nissequogue River State Park.

Fishing, of course, had long been identified with Long Island; first in terms of survival, then for its commercial value. Now it, too, became a sport in both salty ocean and Sound, and in freshwater rivers and ponds as well.

Golf came to America through Long Island, but its passage was so inconspicuous, according to Samuel Parrish, one of its sponsors, that

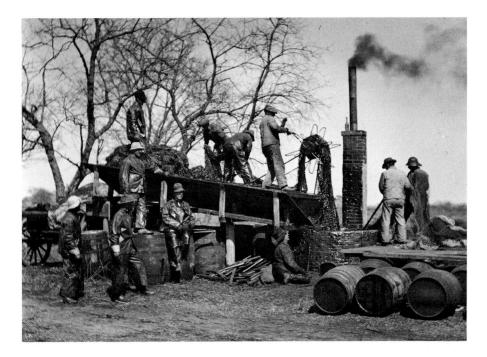

almost two years passed before it was discovered. It was 1891 when a Scottish-Canadian golfer named Willie Dunn was brought to Long Island by Edward S. Mead and William K. Vanderbilt Jr., who had watched him play in France. Dunn designed a twelve-hole course at Shinnecock Hills, which resembled the terrain of Scotland where the sport already was popular. Using 150 Indians from the Shinnecock reservation, the course was built almost entirely by hand, and some Indian burial mounds were left intact to serve as bunkers.

Incorporated the same year, Shinnecock Hills became the first golf club in Long Island and one of the first in America. Its clubhouse, whose white-columned porches overlook both the Atlantic Ocean and Peconic Bay, was the work of the noted architect Stanford White and opened in 1892. Site of the 1986 United States Open, Shinnecock Hills had hosted the second U.S. Open in 1896. Parrish recalled:

In the beginning, so quietly and unobtrusively was golf introduced into this country that it was some time after the Shinnecock Clubhouse had been built and the game was being played in the "Hills" in all its red-coated, white-collared and monogrammed brass-buttoned splendor (a picturesque but for many years past an abandoned feature of the early days of golf, I still have the buttons; the moths the coat) before the game became sufficiently well known to attract the slightest notice from the newspapers....

From 1893 on, however, a veritable craze swept over the country, and the Shinnecock Club became the Mecca for golfing pilgrims from all sections of the country, seeking information before starting in to construct their own links.

Although professional golf tournaments have followed the sun through the southwest in recent times to permit year-round competition, Long Island has hosted some important matches through the years, including three other Opens, one of which Bobby Jones won in 1923 at the Inwood Country Club, and another Gene Sarazen captured in 1932 at Flushing's Fresh Meadow Country Club. The Island's generally flat or rolling topography has lent itself to the sport, and some one hundred public and

ABOVE

The stately Shinnecock Hills Golf Club, designed by famed architect Stanford White, became one of America's first when it opened in 1892. It is the site of the 1986 United States Open.

BELOW

Long Island has been the scene of many notable golf tournaments, such as this one at Deepdale Golf Club, Lake Success, in the 1950s. Player in the center wearing black is champion Sam Snead.

private courses—many with lengthy weekend waiting times—testify to its popularity.

American tennis and Forest Hills were virtually synonymous for more than a half-century until the nation's most prestigious tournament, the United States Open, was moved in 1978 to another Long Island location at Flushing Meadows. Despite this association, Long Island was neither the place where tennis made its American debut, nor the location of the first National Championships. The game first was played on Staten Island, having been brought there from Bermuda in the late nineteenth century by an American tourist named Mary Outerbridge, and Newport was the scene of the first National Championships in 1881.

The Championships, strictly amateur at that time, arrived at Forest Hills in 1915, when the West Side Tennis Club moved to the suburbs from the West Side of Manhattan. Eight years later, with the club's name still intact, the 14,000-seat stadium and familiar Tudor-style clubhouse, which served so long as the focus of tennis in America, were constructed. It was there on the grass at center court that the champions of earlier eras—Bill Tilden, Don Budge, Jack Kramer, Helen Wills, and Alice Marble—served and stroked their way to fame, if not fortune.

While all sports no doubt provide some benefit, a few transcend their purpose to affect society in unintended and, occasionally, significant ways. One such was the homely sport of bicycling. Like many other nineteenth-century innovations, the bicycle came to America from England. The year was 1876 and the bicycle, a strange device with a huge front wheel, was looked on largely as a novelty. But in 1880, an organization was formed that would provide the leadership and political pressure to begin transforming a haphazard arrangement of rough country roads into an integrated system of smooth highways. Named the League of American Wheelmen and called the L.A.W., it exerted a profound influence on New York State and, particularly, Long Island.

With the development toward the end of the century of the "safety" bicycle and the pneumatic tire, replacing the awkward earlier style with its uncomfortable hard rubber, cycling gained tremendous popularity and gave city dwellers a personal interest in road improvement. The effect of the L.A.W. was considerable, as it pointed out in 1895:

Within the last year our State Division has distributed ten thousand illustrated pamphlets, describing the best methods of making and maintaining country roads; it has secured the passage of a law for the erection of guide boards at country road crossings; it has aided in the raising of funds for the construction of the cycle path from Prospect Park to Coney Island (the nation's first); it has successfully opposed the obnoxious bills introduced in the legislature at Albany for the unfair curtailment of wheelmen's rights on the public highways and streets . . . and has issued five thousand tour books for the use of wheelmen and horsemen describing the most delightful and popular tours in the United States.

OPPOSITE ABOVE
A trout fisherman in hip boots tests his skill and luck in the Connetquot River.

OPPOSITE BELOW
Golfers playing into the fall can appreciate the colors of autumn leaves at Bethpage State Park.

BELOW
Helen Wills, who dominated American women's tennis during the Twenties, winning the national singles championship seven times in nine years, is about to serve on an East Hampton court in this 1928 Childe Hassam work.

The impact of this campaign soon became apparent as Kings and Queens Counties embarked on an extensive macadam road-building project, while Suffolk licensed cyclists and used the revenues to construct bicycle paths from Smithtown to Port Jefferson, Riverhead to Greenport, and Amityville to Amagansett, with a network of interconnecting lanes.

By 1898, the craze had so taken hold that the Long Island Rail Road was running specially equipped cars solely to transport bicycles. It also published a guide called *Cyclists' Paradise*, extolling the beauties of the Island and offering tips on the best ways for wheelmen (and wheelwomen) to appreciate them. For example:

Every condition on Long Island is favorable to the cyclist. The record-breaking scorcher finds in the south shore road an ideal century course, smooth, level and almost a straight stretch; the road rider who enjoys hill-climbing with the long compensating coasts, finds these conditions fulfilled on the north shore with a hard roadbed eliminating danger and increasing exhilaration, while the tourist finds on each of the three main roads points of great beauty. The side runs are full of agreeable surprises, with a marvelous diversity of topography.

The brochure contained a map of Long Island's cycling paths and even included an advertising message from the phone company, which contended that "no Paradise for cyclists or any one else would nowadays be complete without telephone service."

Weekends saw thousands of bike riders fanning out on the LIRR's

specials to explore the Island's villages, beaches, woods, and waterways, and to spend their evenings at approved restaurants, their nights at approved hotels, and their money at both. The railroad's promotional talents reached their peak in July, 1899, when it constructed a mile-long wooden runway between the tracks near Farmingdale to test the claim of a cyclist named Charles M. Murphy that he could pedal a bike at the speed of sixty miles per hour. Accompanied by reams of publicity and thousands of spectators, the stunt involved racing behind a timed LIRR train. In just 57.8 seconds, "Mile-A-Minute" Murphy became Long Island's latest hero.

Another sport that produced far-reaching consequences for Long Island and for the nation was auto racing. At the opening of the twentieth century, Europe was far ahead of the United States in the design and construction of cars, particularly high-performance racing vehicles. The new sport was very popular among wealthy spirited young men, who justified their involvement on the grounds that it stimulated serious interest in the development of automobiles and roads.

One of the most involved was William K. Vanderbilt Jr., who raced his Mercedes on both sides of the Atlantic and was determined to upgrade American automobiling. In 1904, he proposed a 300-mile race for international competitors on public roads between Lake Success and Jericho, offering the winner the Vanderbilt Cup—thirty pounds of silver designed by Louis Comfort Tiffany.

The announcement was not received with universal enthusiasm. Many local residents and farmers were concerned about the effect of 100-mile-per-hour speeds on North Hempstead and Jericho Turnpikes, as well as the connecting back roads that would constitute the track. But the event was approved by the Nassau County Board of Supervisors and the Automobile Club of America, and when it was held later that year, the French entry won, a feat that was duplicated in 1905.

By 1906, the race had become established, attracting more than 200,000 fans from throughout the country, many of whom jammed not only the shoulders but the roadways themselves, and two of whom were killed and scores narrowly missed by the careening racers. As a result, the Automobile Club of America withdrew its support for future racing on Long Island's public roads.

In response, Vanderbilt and his associates decided to construct a private, landscaped, 50-mile roadway from Queens deep into Suffolk, not only to accommodate the Vanderbilt Cup Race, but to be used as a public toll road and to test automobile products. The financial Panic of 1907 stalled investors, delaying the project and canceling that year's race. But enough of the world's first concrete highway was completed during the next twelve months to permit incorporating a 9-mile stretch in the 1908 competition. Mounting casualties on the public road portion of the Vanderbilt Cup races over the next few years brought mounting

ABOVE
The Tiffany-designed Vanderbilt Cup Trophy drew worldwide interest to motorcar racing on Long Island.

OPPOSITE ABOVE AND BELOW
The spectacular Vanderbilt Cup Race in 1906 had spectators on telephone poles and roofs watching the cars from Europe and America skid along country roads. When spectators jamming roadways became casualties, the races had to be abandoned.

pressure to end the "slaughter," and the event was abandoned after the 1910 meet.

But the Long Island Motor Parkway lived on. Eventually forty-eight miles long, the first high-speed, limited-access, paved roadway stretched from Horace Harding Boulevard in Queens to Lake Ronkonkoma; it included sixty-five bridges and twelve toll lodges, cost millions of dollars to build, and was used by 150,000 cars annually during the 1920s. The toll, a steep two dollars in 1908, dropped to one dollar and a half in 1912, one dollar in 1917, and forty cents in 1933.

The development of Long Island's extensive public parkway system by Robert Moses made the narrow 22-foot-wide toll road obsolete and, unable to sell it or pay its taxes, Vanderbilt finally turned it over to the counties for $500 and cancellation of a $90,000 tax bill. Surviving is a 13-mile section between Dix Hills and Lake Ronkonkoma; four toll lodges, originally designed by architect John Russell Pope after French country homes and subsequently converted to private use; and fading memories.

As some early twentieth-century daredevils were making history on Long Island's roads, others were creating it above. For while the distinction of being aviation's birthplace belongs to Kitty Hawk, North Carolina, the site of the Wright Brothers' first flight in 1903, the Island can authoritatively claim to be aviation's cradle. Within six years of the Wrights' feats the skies over the Hempstead Plains became the scene of rickety aircraft, fearless pilots, and broken records. Pioneer airman Glenn H. Curtiss got the Long Island aviation industry off the ground on July 17, 1909, when he flew his Golden Flier for fifty-eight minutes over Mineola and Westbury to win $10,000 and the Scientific American Trophy for the first flight of at least twenty-five kilometers (fifteen and one-half miles) by an American. Valentine W. Smith of Far Rockaway recalled:

Contemporary motorists relive the past in their antique auto on a drive along a tree-lined road in Remsenburg.

This airplane looked like an enlarged box kite. The driver's seat projected out in front and the engine with the propellor, set to push forward, was at the back. It was an ideal morning with no wind stirring, and at sunrise Mr. Curtiss wheeled the machine to the east side of the Fair Grounds, and went up a little higher than the tree tops, and circled around for half an hour [sic]. At the end of that time the plane fairly collapsed from the excessive strain, but he had remained in the air just long enough to win the prize of $10,000.

The New York Aeronautic Society had commissioned Curtiss to build and fly that plane, and during the next few weeks one of its members, Charles F. Willard, learned enough under intensive instructions from Curtiss to complete the first "extensive" cross-country flight on August 13: twelve miles from Mineola to Hicksville, where he made a safe forced landing. By year's end, the first airplane built on Long Island, a biplane designed by Frank Van Anden of Islip, and the first monoplane, built by Dr. Henry W. Waldon, were test-flown satisfactorily at Mineola.

These feats and dozens more dazzled crowds who rode, walked, or drove out to the flat, treeless Plains in the ensuing months to view the exploits of the newest American craze—the flying machine. There was a new record for flying passengers (three), the first pilot to cross Long

By covering twenty-five kilometers (fifteen and one-half miles) over the Hempstead Plains in his Golden Flier on July 17, 1909, aviation pioneer Glenn H. Curtiss won ten thousand dollars and put Long Island in the flying business.

Jimmy Doolittle, who was to win fame in World War II for leading a daring carrier-based bombing raid on Tokyo, was a lieutenant when he was photographed with this early Curtiss seaplane; he won the Schneider Cup in it.

Women were not far behind in taking up flying. Harriet Quimby, drama editor of Leslie's Weekly, *was an early aviatrix who learned to fly at the Moisant Aviation School in Garden City.*

Island Sound (Clifford B. Harmon), the first attempt at aerial gunnery (Infantry Lieutenant Jacob Fickel fired two bullets into a ground target from a plane flown by Curtiss), the first air-to-ground radio transmission ("Another chapter in aerial achievement is recorded in the sending of this wireless message from an airplane in flight"), and the first American woman pilot (Dr. Bessica Faith Raiche).

The sport, as it then seemed to be, was so new and the accomplishments so rapid that rarely a week went by without some record being set or broken. And it was all done with such flair. As many as ten thousand Long Islanders would visit the flying fields on weekends to "toot their automobile horns vigorously whenever a daring airman would make even the briefest flight," remembered one spectator. "If a flier bobbed his plane up and down in the air in daredevil fashion, the crowd would applaud vigorously."

Long Island's role in aviation received worldwide acknowledgment in the fall of 1910, when the International Aerial Tournament was held at the Belmont Park Racetrack. The Wright Brothers and Curtiss attended but did not compete, as aviators from England and France challenged those from the United States in a variety of events that included tests of speed, distance, and altitude. The weeklong meet attracted as many as seventy-five thousand daily spectators—at two dollars a ticket—to watch "The Heavenly Twins," Arch Hoxsey and Ralph Johnston, vie for the $5,000 altitude prize by spiraling into the sky until their gas tanks ran dry, their engines sputtered, and they were forced to glide their Wright biplanes to earth. Johnston won and set a new record of more than nine thousand feet.

A year later, the next International Aerial Tournament also was held on Long Island, this time at the Nassau Boulevard Airfield in Garden City. It was noteworthy for two events that foreshadowed the different directions in which air power would affect the twentieth century. One involved pilot Earl Ovington, who made the first air mail delivery by flying six miles and dropping a bag of 640 letters and 1,280 postcards near the Mineola Post Office. The other involved Lieutenants Thomas D. Milling and Henry H. Arnold, who, using the only two planes owned by the Army, spotted troops concealed in the Long Island woods to demonstrate the military potential of aircraft.

It was 1911, and the time for playing games was beginning to run out. America had learned to have fun. But soon there would be other lessons to master. In three years World War I would erupt; in five years the Hempstead Plains would become the site of a military flight training school at Hazelhurst, later Roosevelt Field; in six years an adjacent Army base called Mitchel Field would be created; and in thirty years Lieutenant Henry H. (Hap) Arnold would command the U.S. Army Air Corps during World War II.

CHAPTER SEVEN

Over Here,

OPPOSITE ABOVE

The nation's one-time summer White House and home of Long Island's only President, Sagamore Hill, the residence of Theodore Roosevelt, looks down on a wintry Oyster Bay from its proud promontory. The 23-room Victorian mansion was conceived by young Roosevelt and his first wife, Alice, who died before it was completed.

OPPOSITE BELOW

The setting sun bathes Oyster Bay Cove in pastels as it did when the Roosevelt family hiked and picknicked on its shores. An advocate of "the strenuous life," Roosevelt joined his children in rugged sports and play.

The Hempstead Plains, which would figure prominently as the site of military bases in both world wars, was introduced to the sounds of pounding boots and bugle calls long before the beginning of the twentieth century. It had heard officers' commands and soldiers' curses during the American Revolution, the War of 1812, the Civil War, and, as the location of Camp Black, during the Spanish-American War, as well. Besides Camp Black near Mineola, Long Island's involvement in that brief conflict in 1898 was notable chiefly for Camp Wikoff, at Montauk, and Theodore Roosevelt, whose extraordinary participation as organizer of the volunteer "Rough Riders" cavalry regiment made history and headlines.

Roosevelt, the most famous Long Islander and the only one to become President, enjoyed a long and pleasant association with the area, having first visited it as a child. After being graduated from Harvard in 1880, he bought 155 rolling, wooded acres in Oyster Bay, kept 95 of them, and began construction of a 23-room house to be called Sagamore Hill. The name was taken from Roosevelt's boyhood days, when he was told by a local bayman that the hills once had been occupied by a Matinecock Indian sagamore, or chief.

The rambling Victorian house, typical of the period and yet exceptional like its owner, was conceived by Roosevelt, designed by the New York firm of Lamb and Rich, and built for him and his young bride, Alice Lee. "I wished a big piazza," he said, "where we could sit in rocking chairs and look at the sunset; a library with a shallow bay window looking south, the parlor or drawing room occupying all the western end of the lower floor." But Alice never watched a sunset from the piazza. She died at the age of twenty-two, before the home's completion, following the birth of their first child, Alice.

Roosevelt's mother died the same day, and it was three years before he occupied Sagamore Hill with his second wife, a childhood playmate named Edith Carow. The intervening time, which was to alter markedly the direction of his life, was spent ranching in the rugged Badlands of the Dakota Territory, where the 25-year-old widower sought distraction from his grief.

During the next decade, Roosevelt, a Republican who had been elected to the New York State Assembly at the age of twenty-three, unsuccessfully ran for mayor of New York City and served as a U.S. Civil Service commissioner, New York City police commissioner, and Assistant Secretary of the Navy before resigning in 1898 to form the celebrated "Rough Riders." That group of dashing mounted riflemen was an offshoot of Roosevelt's Dakota days, having been recruited largely from among Western plainsmen and cowboys. The regiment was a great source of pride to him and he wrote a friend that "you would enjoy seeing the mounted drill, for the way these men have got their wild half-broken horses in order is something marvelous."

The Rough Riders, like the other American troops in the Spanish-American War, were afflicted more by disease than by the enemy. Attacked principally by yellow fever, they were unable to combat it in the sultry Cuban climate amid deplorable sanitary conditions. To isolate the disease victims from the general population, it was decided to set up a military hospital at Montauk Point. The development of Fort Pond Bay and extension of the Long Island Rail Road as part of Austin Corbin's grandiose transatlantic port scheme facilitated rapid construction of Camp Wikoff, as the base was named, and enabled troop and hospital ships to dock there rather than going through New York or Brooklyn.

The ships began unloading ailing soldiers even before the camp was ready, as Roosevelt noted:

COL. ROOSEVELT

Tells the story of
THE ROUGH RIDERS
in Scribner's Magazine. It begins in January and will run for six months, with many illustrations from photographs taken in the field.

JANUARY
SCRIBNER'S
NOW READY   PRICE 25 CENTS

For the first few days there was great confusion and some want, even after we got to Montauk the men in the hospital suffered from lack of almost everything, even cots. But after the first few days we were well cared for and had abundance of all we needed, except that on several occasions there was shortage of food for the horses, which I would have regarded as even more serious than a shortage for the men, had it not been that we were about to be disbanded.

Once organized, Camp Wikoff satisfactorily handled 25,000 troops, losing only 126, and Roosevelt approved heartily of its operation. "On the whole," he said, "the month we spent in Montauk before we disbanded was very pleasant."

For Roosevelt at least, the ensuing months were pleasanter still, as his combat adventures made a lasting impact on his political career. His charisma, daring, shrewd sense of publicity, and luck combined, within three years of the war's conclusion, to make him a national hero, governor of New York, Vice-President of the United States, and, on the assassination of William McKinley, the nation's youngest President at the age of forty-two.

But this dizzying rise to prominence did not dilute Roosevelt's love of Sagamore Hill nor his desire to spend time there. It became his summer White House and the place he most prized for cavorting with his six children and numerous young relatives. No affairs of state could divert the President from those commitments. One afternoon when he was discussing tariff rates there with a visiting statesman, a group of boys appeared, announcing: "Cousin Theodore, it's after four."

"By Jove," he said, "so it is. Why didn't you call me sooner? One of

ABOVE
Judging from this photograph, Roosevelt had little difficulty in assuming a distinguished-looking stance when his career soared after the "Rough Riders" exploits. He became governor of New York, Vice-President, and, on William McKinley's assassination, the nation's youngest President at forty-two.

LEFT
A devoted husband and father, Roosevelt resisted allowing the affairs of state to interfere with his family role. From left to right: Quentin, the President, T. R. Jr., Archie, Alice, Kermit, Mrs. Roosevelt (Edith Kermit Carow), and Ethel.

you boys get my rifle." Then, turning to his distinguished visitor, he explained: "I must ask you to excuse me. We'll finish this talk some other time. I promised the boys I'd go shooting with them at four o'clock and I never keep boys waiting."

His proclaimed dedication to the "strenuous life" was carried out at the Oyster Bay estate by riding, hiking, chopping wood, and rowing. Often, these activities were combined during outings at adjacent Lloyd Neck, where, after a 6-mile row, the President and his young chums would hike to a campsite at which he would prepare dinner. Later, around the campfire, he would relate tales from his rich outdoor experiences out West and in Cuba, or recall classics from literature and history.

"I love all these children and I have great fun with them," he wrote. "And I am touched by the way in which they feel that I am their special friend, champion and companion."

Sagamore Hill proved to be the ideal home for a man dedicated to nature and to accumulating the mementos of global excursions. Inside the spacious home, every aspect of Roosevelt's amazingly active life found a niche, from statues of cowboys to elephant tusks and moose heads; few residences ever so revealed their occupants' interests.

Despite his wide travels, Roosevelt was a familiar figure on Long Island, particularly during presidential campaigns. When he was denied the Republican nomination for a third term in 1912 and formed the Bull Moose Party to advance his progressive platform, he got support from his Nassau neighbors, many of them leading Republicans.

"We joined the movement only because we felt Teddy had been cheated at the Republican Convention and many of us idolized the man," explained Sanford Davison, one of the founders of a local "Roosevelt Progressive" club. Although he ran strongly for a third-party candidate, Roosevelt failed to carry his home county in that election, losing in Nassau to Democrat Woodrow Wilson by about 500 votes, while outdistancing incumbent President William Howard Taft, the Republican nominee.

"T. R." continued to live at Sagamore Hill throughout his rich 60-year life, and was buried beneath a simple headstone in nearby Young's Cemetery, Oyster Bay Cove, in 1919.

The vast, flat, treeless prairie called Hempstead Plains, which early settlers found so desirable as a pasture for cattle and sheep, was deemed ideal by early airmen for a flying field, and, whenever war loomed, received top priority as a military training base. Thus, after the Spanish-American War, the tents of Camp Black were replaced by the aircraft hangars of fledgling aviators—until 1917, when the United States declared war on Germany and the Army converted a year-old National Guard base there to Hazelhurst Field.

Named for Leighton W. Hazelhurst, the first noncommissioned officer killed in an aviation accident, the Mineola facility served as the site of a training school for Army and Marine Corps pilots under the tutelage of pioneer fliers called the "Early Birds." Among the trainees was Quentin Roosevelt, youngest of Teddy Roosevelt's four sons, and, according to his father, "the brightest of the children." A few months before the armistice ending World War I, Quentin was killed in a combat mission over German lines. "He died," his father said, "as the heroes of old died; as brave and fearless men must die when a great cause calls." In Quentin's honor, Hazelhurst was renamed Roosevelt Field in 1918.

Just to the south of Hazelhurst-Roosevelt, across Stewart Avenue, that same year an installation called Aviation Field No. 2 became Mitchel Field, after former New York City mayor John Purroy Mitchel, who was killed during aviation training in Louisiana. Used as a training center then, it would achieve its greatest service as an air base during World War II.

In the late summer of 1917, adjacent to the western edge of Mitchel Field, an Army base named for Brigadier General Albert L. Mills was echoing simultaneously to the sound of carpenters' hammers and marching feet. The feet belonged to National Guardsmen from every state in the Union, who were called up to form the 42nd (Rainbow) Division, the first American infantry troops to be sent overseas in World War I. Supervised by Douglas MacArthur, who was to gain fame as the Pacific commander of U.S. forces during World War II and as United Nations commander during the Korean War, these doughboys were virtually adopted by the villagers of Garden City, Hempstead, and Mineola before spearheading American Expeditionary Force assaults in France.

As the troops poured in, local residents and merchants were overwhelmed. "Literally thousands of men thronged the streets," recalled Hempstead historian Felix Reifschneider, "sat on the roofs of trolleys and perched on the steps and bumpers, and packed the taxis besides. Every home made the boys welcome and hospitality was unbounded. Eight new restaurants were built and new stores sprang into existence on all sides."

In Garden City, which was almost totally residential, volunteers pressed to do their bit in entertaining the young soldiers. "One of the biggest jobs at Camp Mills," *The Evening Sun* pointed out in September, 1917, "is the care of visitors. It is estimated that fifty thousand people visited the Rainbow Division last Sunday. The whole problem has been taken out of the hands of the military authorities and handed over to a group of women in the area."

As many as 30,000 doughboys jammed Camp Mills before they began shipping out in December. There were tensions and barroom brawls, but there was affection, too. And after the war, veterans of the Rainbow Division erected a monument to their 2,950 dead and 13,290 wounded in a small park in Garden City on Clinton Road, south of the LIRR tracks.

OPPOSITE ABOVE LEFT
Tent life at Camp Mills, 1917.

OPPOSITE ABOVE RIGHT
A review of the 42nd (Rainbow) Division at Camp Mills, Garden City, 1917.

OPPOSITE MIDDLE LEFT
Camp Upton at Yaphank was the first stop for tens of thousands of draftees during World War I. It was constructed in less than three months during the summer of 1917 and received soldiers by early September.

OPPOSITE MIDDLE RIGHT
Doughboys learned how to fight with bayonets as part of their basic training at Camp Upton. The 77th Division trained here before going overseas.

OPPOSITE BELOW LEFT
Relaxing after a vigorous day of drilling, World War I soldiers listen to a phonograph at the Long Island Army camp.

OPPOSITE BELOW RIGHT
Its proximity to New York City made Camp Upton a popular place to be stationed. On weekends, doughboys often would be met by their wives for some fun in the city.

After the November 1918 armistice, Camp Mills became a major demobilization center, as troops from Europe and many parts of the United States passed through its gates for almost a year en route to civilian status. Among those who did not was Lieutenant William Bradford Turner, an infantryman from Garden City whose heroism won a posthumous Congressional Medal of Honor, one of only ninety-five awarded to soldiers during the entire war.

During the hectic months after America's entry into World War I in the spring of 1917, a Suffolk counterpart to the scene at Camp Mills was being enacted near Yaphank, on a tract now housing the Brookhaven National Laboratory. There, on more than 10,000 acres of flat, swampy, mosquito-ridden land, as many as 15,000 skilled workers and laborers struggled through the hot, wet summer to build barracks for 37,000 soldiers, mostly draftees, who would never forget Camp Upton.

The construction of that Army installation, named after a Civil War general named Emory Upton, was a marvel of logistics and supervision since almost all the workmen had to be fed and housed on the isolated site. Special railroad sidings were laid to facilitate the shipment of lumber and other materials, and a large number of private detectives had to be hired to cope with the influx of crooks who swarmed over the camp. Criminality was so rampant that a U.S. District Court was established at the base while it was being built and it tried more than 1,000 cases in about two months.

Troops began arriving little more than two months after construction started, and by the end of the following month, 30,000 men were being trained at Camp Upton. Among them were members of the 77th Infantry Division, which, composed largely of Long Islanders and New Yorkers, was soon to fight valiantly in the crucial Argonne Forest Battle in France.

One of Upton's more famous trainees was songwriter Irving Berlin, who put together a revue called *Yip! Yip! Yaphank!* that entertained not only his buddies but Broadway audiences. Berlin's experience at the camp led him to compose "Oh, How I Hate to Get Up in the Morning," which survived the war to become a popular song.

Because of its isolation, providing social activities for the soldiers became a major problem. One solution was to let them out, and a shuttle train was run from the camp to the Long Island Rail Road's main line so the men could spend their weekends in New York. It also enabled thousands of relatives and friends to ride in from the city and other parts of the Island for Saturday and Sunday visits.

Like Camp Mills, Upton was converted to demobilization after the war, and tens of thousands of overseas veterans were processed there before returning to their homes. Processed there, too, were thousands of mules that the Army had decided to dispose of at auction. After being sold, they were lassoed, had their government brands removed, were herded into railroad cars, and dispatched to their new owners.

World War I brought varied appeals for enlistments through recruiting posters for the U.S. Navy by artist Howard Chandler Christy.

During the World War II production of This Is the Army, *Irving Berlin sits on a cot and reminisces about his World War I experiences at Camp Upton.*

In 1921, everything else at Camp Upton was auctioned off: barracks, stables, hospitals, warehouses, garages, engines, heating and refrigerating plants, electric substations, telegraph poles, wiring, even lavatories. Structures were moved or torn down and dismembered for parts and lumber. Hundreds of carloads of material were shipped around the country. Successful bidders had sixty days to remove their purchases. And then all was gone. The place became almost as it had been. An era not only had ended, it had disappeared. But the Twenties had arrived. And Long Island was ready to roar.

CHAPTER EIGHT

Fast Times

Through a gazebo, Old Westbury Gardens appears even more elegant. Its unique landscaping draws thousands of visitors annually.

Long Island and the Jazz Age were made for each other. On the North Shore, there was the Gold Coast: millionaire playboys, sophisticated ladies, champagne tastes, lush life. Off the South Shore —three miles off—there was Rum Row: illegal liquor-laden ships, evasive contact boats, machine-gun-toting "go-through guys," watchful Coast Guard interceptors.

It was the Roaring Twenties, and for Long Island it was an era described by unbelievable facts and unforgettable fiction. Glittering parties were held on lawns so extensively lit that the Long Island Lighting Company had to be notified to prevent an overload; dinners for 1,500 guests were held in just one of a mansion's 86 rooms; gardens were so large and delicate that they required the care of 50 workers; housekeepers were so demanding that they supervised the placing of fresh flowers in 200 vases each day.

And in a room over a garage in Great Neck, Francis Scott Key Fitzgerald began to memorialize it all with his novel, *The Great Gatsby*:

There was music from my neighbor's house through the summer nights. In his blue gardens men and girls came and went like moths among the whisperings and the champagne and the stars. At high tide in the afternoon I watched his guests diving from the tower of his raft, or taking the sun on the hot sand of his beach while his two motor-boats slit the waters of the Sound, drawing aquaplanes over cataracts of foam. On week-ends his Rolls Royce became an omnibus, bearing parties to and from the city between nine in the morning and long past midnight, while his station wagon scampered like a brisk yellow bug to meet all trains. And on Mondays eight servants, including an extra gardener, toiled all day with mops and scrubbing-brushes and hammers and garden-shears, repairing the ravages of the night before. . . .

At least once a fortnight a corps of caterers came down with several hundred feet of canvas and enough colored lights to make a Christmas tree of Gatsby's enormous garden. On buffet tables, garnished with glistening hors d'oeuvre, spiced baked hams crowded against salads of harlequin designs and pastry pigs and turkeys bewitched to a dark gold. In the main hall a bar with a real brass rail was set up, and stocked with gins and liquors and with cordials so long forgotten that most of his female guests were too young to know one from another.

Fitzgerald saw in Long Island the stuff that the American Dream was made of, captured its elusiveness on pad with pencil, lived its false promise with his wife, Zelda, as America's Golden Boy and Girl, the gorgeous, talented, irresponsible embodiment of the Roaring Twenties. His experiences and observations were derived from a nineteen-month stay between 1922 and 1924 in a rented stucco house at 6 Gateway Drive, Great Neck Estates. It is still there, in what would constitute the "West Egg," or noveau riche, portion of Gatsbyland, which readers of the book would recognize never quite compared with the very rich milieu of "East Egg" (Sands Point), the home of Gatsby's love, Daisy Buchanan, and her husband, Tom.

Scott and Zelda partied among the rich and mighty at the estate of Herbert Bayard Swope, sportsman and publisher of the *New York World*, and formed a close relationship with writer Ring Lardner, a Great Neck neighbor whom Fitzgerald later eulogized as "that fine medallion, all abraded by sorrows that perhaps we are not equipped to understand." Other literary and theatrical personalities who brightened Great Neck neighborhood soirees in the Twenties included Lillian Russell, Groucho Marx, Leslie Howard, Will Durant, P. G. Wodehouse, George S. Kaufman, Oscar Hammerstein II, and Ernest Truex.

Celebrities abounded on the North Shore then; nor was there any shortage of estates: more than five hundred were occupied during that era, most of them within sight of the Sound or secluded behind high walls in the Old Westbury-Brookville-Muttontown-Locust Valley area. Like ancient emperors, America's corporate and financial rulers scoured the globe for styles, materials, and treasures to live in and with.

Rome's Borghese Gardens were figuratively transported to Glen Cove to enhance Winfield, the showplace of F. W. Woolworth. Built in the Italian Renaissance style, it boasted a marble staircase that, at an estimated two million dollars, probably was the most costly ever constructed. Entry was along a lengthy driveway past the gardens, Roman statuary, and a magnificent pool. The house itself contained fifty-six rooms, including bedroom suites reflecting different historic periods.

Reaching back far further in time to decorate his premises, William K. Vanderbilt II placed columns from the ruins of ancient Carthage at the entrance to his 43-acre summer estate overlooking Northport Bay in Centerport. (The other seasons were spent at his estate in Lake Success, or at his homes in New York and Miami.) The mansion complex and adjacent Hall of Fishes marine museum, both preserved and now open to the public, are Spanish Revival in design and reflective of the Vanderbilts' lavish tastes and wide interests.

The most ornate rooms are one containing an organ whose 2,000 pipes are concealed behind an eighteenth-century tapestry, and Mrs. Vanderbilt's luxurious bathroom-dressing room that has a tub cut from a block of pink Venetian marble and is decorated with gold-plated fixtures.

ABOVE

The chronicler and embodiment of the Jazz Age, F. Scott Fitzgerald lived with his wife, Zelda, in this rented stucco house at 6 Gateway Drive, Great Neck Estates, in 1922 and 1923, absorbing the Gold Coast ambience.

BELOW LEFT

In a plain room above the garage at the rear of the Great Neck Estates home, Fitzgerald began writing The Great Gatsby, *regarded by many as a classic depiction of Roaring Twenties' manners and morals. His friendships with the wealthy and famous gave him access to the lifestyle he described in the novel.*

BELOW RIGHT

Enjoying the good life he wrote about, F. Scott Fitzgerald, Zelda, and their daughter, Scottie, pose aboard a liner in 1926. Scottie later wrote that as a child she thought everyone's parents lived like hers.

The Hall of Fishes did double duty: its roof served as the first tee for the estate's 10-hole golf course, while its interior housed more than 17,000 specimens of marine life collected by Vanderbilt during three decades of worldwide exploration, much of it aboard his 265-foot yacht, *Alva.*

For wealth *and* achievement, few families can compare with the Whitneys, whose ventures in finance, transportation, politics, diplomacy, society, and sports are legendary. The accomplishments began with William C. Whitney, who fashioned a transportation network, accumulated vast wealth, fought the corruption of Boss Tweed, built an estate in Old Westbury, and fathered two sons, Harry Payne Whitney and William Payne Whitney.

ABOVE

In a less serious ‹ in, John Held Jr. was Fitzgerald's artistic counterpart in chronicling the Jazz Age. This watercolor, painted for Life *and entitled* Milkman, Good Morning, *conveys the sophisticated irresponsibility of the times.*

BELOW

The naughty spirit of the Twenties was captured in this humorous illustration entitled Bathing Beauties *by artist James Montgomery Flagg for* Judge *magazine.*

OPPOSITE ABOVE

The Vanderbilt mansion in Centerport, designed by Warren and Wetmore, was augmented by columns from the ruins of Carthage at its entrance, and a golf course.

OPPOSITE BELOW

Interior of the Hall of Fishes at what is now the Vanderbilt Museum in Centerport. William K. Vanderbilt II collected 17,000 specimens of marine life, which are on display here.

The sons branched off but shared a strong interest in Long Island and in racing. Harry Payne remained in the Old Westbury area, married the former Gertrude Vanderbilt, founder of the Whitney Museum of American Art, and raised horses. Their son, Cornelius Vanderbilt (Sonny) Whitney, continued the family involvement in racing and became one of the nation's foremost horsemen. The estate, once comprising some 1,000 acres, largely has become the Old Westbury Golf and Country Club and, along with its striking Tudor-style racing stables, the New York Institute of Technology.

William Payne, who dropped the William, and Helen Hay Whitney, known in her day as "the first lady of the American turf," were the parents of John Hay (Jock) Whitney, who, while going on to a distinguished career as ambassador to the Court of St. James's and publisher of the *New York Herald Tribune*, perpetuated his mother's stake in racing. With his sister, Joan Whitney Payson, he operated the famed Greentree Stable, which bore the same name as his 500-acre estate off Shelter Rock Road in Manhasset. Secluded behind a modest wooden fence, Greentree has remained intact and includes just about everything: indoor tennis courts and swimming pool, conservatory, stables, barns, chicken house, and guest cottages.

The problem of keeping in touch with the family was minimized by Charles Pratt, who, like the Rockefellers, amassed a fortune through Standard Oil. Pratt began buying up property on the Sound near Glen Cove around the turn of the century, and by the Twenties his clan was living on a dozen or so adjacent estates comprising more than 1,000 acres. There even were facilities used in common, such as the stables, garages, and gardens called Pratt Oval, and an indoor tennis and squash complex that has been converted into the Glen Cove YMCA. At one time, Herbert L. Pratt occupied the mansion called The Braes that is now the Webb Institute of Naval Architecture; George D. Pratt resided in the 49-room Tudor revival structure named Killenworth, now a Soviet residence for members of its diplomatic corps; John Teel Pratt was home in the nearby red brick Georgian mansion that has become a retreat for business executives called Harrison House; and Harold Erving Pratt feted social leaders at Welwyn, whose red-tiled roof sheltered a tennis complex and stables and now is part of a Nassau County wildlife preserve.

Not to be outdone, the Morgan family owned two islands, East and West, off what is now Lattingtown. East Island belonged to J. P. Morgan, son of the original robber baron and in some respects his father's son. Access to his 52-room Georgian mansion was across a stone bridge and past a guardhouse that was "supposedly" manned around-the-clock. Supposedly, since on a night in 1915, while Morgan was entertaining the British ambassador, a German sympathizer armed with a revolver and seething with anger at the financier's aid to the Allies, got into the house and, attempting to kill Morgan, succeeded in wounding him. Morgan recovered, but the would-be assassin committed suicide in jail while awaiting trial.

Before and after that incident, violence was as alien to East Island as poverty. Morgan so prized serenity that he grazed a herd of cattle on the front lawn because the scene enhanced his sense of tranquillity. East Island was connected to West Island by a causeway and to their owners by consanguinity: J. P.'s son, Junius Spencer Morgan, built his home, called Salutations, as the Twenties were coming to a close. Among its appurtenances were a dollhouse, used by the Morgan children, that was a miniature Salutations, and a large bank of kennels that housed Mrs. Morgan's show dogs.

Another family that found familiarity bred content was the Guggenheims, Daniel and Harry, heirs to a copper fortune. Daniel arrived first in Sands Point in 1917, purchasing Castlegould, a 300-acre property that included a Tudor-Jacobean mansion built in 1912 for Howard Gould, son of notorious stock manipulator Jay Gould. Howard Gould's wife, actress Viola Katherine Clemmons, had wanted a copy of Ireland's Kilkenny Castle, but he had other plans, and the only resemblance to Kilkenny can be found in the design of the large stables. Mrs. Gould's desires apparently were unfulfilled on several counts, since she obtained a legal separation following a lurid two-year court battle that included allegations involving her relationship with William F. (Buffalo Bill) Cody.

Daniel Guggenheim named the structure Hempstead House, because it overlooked Hempstead Bay, and furnished it in a style befitting a member of one of the nation's wealthiest families. In 1923, when his son, Harry, married his second wife, Caroline Morton, Guggenheim gave him 90 acres of the estate as a wedding gift. Harry immediately set about constructing a medieval Norman manor house on the water, which he called Falaise. Instead of emulating his father's taste, the younger Guggenheim sought to impress through quality rather than size. This appeal to connoisseurship resulted in a second-generation Gold Coast mansion that made Falaise smaller and more livable than Hempstead House, and that made it notable for its transplantation of European art and architectural fragments such as columns, doors, sculpture, and carvings.

Like most Gold Coast estates, its guest list was impressive, drawn from its owner's varied interests, which in this case included horseracing (1953 Kentucky Derby winner Dark Star), publishing (*Newsday*), diplomacy (ambassador to Cuba), art (Solomon Guggenheim Museum), and the advancement of aviation and rocketry. Guggenheim regularly entertained architect Frank Lloyd Wright, financier Bernard Baruch, rocket pioneer Robert Goddard, and presidential aspirant Adlai Stevenson.

One of Falaise's most famous visitors was Charles Lindbergh, who needed a quiet place to write after returning from his epic transatlantic flight in 1927. The result was *We*, a best-selling account of that spectacu-

OPPOSITE ABOVE
Falaise, owned by Daniel Guggenheim's son, Harry, was designed by Frederick Sterner and built on ninety acres that the younger Guggenheim had received as a wedding gift. Co-founder of Newsday, *he lived here with his wife, Alicia Patterson,* Newsday's *first editor and publisher. The estate is now part of Nassau County's Sands Point Preserve.*

OPPOSITE BELOW
Old Westbury Gardens, the former estate of John S. Phipps, was designed by London architect George Crawley and contains paintings by Gainsborough and Reynolds, and furniture by Chippendale.

ABOVE
The Georgian estate of J. P. Morgan on East Island, off Lattingtown, was accessible only by a bridge protected by a guardhouse. But in 1915, a would-be assassin got in.

RIGHT
Castlegould, built for Howard Gould, son of financial manipulator Jay Gould, was bought later by Daniel Guggenheim. Architect Augustus Allen designed the support buildings, including the stables, which resemble Ireland's Kilkenny Castle.

BELOW
Hempstead House, the main structure on the Castlegould estate, was designed by Hunt & Hunt and named by Guggenheim for its site overlooking Hempstead Bay.

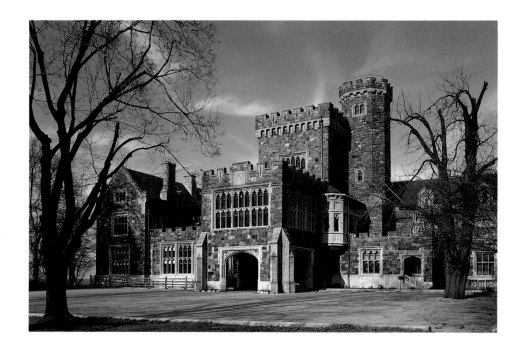

lar feat. Falaise, which Guggenheim shared with Alicia Patterson, his third wife and *Newsday*'s first editor and publisher, was given to Nassau County after his death in 1971, and is open to the public as part of the Sands Point Preserve.

The preserve also includes Hempstead House, which, following Daniel Guggenheim's death, served as an asylum for British children seeking to escape the bombing of London during the early years of World War II, as a facility for the Institute for Aeronautical Sciences, and as a U.S. Navy Special Devices Training Center (where atomic research was conducted), before coming under county aegis.

Other places where the lavish style of the Twenties still can be absorbed include two of Long Island's most magnificent showplaces: Planting Fields, the estate of William Robertson Coe in Oyster Bay, and Old Westbury Gardens, the John S. Phipps estate. Both are renowned for their matchless landscaping, and the structures themselves are outstanding examples of architecture and decor. Coe brought the gate from Carshalton Park in England to guard the entrance to Planting Fields, while at Old Westbury Gardens, paintings by Thomas Gainsborough, Sir Joshua Reynolds, John Constable, and John Singer Sargent hang in rooms furnished with the works of eighteenth-century English cabinetmaker Thomas Chippendale.

Fire, maintenance costs, taxes, and developers' enticements were responsible for the destruction of most of the Gold Coast palaces, including what may have been the most spectacular of all, the estate of banker Otto Kahn in Cold Spring Hills, Huntington. Kahn, whose zeal for social activity matched his drive for wealth and power, sought the highest point on Long Island for his contemplated residence and, on finding it occupied, purchased another site and had it elevated. On it, he built a 126-room, turreted castle, golf course, and formal gardens that made the estate world-famous. The grounds and building later became the Eastern Military Academy, until it went bankrupt in 1979.

Another estate that became an educational institution was Broad Hollow, the home of F. Ambrose Clark and now the State University of New York College at Old Westbury. One of the dynamic personalities of the time, Clark was a noted horseman who not only owned, but trained and rode thoroughbreds on his 500-acre estate. Also an owner of the Singer Sewing Machine Company, he hosted luncheons for 500 guests in his white-pillared, 42-room colonial mansion. But when he decided to throw a party for the visiting Prince of Wales in 1924, Clark evidently felt that the facilities were inadequate, for he had an oak-paneled ballroom built for the occasion.

No longer standing is the French chateau at Harbor Hill, Clarence Mackay's 600-acre Roslyn estate and the site of what may have been the grandest party of them all. Held in honor of the Prince of Wales during his weeklong visit to attend the 1924 International Polo Matches at

Taxes and maintenance costs forced the closing of many of the great Gold Coast estates, some of which have become public institutions. Metal sculpture, titled Sidewinder, *by Allen Bertoldi, decorates the former Childs Frick estate in Roslyn, now the Nassau County Museum of Fine Art* (ABOVE). *Once Broad Hollow, the F. Ambrose Clark estate, designed by Rogers & Zogbaum, is now the State University College at Old Westbury* (MIDDLE). *The Dairy Barn, which once supplied milk to the Whitneys in Old Westbury, currently fills other needs for New York Institute of Technology students as an activity center* (BELOW).

Westbury, the reception was attended by 1,200 guests, who dined on lobster piled six feet high, danced to the music of Paul Whiteman, and inhaled perfume sprayed from the magnificent garden fountains. The winding, mile-long entrance drive was lit by thousands of blue electric bulbs strung through the trees that lined it, and a huge American flag, composed of still more red, white, and blue lights, glowed over the chateau's gabled roof.

The fact that this extraordinary affair was held during Prohibition underscored public contempt for that law; among the celebrants were government officials, judges, diplomats, clergymen, and military leaders. But on Long Island there also was appreciation for the constitutional amendment banning the importation, manufacture, transportation, or sale of intoxicating liquors. Bootlegging became a prime industry in Nassau and Suffolk during Prohibition's 14-year life.

After the Eighteenth Amendment went into effect in early 1920, vast quantities of liquor continued pouring into the United States; of course it did so in a new way. Large yachts and schooners picked up 3,000-case loads from the French islands of St. Pierre and Miquelon, south of Newfoundland, or from many islands in the Caribbean, and anchored off the Long Island coast just beyond the 3-mile limit of federal jurisdiction. There—on what became known as Rum Row—immune from law enforcement, they hung signs from their masts announcing their wares, and awaited the arrival, at dusk, of the contact boats, swift, silent, converted Jersey skiffs which sought to evade the Coast Guard and speed the liquor to shore. With lookouts posted to warn of the approach of patrols, the transfer of the cargo took place according to a well-defined ritual that was fast-paced with a style all its own. To protect against gangsters or undercover agents, sellers often required buyers to confirm their "legitimacy" by producing matching halves of torn dollar bills. With such preliminaries disposed of, prices were agreed upon, orders placed by shouts from ship-to-ship, rolls of bills tossed onto the seller's deck, and cases of liquor loaded aboard the pitching skiffs.

After that, skill and luck determined if the goods were delivered or the rumrunners caught. The contact boats, generally powered by automobile engines with underwater exhausts to minimize sound, hoped to race

back to beaches or secluded docks in Montauk, Fire Island, Cutchogue, Freeport, Greenport, Shelter Island (which still has its Bootleggers' Alley), and other waterfront communities. The darkness helped and so did fog, for the skippers were veteran seamen who knew the local waters well. They soon developed evasive techniques to augment their navigational skills and the swiftness of their small boats. Sometimes they might use an identical but empty vessel to lead the Coast Guardsmen on a false chase, or toss the liquor overboard after attaching the cases to buoys for subsequent retrieval, or as a reluctant, but frequently successful, gambit —commit bribery. Occasionally, when all else failed, the rumrunners simply heaved their cargo into the sea to escape arrest. When that happened, particularly if it occurred close to shore accompanied by the roar of gunfire, alert beachfront residents might rush out to salvage the abandoned liquor.

There were huge profits to be made, and it did not take long for criminals to recognize that the size and complexity of the operation called for businesslike organization. Quicker than one could say "Al Capone," organized crime was born. Investing money in every phase of the illicit business, the newly formed mobs even had their contact boats built by the same shipyards that made the Coast Guard craft, enabling them to obtain the specifications of the government ships; they could then install engines capable of outdistancing them.

But the Coast Guard was regarded by the rank-and-file bootleggers as a far less formidable foe than the "go-through guys." These were professional robbers and killers who, riding the speediest boats and carrying deadly Thompson submachine guns, would "go through anything" to get what they wanted. What they wanted were the fat bankrolls used to buy the contraband, and to get them, like an updated version of the murderous pirates who roved Long Island waters in an earlier century, they would pull over the contact boats and rob them at gunpoint. The contact-boat crews were especially vulnerable; normally they went unarmed in order to mitigate their sentences if caught and convicted of rumrunning.

One of the most popular eastern Long Island bootlegging terminals was Greenport, ideally located because of its access to the open sea, to the secluded coves of Shelter Island and the North and South Forks, and to Jericho Turnpike, which led to New York. On shipment nights, the community's dock area literally would be taken over by mobsters who stood guard while the cargoes of illegal liquor were unloaded from the contact boats and placed aboard trucks for the predawn run to the city. Finding loaders was no problem: most townspeople able to lift and carry cases were eager to do so for twenty dollars—the equivalent of a few days' pay. Once ready to move, the convoy fell into position: a line of trucks sandwiched between escort cars filled with armed gangsters.

The precautions were not exaggerated. Rival gangs and hijackers would lie in wait along Jericho Turnpike and other major routes to ambush the

Prohibition evaders and agents played an ongoing game of cat-and-mouse throughout the existence of the Prohibition law. (OPPOSITE ABOVE) *This one-time private yacht,* Edith, *from which customs agents are unloading contraband booze, was carrying $75,000 worth of illegal liquor when it was stopped by Coast Guardsmen.* (OPPOSITE BELOW) *One dirty trick that did not quite work involved hiding 3,000 bags of bottled whisky amid the coal aboard this coal steamer.*

BELOW
The Prohibition laws were violated so openly that they inspired songs. This is the cover of the sheet music for "Everybody Wants a Key to My Cellar," a number popularized by Bert Williams.

caravans by blocking the road with stalled vehicles or ramming them with empty cars. There would be warning gunfire and, if the hijackers encountered resistance, violence; stealing the trucks and their contents was a high-stake, high-risk business.

Obviously unable to complain to the authorities, the bootleggers devised new methods to make their deliveries. One was to send high-powered cars, outfitted with false bottoms to conceal the liquor and with shock absorbers to prevent sagging, at breakneck speeds on Vanderbilt's private Long Island Motor Parkway. Local police and federal agents also had to be evaded, but with corruption widespread, payoffs frequently insured a lack of interference. In instances where some officials, notably Nassau District Attorney Elvin N. Edwards, sought to carry out the unpopular law, little public support existed.

Most of the antibootlegging pressure on Long Island came from the churches and the Ku Klux Klan; the latter, having been revived nationally in 1915 after its seeming demise in 1869, enjoyed extensive backing. In Nassau and Suffolk during the early Twenties, one out of every eight residents was a member of the Klan. Espousing "law and order" along with vicious attacks on Catholics, Jews, the foreign-born, and blacks, the Klan strongly pressed for enforcement of Prohibition and eagerly provided manpower to assist officials in patrolling highways and performing other parapolice work.

When a special constable named Ferdinand Downs was killed by bootleggers in Southampton, the Klan made a major issue of the crime and called for 10,000 members to attend his funeral. Although that goal was not reached, more than 2,000 mourners did show up to demonstrate their indignation, along with paying their last respects. More significantly, after Patrick Ryan, a Catholic from New York City, was charged with Downs' killing, he contended that he could not get a fair trial locally and succeeded in gaining a change of venue to Kings County. In granting the motion, a State Supreme Court justice said: "There exists in Suffolk County great hostility toward Roman Catholics and a feeling of bias, prejudice and passion exists and is expressed against the defendant whenever men congregate."

The Klan's anti-Semitism was not limited to speeches. After a Jewish druggist in Freeport was cleared by police of having attacked a little girl in the summer of 1924, the Klan ordered him to leave town and, when he refused, kidnapped him on a village street and left him in Hicksville. The victim, Ernest Louis, then sold his store and moved, explaining that the harassment had destroyed his business.

Although in recent years the Klan's national activities have been directed primarily against blacks, in the Twenties on Long Island it was the foreign-born who were regarded as a threat to the "American way of life." They constituted more than 20 percent of the Nassau and Suffolk population, while blacks comprised only about 2 percent. Antiblack activists concentrated on preserving existing housing patterns, which meant, for example, seeking to keep blacks out of predominantly white Roosevelt, or insuring that blacks in Freeport lived only in the Bennington Park section.

Freeport was a stronghold of KKK sentiment, and the organization had little difficulty in demonstrating boldly or in gaining an audience. On September 20, 1924, an estimated 30,000 spectators lined the village streets to watch a parade of 2,000 Klansmen and Klanswomen led by Freeport Police Chief John M. Hartman. Floats called on the citizenry to "Teach the Bible in Public Schools," "Protect American Womenhood," and maintain "Clean Politics." In Suffolk, 25,000 men, women, and children attended a Klan rally near Central Islip in the summer of 1923 to hear a minister describe Jews and Catholics as dangerous to the United States and to witness the initiation of 1,500 new members.

There was remarkably little opposition to the Klan's cross-burnings and other hate-mongering activities by public officials. What protests did arise usually came from victimized groups, such as when the Knights of Columbus and synagogue members criticized the Freeport school board for accepting a flag and flagpole from the Klan.

By 1926, the KKK had begun to decline in influence on Long Island. This was evident in local elections in Greenport, Babylon, and Sag Harbor, where anti-Klan candidates were successful, a fact noted in *The New York Times*: "Long Island seems to be recovering from its belief in the Ku Klux Klan. . . . Thus has good sense returned to Long Island, and its people have resumed the display of their accustomed intelligence."

The Klan's promotion of nativism held some appeal on Long Island, particularly to old-line families—the white Anglo-Saxon Protestants who resented the intrusion of newcomers and feared the threat they represented to their traditional domination of the area's institutions. So long as Catholics and Jews had only been sprinkled among the population, these feelings had been kept relatively in check, although aspects of anti-Catholicism and anti-Semitism came to America with the first settlers. But the immigration expansion that began with the Irish and Germans in the mid-nineteenth century and became an explosion with the Italians, Poles, Russians, and Jews in subsequent decades, triggered far more active hostilities.

Catholics became part of Long Island's history as early as 1683, when the Duke of York, a Catholic, appointed Catholic Thomas Dongan to replace the tyrannical Edmund Andros as royal governor of New York. Long Island's first Mass probably was celebrated by Dongan's chaplain, Jesuit Father Thomas Harvey, when the governor arrived in Sag Harbor en route to his new post.

The Catholic influx was sporadic in the beginning. In the 1750s, a few French immigrants from Nova Scotia, called Acadians, made their

The Klan focused its Long Island campaign of hatred on the foreign-born, Catholics, and Jews in those days.

way to Long Island after a stay in New York and settled in various Suffolk villages. But so few Catholics were living in the Thirteen Colonies at the time the United States was formed, that when the first diocese was established in Baltimore in 1789, it embraced the entire nation. As Catholics, primarily from Ireland, began to enter the country in greater numbers, three more dioceses, including one for New York, had to be created in 1808.

On Long Island, Catholic communities developed at both ends. In Brooklyn, this led to the formation in 1823 of the Island's first Catholic church, St. James, at the present site of St. James Cathedral in the Borough Hall section. In eastern Suffolk, after several years of prayer meetings, Catholics in Sag Harbor purchased a former Methodist church in 1838, and converted it into what apparently was Long Island's second Catholic church and Suffolk's first. This was accomplished with financial support from a prominent Protestant, offsetting considerable antipathy from other Protestants.

The Catholic population was augmented during the following decade when large numbers of Irish were employed to lay Long Island Rail Road track from Brooklyn to Greenport. Swelled significantly by migration following the destruction of the potato crop in Ireland, the Catholic community had grown large enough by 1853 to warrant the creation of the Diocese of Brooklyn, consisting of Kings, Queens (which then included Nassau), and Suffolk Counties.

The next hundred or so years became the most significant in Catholic history on Long Island. Vast numbers of Italian and Polish immigrants poured into Brooklyn and Queens toward the turn of the century and watched their children and grandchildren populate Nassau and Suffolk during the post-World War II exodus to the suburbs. From representing a vulnerable minority on Long Island in the mid-nineteenth century, Catholics became a powerful majority in the mid-twentieth, a circumstance reflected by the establishment in 1957 of a new diocese for Nassau and Suffolk. Seated at St. Agnes Cathedral, the Diocese of Rockville Centre now has more than one million communicants, making it the nation's largest after Brooklyn.

For many Italians, Long Island provided the opportunity to transplant the ambience of their native land to the estate of a Gold Coast magnate. As the nineteenth century came to a close, some of New York City's most affluent families had decided to live or entertain on Nassau's North Shore and they needed skilled landscapers and gardeners to help them emulate the sumptuous showplaces of Europe. One of the places they drew on for expertise was the Italian town of Durazzano, whose residents flocked to America and settled in the rural community of Westbury. They worked on the estates, planting trees and shrubs, hedges and flowers. Those who were not required on the estates soon found employment in the flourishing nursery business, particularly with a leading firm named Isaac Hicks and Sons. Immigrants from Italy also settled in Long Island villages such as Glen Cove, Oyster Bay, and Inwood, going into construction work or, later, becoming barbers, shoemakers, and tailors.

Although, like most immigrants, Italians tended to be clannish and preoccupied with their own institutions and societies, they soon discovered that their interests would be ignored by the Protestant hierarchy unless they learned to exert political pressure. In Westbury, for example, Italian-Americans were furious during World War II when the village board, citing Italy's Axis status, curtailed the annual festival honoring Our Lady of the Assumption, the community's most colorful ethnic celebration. When the war was over, they channeled their anger and frustration into politics and soon found they could gain representation within the power structure and, ultimately, control of it.

The postwar rush to the suburbs found Americans of Italian descent buying homes in such areas as Franklin Square, Elmont, East Meadow, Levittown, Hicksville, Deer Park, Copiague, North Babylon, and Commack. By 1980, they clearly had become the predominant ethnic group on Long Island and were exercising significant political influence in Nassau and Suffolk, both in elective positions and behind the scenes.

Another major ethnic group that encountered difficulties on Long Island both because of their foreignness and their Catholicism was the Poles. They also arrived in substantial numbers toward the turn of the century, finding work as farm laborers, often in the employ of German immigrants who had settled a generation or two earlier.

In time, they gravitated toward eastern Suffolk, where they purchased land, grew potatoes, and populated Riverhead, which they dubbed "Polish Town, USA." Attempts to keep the ethnic heritage alive are concentrated at St. Isidore's Church, erected there in 1907 and named for the

ABOVE
Catholics, who constitute the largest religious group on Long Island by far, gained significant numbers during the Twenties. St. Agnes Cathedral is the seat of the Diocese of Rockville Centre, the nation's largest diocese after Brooklyn.

BELOW LEFT
Jews comprise Long Island's largest ethnic group after Italians. In 1898, Jews who went to work in a Sag Harbor watch plant formed Temple Adas Israel, the oldest synagogue in Nassau or Suffolk.

BELOW RIGHT
The oldest Episcopal Church building on Long Island is Caroline Church, Setauket, which was founded in 1729. Its Revolutionary War bullet wounds are still visible.

patron saint of farmers. The Nassau counterpart is St. Hedwig's Church in Floral Park, built in 1903.

Jews were among the earliest Europeans to seek a home in Long Island and, consistent with the treatment they have received throughout their long history, met with resistance and hostility. A group of twenty-three Jews who had fought with the Dutch and earned permission to trade in New Netherland were challenged on their arrival in 1654 by New Amsterdam Governor Peter Stuyvesant. Directed by his superiors to grant the Jews admission to the Dutch territory, which included Long Island, Stuyvesant acquiesced, but imposed severe restrictions on their rights to own property, open stores, worship publicly, and perform skilled labor. One of the group, Asser Van Swellem Levy, demanded, persisted, and eventually won equal rights for himself and his co-religionists.

Levy made his summer home in what is now Long Island City, bought property elsewhere on Long Island, and saw his son's family settle in East Hampton in 1730. In 1750, another Jewish pioneer, Aaron Isaacs, a Sag Harbor merchant, married Mary Hedges of East Hampton, became a convert to Christianity, a father, and, later, grandfather of John Howard Payne, author of "Home Sweet Home."

During the nineteenth and early twentieth centuries there were pockets of Jews who appeared in the most unlikely Long Island communities. In Sag Harbor, for example, they went to work at the Fahys Watch Case Company and built Temple Adas Israel in 1898, the oldest existing synagogue in Nassau or Suffolk. In Lindenhurst, then called Breslau by its German founders, they worked in a button factory or used the village as the hub for peddling in western Suffolk. In East Setauket, they were employed in the J. W. Elberson rubber factory and formed the Congregation Agudath Achim, now the North Shore Jewish Center.

Jews, who settled in New York City in vast numbers on their arrival from Europe, generally remained in the five boroughs until the 1920s. When they did move, many made their homes within relatively easy commuting distance of the city, in such communities as Great Neck, the Five Towns (Woodmere, Hewlett, Cedarhurst, Lawrence, and Inwood), Lynbrook, Freeport, Hicksville, and Long Beach. But it was not until the post-World War II migration that they moved in sufficient numbers to comprise almost 20 percent of Long Island's population, and become its second largest ethnic group, after Italians.

German immigrants came to Long Island earlier than most Europeans, settling in the Hempstead Plains in the 1850s to coax vegetables out of the dry fields. Completion of the Long Island Rail Road to Hicksville prompted a real estate mini-boom there as newly arrived Germans came out from New York City and Brooklyn, liked what they saw, and began buying lots and homes.

In the ensuing decades, German farmers moved into many areas of western Nassau, such as Floral Park (named for its nurseries), New

In East Setauket, Jewish employees of a rubber factory established Agudath Achim Synagogue, now the North Shore Jewish Center.

Hyde Park, Elmont, Freeport, and Franklin Square. Their institutions, particularly the Lutheran Church, soon followed, and today more than one hundred Lutheran churches serve Long Island congregations of German and Scandinavian extraction. One of the area's best-known Lutheran facilities is the Mill Neck Manor School for Deaf Children, which occupies the stately English Tudor mansion formerly owned by Robert L. Dodge.

Of course, the earliest Europeans to colonize Long Island were the Dutch and English. Although refugees from religious oppression in the Old World, they became the arbiters of religious orthodoxy in the New. The Long Island Dutch worshiped in the Dutch Reformed Church as far back as 1654, when their leader, Peter Stuyvesant, directed the Reverend Johannes Theodorus Polhemus to organize three congregations in what is now Brooklyn. Two of the three are still functioning as part of the Reformed Church in America, although after the British took over Long Island from the Dutch in 1664, Dutch immigration eased, Dutch influence waned, and the growth of the Dutch Reformed Church was slowed.

The Puritan sect, which developed in opposition to the Church of England, dominated the English settlements on Long Island, as it had in New England. The initial religion to be brought from Europe to the Island, its first churches, in Southold and Southampton, were established in 1640. The Presbyterian and Congregational denominations evolved from the Puritans and continue to be active throughout Nassau and Suffolk.

Religion and politics were inextricable during colonial days, as church leaders helped write and enforce civil laws to support their religious tenets. Thus, church attendance was made compulsory at the risk of fines, corporal punishment, or even banishment.

In reaction to the harshness of the Puritans, other sects gained adherents during the eighteenth and nineteenth centuries, giving Long Island a religious pluralism with the addition of Methodists, Baptists, Episcopalians, and, despite severe harassment, Quakers. For the Episcopal Church, particularly, the growth of parishioners on Long Island has special meaning. It led to the Island's designation as a diocese, adorned by the Gothic Cathedral of the Incarnation in Garden City, which serves as the seat.

But the story of religious evolution on Long Island is replete with contradictions. The Puritans fled persecution in England only to inflict it on "non-believers" in their new homeland. This insistence on conformity led to the growth of denominations which espoused less stringent behavior and appealed to more liberal worshipers. Yet, it was many of these very churches that later supported attacks on twentieth-century "outsiders," the immigrants whose religious beliefs differed from their own.

That bigotry and intolerance lurked just below the surface of Long Island society became evident from the broad implicit support given to the Ku Klux Klan. And it is difficult to examine the period without recognizing the reluctance of Long Islanders to confront the prejudice and mean-spiritedness in their midst. It was a sordid chapter that revealed the depths to which the American character can descend.

Still, before the decade ran out, a brief, simple, yet extraordinary event would enable the nation to redeem its spirit. It was an exploit seized upon by the public to symbolize the traditional values—courage, grit, decency, self-reliance, humility, and faith—that they regarded as uniquely American.

BELOW
Charles A. Lindbergh talks over flight plans with Commander Richard Byrd, who had flown over the North Pole, and Clarence Chamberlin, another noted flier, before starting his epic journey to Paris. Byrd and Chamberlin were preparing their own transatlantic flights when Lindbergh succeeded.

OPPOSITE ABOVE
Brave and modest, young Lindbergh represented an antidote to the gaudiness and decadence of the Roaring Twenties and became an instant hero following his unprecedented solo flight across the Atlantic in 1927.

OPPOSITE BELOW
The Spirit of St. Louis *"flying" in its honored location in the National Air and Space Museum in Washington, D.C.*

It began on the misty morning of May 20, 1927, when a lanky, 25-year-old mail pilot from the Midwest left Long Island in an over-loaded plane called the *Spirit of St. Louis* seeking fame and the $25,000 prize offered for the first nonstop flight between New York and Paris. The challenge of crossing the Atlantic had captured the attention of the world, and the dramatic takeoff was described by Russell Owen, correspondent of *The New York Times*, as follows:

A sluggish, gray monoplane lurched its way down Roosevelt Field yesterday morning, slowly gathering momentum. Inside sat a tall youngster, eyes glued to an instrument board or darting ahead for swift glances at the runway, his face drawn with the intensity of his purpose.

Death lay but a few seconds ahead of him if his skill failed or his courage faltered. For moments, as the heavy plane rose from the ground, dropped down, staggered again into the air and fell, he gambled for his life against a hazard which had already killed four men.

And then slowly, so slowly that those watching it stood fascinated, as if by his indomitable will alone, the young pilot lifted his plane. It dipped and then rose with renewed speed, climbing heavily but steadily toward the distant trees.

The spirit of unconquerable youth had won, and "Slim" Lindbergh was on his way to Paris.

Thirty-three and one-half hours later the shy, boyish aviator landed in Paris to a hero's welcome, detonating a binge of pride throughout the United States. Lindbergh's daring and modesty had provided an ideal antidote to the cynicism and self-indulgence of the Jazz Age. But the memory would have to last, for Americans soon would be searching vainly for something to cheer about. The stock market was going up only so it would have farther to fall. Prosperity still was booming, but the Great Depression was just around the corner.

CHAPTER NINE

Turning the Corner

Robert Moses, the controversial master builder who altered the face and pace of Long Island with his parks and parkways, poses in 1965 with Harry Guggenheim, Newsday's first president, in front of a painting depicting some of his innumerable construction projects.

Ironically, Long Island's failure to develop its commerce and industry spared it from a worse fate during the Great Depression. Still largely residential and agricultural, Nassau and Suffolk were less vulnerable to the effects of economic collapse than their urbanized neighbors. And Suffolk, even better suited than Nassau by its geography and history to exploit the land and the sea, was able to weather the crisis more easily.

Yet, it was a time of travail, particularly for commuters and construction workers whose livelihoods were jeopardized by paralysis and bankruptcy in manufacturing, wholesaling, retailing, and building. For despite the small-town character that permeated much of the Island east of Queens, the first third of the twentieth century was a period of transition, especially in Nassau, and of movement away from the traditional farm economy of the past toward the suburban growth of the future.

The two principal factors boosting Long Island's development at this time were railroads and roads. The opening of Pennsylvania Station in 1910, and the electrification of Long Island Rail Road service to Hempstead in 1908 and to Babylon in 1925, had enhanced greatly the ease of commuting by train to jobs in New York City. By 1930, 30,000 Nassau residents were doing just that.

While the railroad was moving commuters into the city, and thus inducing New Yorkers to consider moving to Long Island, an inadequate system of roads on the Island was having just the opposite effect on potential residents. City dwellers, including those from Brooklyn and Queens, seeking a restful Sunday in the country during the 1920s, found instead a bumper-to-bumper ordeal over the few narrow, potholed roads that connected Nassau and Suffolk with the rest of the nation. These conditions apparently had the tacit support of many Long Islanders who perceived that any improvement in road transportation would send unwelcome multitudes pouring into their midst from New York. Consequently, there was little encouragement—and massive resistance— when Robert Moses sought to implement his vision of a vast checkerboard of Long Island parks and an interconnected system of parkways through which to reach them.

Moses, a controversial combination of idealist and manipulator, public servant and personal power seeker, left an ineradicable imprint on Long Island, probably affecting more lives in more ways than any individual in or out of local government. Legendary by middle age because of his enormous accomplishments, Moses' reputation subsequently became tarnished, his policies called into question.

This decline apparently reflected a change in public attitudes toward the efficacy of automobile travel. Moses, as the most forceful proponent of more bridges, more expressways, and more parkways, once had been praised as Long Island's "Colossus of Roads." But as his emphasis on private—as opposed to mass—transit failed to alleviate traffic problems, his status fell as motorists' tempers rose. And this disenchantment with his judgment was accompanied by increasing distaste for his authoritarian manner and prickly personality.

Moses' presidency of the Long Island State Park Commission, a post from which he was to wield lifelong influence, came about in 1924 through Governor Alfred E. Smith, who had a profound effect on his appointee's career. Moses soon transformed this paper office—the only Long Island state park at that time was an unused portion of beach on Fire Island—into one of New York's most powerful governmental agencies. But not without struggle.

One of Moses' first goals—to convert the former East Islip property of George C. Taylor from a private hunting preserve to a public park—met potent opposition from the wealthy, influential sportsmen who enjoyed its use. It was only through Smith's backing, along with a $262,000 cash gift from philanthropist August Heckscher, that Moses was able to win a crucial legal victory, establish the state's right to appropriate property in such instances, and create Heckscher State Park.

A key incident in the protracted battle came when one of the landed gentry complained to the governor that if Moses succeeded, the area would be "overrun with rabble from the city." A fiercely proud product of New York's Lower East Side, Smith snapped, "Rabble? That's *me* you're talking about!" He gave Moses his total support. Later, Moses ran into similar hostility from elite North Shore estate owners who sought to block his proposed Northern State Parkway because it would run through their land. This time, however, a "compromise" was worked out. The result—the Northern State Parkway that took a suspiciously erratic course in the vicinity of the Old Westbury estates.

If Moses occasionally backtracked or sidestepped, his direction otherwise was straight ahead; his only velocity—top speed. In 1929, he saw Heckscher State Park open in June, the Southern State Parkway in July, and the Wantagh Causeway and Jones Beach in August. Each year brought new plans, new groundbreakings, new completions. In 1934, Bethpage State Park and Bethpage State Parkway were built; in 1935, the Meadowbrook Causeway; in 1936, the Heckscher State Parkway Spur.

ABOVE

Only the light poles look familiar in this 1930 photograph of the Southern State Parkway near Valley Stream. The absence of a divider, and a makeshift sign banning commercial traffic seem particularly out of place.

BELOW

In 1931, Robert Moses, second from right, was heading the Long Island State Park Commission, and Franklin D. Roosevelt, wearing his favorite Panama hat, was governor of New York. Occasion was the cornerstone-laying of Northern State Parkway.

There was other major highway construction, too. While the parkways barred trucks and skirted the villages, Nassau County concentrated on improvements to roads bearing commercial traffic between communities: the first section of Sunrise Highway was opened in 1928, and Merrick Road, Jericho, Hempstead, and North Hempstead Turnpikes were widened and paved.

This was a period of tight money, of Depression. And these vast public projects provided jobs. One of the most extensive uses of the New Deal relief rolls involved Bethpage State Park, where jobless architects

During the Depression, inexpensive camping at Heckscher State Park was a particularly popular way to vacation. This was the scene there in August, 1933.

were hired to plan the clubhouse and 1,800 unemployed workers to build it along with auxiliary units, four 18-hole golf courses, and the polo field. The government operation even involved the take-over of an idle factory to make new furniture for the clubhouse.

For laborers, there was heavy construction work on roads and drainage systems, post offices, military installations, and a new courthouse complex at the site of the old Mineola Fair on the south side of Old Country Road. And out-of-work white-collar employees were used to take an inventory of structures for the American Historic Buildings Survey, draw up a countywide lot and block map, paint murals on the walls of the old Nassau County courthouse on Franklin Avenue in Garden City (frequently misidentified as the Mineola courthouse), and establish a junior college—Nassau Collegiate Center—in the former Curtiss aircraft factory in Garden City.

At the same time, Nassau and Suffolk bankers were hard-pressed to keep going. Failures at the Bank of North Hempstead in Port Washington and the Long Beach Trust Company, and the imminent closing of the First National Bank of Rockville Centre, precipitated the formation in early 1932 of the Nassau County Clearing House. Meeting in emergency sessions, representatives of 60 banks cushioned the impact of First National's closing by working out protective arrangements with the Bank of Rockville Centre. After President Franklin D. Roosevelt declared a national "Bank Holiday" in March, 1933, to forestall panicky withdrawals by fearful depositors, Nassau emerged with several closings but without financial chaos. In Suffolk, the situation was even less severe. Although 6 of about 50 commercial banks failed to reopen on schedule, they did eventually, and without the loss of a single dollar.

In addition to the effects of unemployment and bankruptcy, the Depression stopped Nassau's real estate and housing boom in its tracks. Residential construction in such burgeoning villages as Rockville Centre and Freeport declined so drastically that the value of new homes built during the entire year of 1934 was less than that put up in a single month a decade earlier.

In Suffolk, too, real estate values plunged, and undoubtedly the biggest loser was the biggest plunger, a flamboyant, multimillionaire-speculator named Carl Fisher. The creator of Miami Beach, Fisher sought to duplicate his success at Montauk, which he envisioned as the "Miami Beach of the North." In 1926, he spent $1,000,000 to build the 200-room Montauk Manor, constructed a glass-roofed indoor tennis complex, yacht club, polo field, movie theater, and golf course, and adorned his superplayground with a seven-story office building. But a devastating hurricane later that year caused expensive damage to Fisher's Miami Beach holdings, and the 1929 stock market crash cut deeply into his remaining assets so that by the early 1930s he could not prevent his Montauk Beach Development Corporation from going into bankruptcy. All that remains of the dream are two of Montauk's most familiar landmarks—the Manor and that strange-looking, out-of-place, seven-story building.

The hurricane that struck southern Florida in 1926 never reached Long Island, but in 1938 another one did, and those living on Long Island then will never forget it. It came with little warning in the afternoon of September 21 and hit the Westhampton Beach area with terrible ferocity. Abnormally high tides, topped with huge breakers, sent 50-foot waves

A Long Island landmark and monument to an unfulfilled dream is the Montauk Manor Hotel. Built in 1926 at a cost of $1,000,000, it was intended as the capstone of developer Carl Fisher's "Miami Beach of the North," but fell victim to the Depression.

OVERLEAF
Jones Beach, one of the earliest of Robert Moses' projects, opened in the summer of 1929 and became popular immediately. By the Fourth of July, 1952, when this photograph was taken, the only space left was in the ocean.

roaring across the dunes, crushing hundreds of homes, tossing cars as if they were cartons, ripping new inlets into Quantuck and Shinnecock Bays, and killing at least 70 people, including 28 in Westhampton Beach alone. Power and telephone lines were out for days in some eastern Suffolk villages, travel was impossible as roads lay buried under several feet of water, sand, and mud, and many of the houses left standing were damaged beyond repair. Winds were clocked in excess of 100 miles per hour, and few communities were unscarred by the disaster.

The 1938 hurricane struck the South Shore of eastern Long Island with devastating force as this scene of destruction in Westhampton demonstrates. More than 70 people were killed during a few hours on September 21.

Besides being assailed by nature, Long Island was the scene those days of another kind of affliction. In the summer of 1937, stunned villagers watched as swastika-wearing, jack-booted members of the German-American Bund marched behind a brass band through Yaphank to Camp Siegfried, a 45-acre site of Nazi demonstrations and propaganda. Streets were named for Hitler, Goering, and Goebbels; bungalows were festooned with Nazi paraphernalia and photographs of the German dictator and his lieutenants; and books such as *Mein Kampf* and anti-Semitic pamphlets were offered for sale.

The Bund, formally the Amerikadeutscher Volksbund, had infiltrated and then taken over the German-American Settlement League, Inc., an organization that operated a communal settlement near a Yaphank lake. Under the leadership of Fritz Kuhn, a German engineer who aspired to

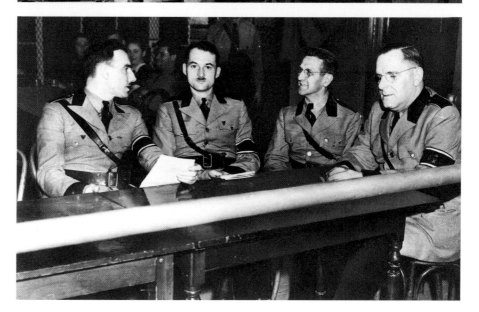

become an American führer, the summer campsite was transformed into a miniature Germany, a place where sympathizers of the Third Reich could eat frankfurters, drink beer, and expose their children to Nazi indoctrination, martial training, and racial and religious hatred.

By the summer of 1938, Camp Siegfried was attracting as many as 50,000 spectators on a Sunday afternoon to watch close-order drill to the sound of German Army marches and hear Kuhn extol this "Aryan paradise and part of Germany in America." But the end of paradise was already in sight. Several members of the German-American Settlement League were charged with failure to file membership lists with the state government, and, perhaps worst of all, the Suffolk County Alcoholic Beverage Control Board refused to renew Camp Siegfried's beer and wine license. By 1939, Kuhn, convicted of grand larceny and forgery, was seeking converts in Sing Sing Prison. The Bund hung on through the courts until the United States declared war on Germany and seized the organization's assets.

Although Long Islanders expressed curiosity and displeasure in the mid-1930s about the Nazis in their midst, they showed only limited concern about those in Germany and the impact they soon would have on everyone's life. The Depression was still making its presence felt, and whatever political interest Long Islanders had was focused largely on the domestic scene.

On Long Island, particularly in Nassau, politics in the modern era has been determined by fear of one machine and acceptance of another. Nassau's electorate has reacted to the possibility of control by New York's *frequently* corrupt Democratic organization by preferring the control of its own *occasionally* corrupt Republican organization. It was imminent rule by New York City at the turn of the century that led to the county's formation. At a Mineola meeting called in 1898 to create Nassau by withdrawing from Queens the towns of Hempstead, North Hempstead, and Oyster Bay, a resolution was adopted unanimously. Containing what since has become for Republican candidates an obligatory swipe at the reputedly omnivorous octopus to the west, the resolution asserted that independence for Nassau was essential "to carry into effect the desire of the people to have a county free from entangling alliance with the great city of New York."

In the early years of the twentieth century, Republicans and Democrats swapped domination of the Nassau County Board of Supervisors—then composed of the chief executives (supervisors) of the three townships—as the Democrats stressed GOP "extravagance" and the Republicans warned of the "Tammany tiger." But within a few years, a wealthy oysterman and state assemblyman from the Five Towns, named G. Wilbur Doughty, became the man to deal with in western Nassau. Doughty's anti-New York City credentials were impeccable: he actually had gotten Inwood, his hometown, taken out of Queens and placed in Nassau.

In 1912, the GOP was split throughout the nation by the decision of former President Theodore Roosevelt to frustrate the presidential reelection bid of his one-time favorite and fellow Republican William Howard Taft. Roosevelt did it by running for President himself as an independent under the banner of the Progressive (Bull Moose) Party. Republicans everywhere were forced to choose between their party's incumbent candidate, Taft, and the popular ex-President who was campaigning against him. Nowhere was this controversy more divisive than in Nassau, where Roosevelt lived and enjoyed the support and friendship of prominent Republicans. When the election returns came in, it was clear that both Roosevelt and Taft had lost to Democrat Woodrow Wilson. What became evident only later was that Doughty had *really* won. The internal GOP strife helped Wilson to carry Nassau county, and enabled Doughty to take over the leadership of the stricken local Republican organization.

Shrewd and tough, Doughty assured his dominance by getting the State Legislature to require that representation on the Board of Supervisors be proportional, according to the relative population of the towns. This gave the Town of Hempstead, which happened to be Doughty's bailiwick, an additional seat, which he immediately filled with himself. Now armed with both public office and political power, he had little difficulty in asserting his will. Doughty formed an alliance with Andrew (Uncle Andy) Weston, a successful contractor and Republican leader, that brought Weston millions of dollars in highway and bridge contracts, usually without competitive bidding, as well as an indictment in 1922 for handing in false claims. The indictment was quashed.

Weston went on to become a millionaire-builder whose projects ranged from the Canadian border to the Alabama swamps. Doughty survived his own indictment in 1920, charging that he had tipped off gambling houses of impending raids (it was quashed), and groomed his nephew, J. Russel Sprague, a Lawrence police justice, to succeed him.

When Doughty died in 1930, Sprague was ready and took over as Hempstead's supervisor-at-large, but he had to endure five years of infighting before he could assume his uncle's party mantle. In overcoming older and more experienced Republican politicians (Sprague was a comparatively young 43 when Doughty died), he had the considerable clout of Weston behind him. Created very much in Doughty's mold, Sprague did nothing to interrupt the beneficial arrangements that the contractor had enjoyed with his uncle. Materially, as well as politically, the Sprague-Weston relationship paid off for both. In later years, with Weston's help, Sprague made more than $500,000 on a $2,000 investment through secret harness-racing stock manipulations.

Pragmatic but farsighted, Sprague had a talent for organization and a feel for the future. His skills became apparent in the 1936 elections. The Republicans won handily in Nassau, despite losses almost everywhere else in the nation because of President Franklin D. Roosevelt's landslide conquest of Alfred M. Landon.

The 1936 election also marked the passage of the Nassau County Charter, a blueprint for modernizing county government by consolidating authority and responsibility under one official, to be called the county executive, and centralizing into new county departments many of the services formerly handled by towns and villages. It was a substantial personal victory for Sprague. He had championed the charter over the objections not only of Democrats but of many fellow Republicans who were concerned about the effect on tradition, local rule, and, of course, patronage. Once again the "Tammany tiger" was paraded into the Nassau arena and did its job: in leading the fight for adoption, Sprague described the charter as "a positive guarantee against future annexation to New York City without consent of our own people."

The charter went into effect in 1938 and, perhaps predictably, Sprague became Nassau's first county executive, a post to which he was reelected four times before retiring in 1952. Normally reserved and businesslike in appearance as well as manner, he had a politician's knack of projecting charm when necessary, a quality that made him a formidable candidate in addition to being a consumate boss.

Under Sprague's direction, Nassau's Republican organization gained a nationwide reputation for unanimity and efficiency. Loyalty was demanded and rewarded, although Sprague could forgive former political enemies, provided they were Republicans, when it suited the party's and his own purposes. He gained substantial status from his relationship with Thomas E. Dewey, although the former racketbuster failed—with Sprague's backing—in his 1938 attempt to unseat Democratic Governor Herbert Lehman and in his 1940 bid to become the GOP candidate for President. But Sprague's faith was vindicated when Dewey was elected governor in 1942 and swept the Republican presidential nomination on the first ballot in 1944. A decade later, in 1952, now wielding even wider influence as a Republican national committeeman, Sprague was an early passenger on the bandwagon of Dwight Eisenhower, when the popular general became the first Republican President in twenty years.

National politics did not diminish Sprague's interest in local party

BELOW

J. Russel Sprague, left, first Nassau county executive and the party leader who made the county's Republican organization the envy of politicians throughout the nation, accompanies New York Governor Thomas E. Dewey, the 1948 GOP presidential candidate, on a campaign swing through New Jersey.

OPPOSITE

Prematurely pleased with early returns on election night in 1950, W. Kingsland Macy, left, Suffolk Republican power and two-term congressman, later learned that he had lost his reelection bid to a little-known Democrat named Ernest Greenwood. With Macy, who continued wearing high, starched collars long after they had gone out of style, is Surrogate Edgar Hazelton of Huntington.

matters. Foreseeing the need to broaden the Nassau Republican organization's traditional Anglo-Saxon, Protestant hierarchy, he opened leadership posts to others, especially Italians, who were destined to become the county's largest ethnic group.

While the Doughty-Sprague dynasty was determining the political direction of Nassau, a colorful, old-fashioned, vengeful Republican boss was doing the same for Suffolk. Unlike his Nassau counterparts, however, W. Kingsland Macy was not reared for politics; his interest arose from a dispute with Robert Moses. Scion of a wealthy Nantucket whaling family, Macy was brought to Islip at the age of three, went through Groton and Harvard, ran a wholesale grocery firm, and was a partner in a Wall Street brokerage house before being politicized by the controversy over Moses' plan to transform the hunting preserve on the former George C. Taylor estate into a park.

Macy's zest and leadership in that fight led to an invitation in 1926 to become Suffolk County Republican chairman. He accepted and promptly buttressed his new role by purchasing a string of eight weekly newspapers. A committed conservative in ideology and dress, he favored high, starched collars and vitriolic exchanges. But he did not shun publicity and engaged in highly visible hostilities with Democrats and Republicans alike: from Franklin D. Roosevelt and Alfred E. Smith to Fiorello LaGuardia and Thomas E. Dewey.

As county and, in 1930, state GOP chairman, Macy attacked the scandalous administration of New York Democratic Mayor James J. Walker, and he was instrumental in launching the Seabury Commission investigation that paved the way for Walker's resignation. Macy's zeal and ambition were exceeded only by his inability to forgive or forget, a characteristic that led to an ongoing feud with Dewey and his own descent into political oblivion.

Dumped as state chairman in 1934, Macy was appointed to a 12-year term on the Board of Regents in 1941 and became enraged when Dewey, then governor, sought in 1948 to limit the board's power. Macy was determined to eliminate the popular governor from the state scene by frustrating Dewey's renomination in 1950, reportedly by making Dewey the Republican candidate for U.S. Senator.

On the eve of the 1950 GOP state convention, Lieutenant Governor Joe R. Hanley, who had been expected to run for governor, wrote a letter to Macy stating that Dewey had promised to clear up Hanley's personal debts if Hanley ran for the Senate and allowed Dewey to seek reelection. The letter wound up in Democratic hands and its blunt language stunned even professional politicians. "Today I had a conference with the governor in which certain unalterable and unquestionably definite propositions were made to me," Hanley stated. "If I will consent to take the nomination for the United States Senate, I am definitely assured of being able to clean up my financial obligations. . . ."

Macy denied leaking the letter to the Democrats and later won a libel suit against the *New York World-Telegram and the Sun* for an article contending that he had threatened to make the "Hanley letter" public unless he got the Senate nomination himself. Macy unsuccessfully had sought such a nomination in 1940 and 1944.

However, the Democrats gave the letter wide circulation during the 1950 campaign, in which Dewey was reelected governor and Hanley was defeated for the U.S. Senate. But the biggest loser was Macy. Running for a third term in Congress to a seat he had won by an overwhelming margin in 1948 from a district that had a 7-1 Republican advantage, Macy lost by 138 votes out of 152,500 to a little-known former schoolteacher named Ernest Greenwood.

The extraordinary outcome was attributed to the "Hanley letter" and disclosures by *Newsday* of widespread gambling and other irregularities in Macy's Suffolk jurisdiction. Macy announced his retirement as Suffolk Republican chairman, then changed his mind, and was defeated 411 to 6 by County Clerk R. Ford Hughes at a county committee meeting. The unforgiving, one-time GOP power suffered his final humiliation in 1953, when a vindictive Dewey refused to reappoint him to the Board of Regents.

For *Newsday*, the end of "King" Macy's reign represented a major victory, the culmination of a lengthy and bitter campaign to oust a longtime political boss whose conservative policies frequently clashed with those of the young, progressive, and brash newspaper. It was a particularly sweet triumph for Alicia Patterson, *Newsday*'s first editor and publisher, who had been portrayed in Macy's weeklies as an evil witch named "Malicia" and had been called before a congressional committee at Macy's behest to answer unsubstantiated charges that *Newsday* had financed Greenwood's campaign.

Newsday's arrival was rather inconspicuous. Born in a converted Hempstead garage, its first issue of 32 pages was run off (on secondhand presses) on September 3, 1940, for a circulation of 15,000, who paid three cents to read it. The garage had housed the short-lived *Nassau Daily Journal*, which Harry F. Guggenheim, Miss Patterson's third husband and *Newsday*'s first president, had purchased for $50,000 because, as he told the former playgirl, "everybody ought to have a job; people who make a business out of pleasure seldom are happy."

The feisty tabloid's survival and unimagined success was a tribute not only to Miss Patterson's daring, imagination, and tenacity, but to her passion for newspapering, a drive unknown to most of her socialite friends who assumed that *Newsday* was simply a rich woman's toy. ("How nice of your husband to give you such a pleasant wedding present," one told her.) What they did not realize was that as the fifth generation of a newspaper-publishing family and daughter of the founder of the New York *Daily News*, she long had dreamed of running a paper and hoped it would be her father's. (The hope evaporated in 1945, when her father,

NASSAU'S COMPLETE DAILY
32 Pages — 3 Cents
Weather on Page 30

Newsday

FINAL EDITION
Tuesday, Sept. 3, '40
Vol. 1 . . . No. 1

U. S. GIVES BRITISH 50 WARSHIPS

Gets Naval, Air Bases in Return

Story on Page 4

Tear Gas Battle on North Shore

Story on Page 2

↑ He's Happy

And he has reason to be happy, having just pocketed the $1,000 first prize in our What's-In-A-Name contest. Tied with two others, Larry Brown won in a playoff of essay-writing. Brown, an East Hempstead engineer, plans to make some other people happy with his prize-money by paying off debts. His wife, Hazel, and 2½-year-old daughter may have some ideas of their own about spending the money. Other pictures and stories on Pages 3 and 5.

← He's Not

And he has his reasons, too. Today was the end of his summer freedom. Back to school he went, feet shuffling, chin down. When he got there, Kenneth Benson, 8, of State St., Merrick, plumped down on the steps, hoping for some miraculous reprieve. None came. Finally he shook off the faraway look and dragged his brand new school bag in the North Merrick Grammar School. School story on Page 3.

Will F. D. R. Gain or Lose in County? See Page 2

Joseph Medill Patterson, changed his will after a dispute over President Roosevelt whom she admired and he detested.)

Extraordinary events would shape the future of the newspaper, which, in turn, would have its own impact on the future of Long Island. Surviving World War II, with its paper, gasoline, and manpower shortages, was to prove even more crucial to *Newsday* than anyone might have imagined, for that positioned the newspaper to take advantage of the mass postwar movement of potential readers to the suburbs.

Although Miss Patterson's first editorial promised that "our first, second and final object is to present the news," in its early days the paper seemed poised on the brink of advocacy. If readers sometimes confused its news stories with its editorials, they never misunderstood its intent. Some of its early campaigns may have found unyielding authorities and even unsympathetic subscribers; but when young, uncertain, impatient veterans and their families later poured onto the Island, they appeared to sense an ally in this cocky, unconventional newcomer that seemed so eager to challenge virtually anything and anyone.

By starting a Suffolk edition in 1944, *Newsday* became the first Long Island newspaper to publish for both Suffolk and Nassau residents. This gave it a unique bicounty role that no governmental or public interest agency was filling; its concern transcended divisions and borders—it saw the two counties as a single Long Island.

When *Newsday*'s first issue rolled off the presses in 1940, Miss Patterson joined a small and hardly secure group of Long Island editors who could trace their heritage to David Frothingham, a young Massachusetts printer responsible for the Island's first journal, the *Long Island Herald*, whose initial issue was published in Sag Harbor on May 10, 1791. Although it printed little local news, the *Herald* was hardly reluctant to tackle controversy, and ran sharply worded editorials accusing President John Adams of operating the young democracy as if it were a monarchy. The paper also published some foreign and domestic news reprinted from other newspapers, as well as essays, poems, and local advertisements.

Frothingham closed the *Herald* on December 17, 1798, and, at the urging of Republican Aaron Burr, took over the New York City *Argus*. By switching papers, Frothingham achieved public notoriety, but journalistic fame, for his conviction under the newly enacted Sedition Act. The suit was brought by Federalist Alexander Hamilton over a letter published in the *Argus* in 1799 accusing him of having sought to suppress a Republican paper called *Aurora*. Frothingham was fined and imprisoned.

Sag Harbor was the scene of much of Long Island's early journalism. In 1804, Alden Spooner, a resident of Connecticut and descendant of *Mayflower* Pilgrim John Alden, began work at the *Suffolk Gazette* as its sole employee. "It will appear curious to any printer," he wrote, "to be told that I printed the *Suffolk Gazette* about two years, without the assistance of any person whatever—not even a boy! I was editor, printer, publisher, clerk and errand boy."

In 1811, Spooner bought a Brooklyn paper called the *Long Island Star*, which had been founded two years earlier. A weekly, like most of the early papers, it underwent a series of name changes and became a semi-weekly and a daily while remaining in the Spooner family until 1863, when it was discontinued. Among the *Star*'s employees was a teenager named Walt Whitman. He had been an apprentice in the composing room of another Brooklyn paper, the weekly *Long Island Patriot*,

One of Long Island's earliest newspaper publishers, Alden Spooner is shown in a portrait painted in 1832 or 1833 by Hubbard L. Fordham, about the time that Spooner hired young Walt Whitman as a printer's devil for his Long Island Star. *Spooner had bought the* Star, *which was published in Brooklyn, in 1811; it remained in the Spooner family until 1863.*

where he began working at the age of twelve. Spooner reportedly considered Whitman, who was obviously a late bloomer, as "an idle boy," and, according to one version, said that "if he had been stricken with fever and ague, the boy would have been too lazy to shake."

Despite such disparagement, Whitman, at nineteen, went on to found *The Long-Islander* in Huntington, which he left after about two years, although the paper still exists. Its first issue was noted by the *Enquirer*, a Hempstead weekly, which said that "from its columns we judge that its publisher (Mr. W. Whitman) has spared no pains to make it acceptable to the reading community."

In 1846, when he was twenty-six, Whitman became editor of the *Brooklyn Daily Eagle*, an influential daily established five years earlier. Under Whitman, the *Eagle* generally took a liberal line that reflected the Democratic-Republican philosophy, advocating humanitarian principles and civic improvement. As editor, Whitman covered news events, wrote editorials, and reviewed books, plays, operas, concerts, lectures, and art exhibits. The *Eagle* became a Brooklyn standby for another century, but Whitman was fired some two years later over his support of the Wilmot Proviso, which opposed the extension of slavery into any territories acquired through the Mexican War. After losing his job, the man who was to become one of America's greatest poets was hired as editor of the *Brooklyn Freeman*, a free-soil newspaper that he quit a year later when its editorial policy changed.

Although several daily newspapers, including Horace Greeley's *New York Tribune* and *The New York Times*, were in circulation before the Civil War, Long Island did not get its own daily until after World War I. Founded on March 7, 1921, in Rockville Centre by James E. Stiles, who had begun publishing weeklies in 1914, the *Nassau Review* began with 8 pages; by 1927, fed by the real estate boom, it became *The Nassau Daily Review*, with 24 pages and a circulation of more than 10,000.

The only local daily until *Newsday*'s arrival in 1940, Stiles' standard-size paper, by then the *Nassau Daily Review-Star*, found itself surpassed in circulation within two years by the upstart tabloid. Paralyzed by a lengthy strike in 1947, the beset *Review-Star* was bought by chain publisher S. I. Newhouse and merged in 1953 into his *Long Island Daily Press*, a Queens-based operation. In the 1960s, the now established tabloid overcame a brief challenge from *The Suffolk Sun*, a Cowles Communications paper put out in Deer Park for three years before it closed shop in 1969. Newhouse in 1977 folded the *Press*, leaving the Long Island newspaper field open to *Newsday*.

If Long Island has proved economically inhospitable to some newspapers, it has provided a healthy climate for much of the aircraft industry. When American involvement in World War II became increasingly likely, the nation began its military preparedness program. And it looked to the "Cradle of Aviation" for help.

By the end of the 1930s, there were about 5,000 people working in Long Island airplane plants, a figure that soared to almost 90,000 during the war. In 1939, about 700 employees of the Grumman Aircraft Engineering Corporation, formed in 1929 by Leroy Grumman and Leon (Jake) Swirbul, were turning out fighters and scout bombers for the Navy from the company's new plant in Bethpage; in nearby Farmingdale, at what had been the Seversky Aircraft Corporation, 1,500 employees of the recently formed Republic Aviation Corporation were making pursuit planes for the Swedish government and the U.S. Army.

After the Japanese bombed Pearl Harbor on December 7, 1941, these two manufacturers went into an all-out production schedule that, combined with the effectiveness of their planes, has been credited with changing the course of the air war over both the Pacific and Europe. For Grumman, the F4F Wildcat, its successor the F6F Hellcat, and the TBF-1 Avenger, with their folding wings, became not only the Navy's standard carrier-based fighters and torpedo bombers, but legends.

During the first five months of 1944, only 71 Hellcats were lost in destroying 444 Japanese planes in air combat and another 323 on the ground. A month later, during the battle of the Marianas, Hellcats shot down 346 enemy aircraft in one day—the war's greatest aerial victory —while losing only 30 of their own. And one Navy squadron reported that it had lost only one Avenger in sinking 14 enemy ships. It was such performance that endeared the company to American pilots and led Vice Admiral John S. McCain to tell a Washington labor conference that "the name 'Grumman' on a plane or part has the same meaning to the Navy that 'Sterling' on silver has to you."

What Grumman was doing to the Japanese in the Pacific, Republic was doing to the Nazis in Europe. Its P-47 Thunderbolt fighter-bomber knocked the Luftwaffe out of the sky at the rate of better than four-to-one. By war's end, Republic had grown to be the world's largest producer of fighter aircraft. More than 23,000 workers—60 percent of them women—had turned out over 9,000 Thunderbolts at the expanded Farmingdale complex, while another 6,000 were made at factories in Indiana. At Grumman, the record was even more astonishing. With 25,000 employees, the company put better than 17,000 planes into the hands of the Navy. To keep production at top speed, Grumman provided a nursery school, job counseling, and even a trucking service that repaired workers' cars and ran errands for them. By giving employees bonuses for keeping production costs down, the corporation pioneered a new type of incentive system that reduced the per-plane price of the Hellcat from $50,000 to $35,000 (a saving to the Navy in 1944 of more than $127 million).

There was also the Sperry Gyroscope Company, whose 32,000 workers made bombsights, automatic pilots, radar equipment, and other flight-related instruments at plants in Lake Success and Garden City. More than 4,000 employees worked for the Fairchild Camera and Instrument Corporation, and other thousands were hired by the Long Island aviation industry's largest subcontractor, the Liberty Aircraft Products Company in Farmingdale.

The overwhelming majority of Long Island war workers had never seen an assembly line. Many of the housewives never had a job before, but they poured into the factories, learned skills, and altered their lifestyles. Altered, too, was the landscape and character of Long Island. The war effort had changed forever its rural-residential ambience, splattering the flat fields with vast factories, exposing its recesses to commuting city dwellers, and creating a pent-up demand for its living space that would erupt in succeeding decades.

Long Island's location made it particularly sensitive to fears of bombing and submarine and naval attack; while there was a lot of excitement and some anxiety, no action was taken. Anti-aircraft batteries were set up in remote areas of Nassau's South Shore and Suffolk's East End, but never fired at an enemy. Civilians volunteered as aircraft spotters, learned how to distinguish between a German Messerschmitt and a British Spitfire, but did not see either. Still, the beaches bore grim reminders that the war was being fought only miles away. Gobs of oil, charred timbers, and bits of life jackets floated onto the sand from torpedoed ships. Coast Guardsmen patrolled the many miles of shoreline.

One of them was Seaman 2/c John C. Cullen. Shortly after midnight on June 12, 1942, he left the Amagansett Lifeboat Station in a thick fog to begin walking his three-mile post. Unarmed, in accordance with regulations, he had gone only a few hundred yards when he spotted three figures on the beach. The 21-year-old Coast Guardsman challenged them, and the men said that they had been fishing when their boat ran aground. Cullen told them that they would have to accompany him to the Coast

Over Europe, P-47 Thunderbolts, made in Farmingdale by the Republic Aviation Corporation, took a heavy toll of Nazi aircraft and armored vehicles. These P-47N models, a long-range version, were flown principally in the Pacific. Republic was the world's largest producer of fighter planes.

LEFT AND BELOW
*One of World War II's most
extraordinary episodes took place on
a beach near Amagansett, where four
Nazi saboteurs were put ashore by
submarine in 1942. Two Coast
Guardsmen and a U.S. Navy officer,
center, examine the place where
explosives were buried. Four other
agents were dropped off in Florida.
All but George Dasch* (SECOND FROM
BOTTOM) *and Ernst Peter Burger*
(BOTTOM) *were executed. Other eyes,
belong to Edward Kerling, Werner
Theil, Heinrich Harm Heinck, and
Richard Quirin.*

Guard station and file a report. At that point, a fourth man, dragging a large canvas sack, walked out of the surf.

Suspicious, Cullen turned to go but was stopped by one of the men who first threatened him and then, after a discussion in German with his companions, offered him a bribe. Cullen quickly took the money and ran back to his station to report the incident to skeptical officers. Within minutes, Coast Guardsmen were combing the beach and within hours, after first a pack of German cigarettes and then crates of explosives and German uniforms were unearthed, one of the most extensive spyhunts in American history was under way.

The four men were Nazi saboteurs who had been landed off the Amagansett beach by the U-202 in a fantastic and daring plot to destroy hydroelectric and aluminum plants, bridges and canal locks, railroad tracks and terminals, and New York City's reservoirs. Four other agents, assigned similar missions, were put ashore in Florida five days later.

The scheme had been worked out with a thoroughness worthy of Ian Fleming. "In the next six weeks," the eight were told during their first day of training, "you will become new men, with new identities, confirmed by birth certificates, draft cards and driver's licenses. When you destroy a machine or a factory or blow up a bridge, your work will not look like an accident. It will be sabotage and it will look like sabotage and the Americans will know that we are among them!" Carefully drilled, the eight English-speaking saboteurs were given $175,000 in American currency, clothes bearing American labels, explosives disguised as lumps of coal and blocks of wood, incendiary bombs enclosed in pen and pen-

Camp Upton at Yaphank, which had served as an Army base during World War I, was reactivated to train soldiers during World War II. Barracks were hurriedly constructed in 1940, and later that year draftees were trying on their new military garb.

cil sets, and handkerchiefs with the names of contacts written in invisible ink.

By the time the Coast Guard, Army, Navy, and FBI figured out what was happening, the four agents who had come ashore on Long Island were in New York City hotel rooms, having taken the 6:51 A.M. Long Island Rail Road train from Amagansett to Pennsylvania Station. What might have happened if their leader, George Dasch, had not surrendered to the FBI in Washington a week later, is speculation. What did happen was that his seven accomplices were rounded up, tried, convicted, and, in the case of six, electrocuted. Dasch and Ernst Peter Burger, an SS lieutenant colonel, testified for the government, were sentenced to prison, and, in 1948, sent back to Germany. Cullen, a Long Islander, was awarded the Legion of Merit and a special citation from President Roosevelt.

While Operation Pastorius—as the Nazis named the plot in wry homage to Franz Pastorius, considered America's first German immigrant—was surely the most spectacular war story to be enacted on Long Island, the hundreds of thousands of men and women stationed in Nassau and Suffolk undoubtedly have their own recollections.

Long Island was filled with members of the armed forces. Camp Upton was reactivated, the Army Air Corps trained pilots and ferried planes to Europe from Mitchel Field and Westhampton, which had been converted from a commercial airport. Camp Hero at Montauk housed long-range artillery, the Montauk Manor had sailors from the torpedo-testing unit at Fort Pond Bay, and the United States Merchant Marine Academy at Kings Point trained officers for the maritime service.

When World War II ended in 1945, the Navy station at Lido Beach, which began turning sailors to civilians at the rate of 2,000 a day, symbolized Long Island's rush into peacetime. The pace was frantic; everyone was so anxious to resume their lives, to return to normalcy. What nobody realized was that within a decade Long Island would be changed more drastically than at any time in its history.

CHAPTER TEN

Taking Stock

The popularity of shopping malls altered the face and economy of postwar Long Island. In 1996, Roosevelt Field doubled its capacity by adding a second floor of shops.

During the last half of the twentieth century, Long Island underwent an extraordinary transformation, altering its image from drowsy to dynamic to, some might even say, ditsy. Nassau and then Suffolk became the prototype—for better *and* worse—of the national drift. The Island served as a sometimes deliberate, often inadvertent, laboratory, where watershed industrial, technological, social, cultural, and political experiments succeeded and failed, yet repeatedly presaged the course of America itself.

Long Island's most significant contribution to the nation, no doubt the world, was contemporary suburbia. If the suburbs could be considered an invention, Long Island would hold the patent, having pioneered the essential suburban components: housing developments, shopping malls, and parkways. It provided real trees and grass to concrete-weary city dwellers, and at least the illusion of tranquillity and security. If it was a bit short on culture and became too long on traffic, in the beginning nobody seemed to mind. It was the prototype of the new American dream, and well before the century's end, suburbia was the nation's most popular address, the residence of choice of more Americans than either the cities or rural areas.

While at one time derided as a breeding ground for materialism and habitat of conservatism, Long Island has, in fact, been the catalyst for a host of progressive innovations and environmental reforms. It has been responsible for taking prayer out of the public schools, farmland out of the grasp of developers, cigarette smoke out of restaurants, and detergents out of washing machines. It can boast among its native born Billy Joel and Billy Crystal, Dr. J. and Dr. Watson, Willem de Kooning and Alfonse D'Amato. It produced and nurtured writers and painters, musicians and scientists, comedians and Hall of Fame athletes. Along with these icons, however, it must be answerable for such contributions to pop culture as "Long Island Iced Tea" (vodka, gin, rum, and triple sec are among the ingredients), schlockmeister Howard Stern, and Amy Fisher and Joey Buttafuoco.

This recent notoriety contrasts sharply with the Island's no-nonsense wartime persona and with the frenetic growth of ensuing decades. The end of World War II, the most devastating conflict in human history, found Long Island following the biblical admonition to turn swords into plowshares with near-literal obedience. In Nassau at Lake Success, the Sperry Gyroscope

Company, which had produced the bombsights that helped level the Axis enemies, was converted into the temporary headquarters of the United Nations. In Suffolk at Yaphank, the Brookhaven National Laboratory was constructed to develop the peaceful uses of atomic energy in place of the military training base Camp Upton.

Such dramatic symbols of hope had their counterparts in the hearts and minds of millions of veterans, who, having savored victory and then peace, were eagerly looking forward to the promise of fuller, richer, more rewarding lives. Foremost among their goals was the wish to move out of their parents' cramped urban apartments and create families of their own in new settings with new perspectives and new opportunities. What these young people wanted was a home of their own, a room for the kids, a yard for the dog: their share of the American dream.

But the war's demands on men and materials had virtually halted homebuilding. In this rare conjunction of scarcity and desire, Long Island became the site and William Jaird Levitt the leader of an enterprise that would alter forever the lives of hundreds of millions of people around the globe.

Levitt was thirty-eight years old, a college dropout, Navy veteran, and president of Levitt & Sons, Inc., when he and his brother Alfred, an architect, envisioned the creation, literally from the ground up, of an entire residential community: a place of homes, schools, playgrounds, swimming pools, community centers, shopping centers, even churches. And, it would be affordable. Levitt had already built on Long Island with Alfred and their father, Abraham, an attorney; before the war they had constructed houses in Rockville Centre and the more upscale "Strathmore" developments on the North Shore. But the grand scheme took shape in Norfolk, Virginia, where the company erected thousands of rental units for wartime shipyard workers using mass-production techniques that drastically reduced the time, and thus the cost, of construction.

Adapting the automobile assembly-line concept of Henry Ford, Levitt brought construction specialists to his homesites. More than 15,000 of them—carpenters, masons, plumbers, electricians, painters, and landscape gardeners—performed their roles in sequence. Heavy machinery operators, using Levitt equipment, dug trenches for foundations. Levitt cement mixers, using Levitt cement, poured rows of concrete slabs. Precut piles of lumber appeared as if by magic in front of each site at the appropriate time for squads of carpenters specializing in framing, sheathing, roofing, and shingling. The result was dazzling: the completion of thirty-five houses a day at costs that were $2,000 below those of competitors.

These spectacular accomplishments were not entirely the consequence of ingenuity in building. The Levitts did not use union labor; they did not provide basements; they used unconventional "radiant" heating; they demanded that appliance manufacturers sell directly to them; they did not give customers a choice of colors; and the only non-Caucasians allowed to occupy Levitt homes had to be "domestic servants."

Not all of these conditions and concessions were known on May 7, 1947, when *Newsday* headlined: 2,000 $60 RENTALS DUE IN L.I. PROJECT. The $16 million project, financed by the Federal Housing Administration (FHA), was proposed for a 500-acre tract of flat, treeless potato fields and vacant property south of Hempstead Turnpike in a sparsely settled area of Nassau fancifully called Island Trees. The plan was greeted with almost hysterical enthusiasm; within three weeks, Levitt received more than 6,000 written applications, and he promptly announced the purchase of enough property to accommodate another 2,000 units.

The only hitch was a Town of Hempstead building code provision that required basements. With *Newsday* unashamedly lobbying with editorials and "feature stories" for elimination of the requirement, more than 800 veterans and their spouses, many carrying babies, jammed the town hall and overflowed into the street when the board met for a hearing on the issue. The officials repealed the provision unanimously in just twenty minutes. To have done otherwise would have ended their political careers. Shouted one uniformed ex-GI: "Cellar or no cellar doesn't mean anything to me or anyone else here. We want the houses!" Roared another: "No cellar beats one room in an attic where you freeze to death for $45 a month!"

Construction began immediately on the four-room Cape Cod models with refrigerators, ranges, washing machines, and expandable attics. Only four months later, the first 200 families moved in. Three months later, Levitt gave the new community a new name: Levittown. This prompted residents to form Levittown's first civic association, defiantly named the Island Trees Community Association. Residents had other complaints, as well, particularly when Levitt hiked the rent to $65 and upped the "absolute maximum" purchase price from $6,990 to $7,990. But people rented and bought.

By the time he was finished, Levitt had built 17,447 homes, nine community swimming pools, a community hall, playgrounds, ball fields, village greens, and shopping centers. He planted more than 500,000 trees and set aside property for houses of worship—enough for a community of 83,000 people, which is what it became.

And Levittown became far more. It set the pattern for other developments on Long Island and for other Levittowns elsewhere: in Pennsylvania, New Jersey, Maryland, even Europe. It opened the door of affordable housing to war veterans and opened the floodgates to a mass exodus from the city. It was the symbol of postwar suburban growth and the stereotype of postwar suburban lifestyle.

The legacy of William Jaird Levitt was mixed. From the estimated $1,000-per-house profit his company derived from Levittown, he developed a home-building empire that brought $90 million when he sold it to International Telephone and Telegraph in 1968. He accumulated immense personal wealth and spent lavishly: a mansion on sixty-eight acres in Mill Neck, a collection of Impressionist paintings, and a magnificent yacht. But he also gave profusely: to the State of Israel, to North Shore University Hospital, where he died of kidney failure in the Levitt Diagnostic Center at the age of eighty-six in 1994. Yet the business acumen that built his fortune and reputation in the Forties and Fifties and Sixties, deserted him in the Seventies and Eighties, when a series of ill-conceived undertakings and questionable dealings in Florida, Iran, Nigeria, and Venezuela cost him not only his North Shore estate but his right to ever again put up a house in New York State.

While he may have been a visionary when it came to housing, Levitt was hardly a social or political idealist. His whites-only covenant, although arguably an outgrowth of the racist policies of the FHA, contributed to the discriminatory nature of suburban life. His actions in the Fifties, such as denying a meeting hall to the Committee to End Discrimination in Levittown

Where suburbs take root, can shopping malls be far behind? Not in the Long Island of the Fifties, as this night scene at Roosevelt Field confirms. The Roosevelt Field mall was one of the nation's first attempts at one-stop shopping.

and seeking to evict two families who allowed black children to play in their yards, clearly transcended mere real estate practice. But he hardly stood alone. At the time, *Newsday* lent him its support, editorializing: "Organizations which appear to be either Communist-dominated or Communist-inspired have been attempting to raise a racial issue at Levittown."

In the final analysis, those who bought Levitt houses (generally with the aid of cheap, long-term FHA and Veterans Administration mortgages) seem to have done considerably better than those who conceived them. Far from becoming the slum that many had predicted, expansions, extensions, innovations, and a healthy market have boosted prices of some homes into the $200,000 range. The criticism of "ticky-tacky" sameness that was heaped on Levittown in its early days can no longer be substantiated. One cannot find two houses that look alike.

Tantalized by the success of Levittown, Long Island builders quickly shifted their focus from the upscale to the mainstream market. And they were not disappointed: buyers by the tens of thousands, mostly from Brooklyn and Queens, lined up to become the newest suburbanites. In the Fifties the growth seemed unending. Long Island's population, 604,103 in 1940, increased almost 60 percent by 1950, then more than doubled to nearly 2 million by 1960. Nassau, closest to New York City, was the initial target. Its population soared by 65 percent in the Forties and 93 percent in the Fifties, before settling down—when space ran out—to a slim 10 percent in the Sixties. The rush to Suffolk came only slightly later. Its population jumped 40 percent in the Forties, 142 percent in the Fifties, and 69 percent in the Sixties. The extraordinary influx made Nassau the fastest growing county in the United States during the Fifties; in the Sixties that title fell to Suffolk. Since the mid-Seventies the population of Nassau has been stable at about 1.3 million, while the population of Suffolk has risen from 1.2 million to approximately 1.35 million.

This unprecedented movement modified far more than the Long Island landscape, creating vast changes—some obvious, others unforeseeable. One of the first changes occurred in consumer business. The new Long Islanders needed goods, but the established merchants were located in the old towns, inconvenient to the newcomers, and incapable of coping with traffic and parking demands. New shops followed their potential customers and clustered together; they provided parking facilities and other amenities, and thus became shopping centers. The largest shopping centers enclosed themselves like cocoons and became shopping malls: Roosevelt Field, Smith Haven, Sunrise, and Walt Whitman.

Amid this swirling change, some communities, particularly the established, commuter-oriented villages in western Nassau, such as the Five Towns (Hewlett, Woodmere, Cedarhurst, Lawrence, and Inwood), Rockville Centre, Lynbrook, East Rockaway, Roslyn, East Williston, Garden City, Mineola, Port Washington, Manhasset, and Great Neck, retained their traditional, prewar character. In her tender, insightful memoir, *Wait Till Next Year*, Pulitzer Prize–winning author Doris Kearns Goodwin captured the distinctive small-town ambience of Rockville Centre, with its "century-old Village Hall . . . set in a green square with a Civil War cannon near the front door."

The house in which I grew up was modest in size, situated on less than a tenth of an acre, and separated from the neighboring houses by the narrowest of driveways and a slender strip of grass. For my parents, however, as for other families on the block, the house on Southard Avenue was the realization of a dream. My family had moved to Rockville Centre from the crowded streets of Brooklyn in the late 1930s, early pioneers of that vast postwar migration which was to transform America into a nation of suburbs, and bring to once-bucolic Nassau and Suffolk counties a population as large as that of sixteen of the forty-eight states. Here they would have a single-family home, a private world for themselves and their children, which they could make their own— furnish, repair, remodel—something which only a few years before had seemed the prerogative of the impossibly affluent. They took visible pleasure in every room, the gabled roof, the small enclosed porch that looked out onto the street, the breakfast nook that stood in an alcove off the kitchen, and most of all in the tiny front lawn amid which our house was set. They had land, grass, soil of their own. The great American ambition.

However, beyond such stable and tranquil enclaves, the kinetic pace created immense demands. More people meant more services: more schools, more roads, more trains, more sewage disposal, more hospitals, more electric power. But the population explosion caught Long Island officials with their plans down. The growing pains were acute and efforts to deal with problems engendered by the burgeoning population often were accompanied by bitter controversy, extraordinary costs, patent mismanagement, and flat-out corruption. Poor planning, faulty construction, inefficient administration, and even tragedy and scandal became almost routinely associated either with Suffolk's Southwest Sewer District, Nassau's County Medical Center, the Long Island Rail Road, or Long Island Lighting Company's Shoreham Nuclear Power Station.

In the early Seventies the disposal of sewage was a desperate necessity in Suffolk and unscrupulous contractors found an opportunity of the first water.

The resulting mess aborted the political career of Republican County Executive John V. N. Klein, whose misplaced trust and sloppy oversight cost him renomination, and, in the belief of many, a potential seat in the Governor's Mansion or the U.S. Senate. Klein, the son of a prominent judge, had risen dramatically in Suffolk politics and earned international acclaim for pioneering a widely copied farmland preservation program that has saved thousands of acres from commercial and residential development. Although Klein was reared as a lawyer to practice politics, he subsequently claimed to have found more fulfillment in his second career as a politician practicing law.

More people in the postwar push also meant more commuters, and more passengers for the overburdened and chronically ailing Long Island Rail Road. In 1950, within the span of nine months, two devastating crashes on the nation's largest commuter line took more than 100 lives and maimed additional hundreds. The collisions—the first, on February 17 at Rockville Centre, killed 29 and injured 75; the second, on Thanksgiving Eve, November 22, at Richmond Hill, killed 77 and injured 334—chilled Long Islanders and led to major safety measures. In early 1988 the centenarian railroad took a major leap into the present by electrifying its diesel service eastward to Ronkonkoma, cutting more than a half hour of travel time to Pennsylvania Station and eliminating, at least for those passengers, the irksome change at Jamaica.

Although the Long Island Rail Road doubtless played a significant role in the development of suburbia, its importance tended to diminish as Nassau and Suffolk spawned their own economy. As increasing proportions of Long Islanders became employed on the Island, they chose to drive to work rather than commute by train to New York City, as an earlier generation had done. This, of course, put an immense strain on the highway system, which had served largely for weekend excursions into the country. Long Island's best roads, the parkway system created by Robert Moses, had been built to reach Moses's state parks, and thus were only indirectly useful; they were also off limits to trucks.

The response was to build more roads and widen or lengthen existing ones, such as Sunrise Highway and Jericho Turnpike. The Island's long, narrow shape dictated West–East routes and the major postwar transportation project became the Long Island Expressway, whose early promise quickly turned to notoriety. Running from the Queens-Midtown Tunnel to Riverhead, the frequently clogged artery finally reached its eastern terminus in 1972, eleven years behind schedule and $80 million over cost estimates.

The Fifties and Sixties may have been the "go-go" decades in the financial world, but that was not the name Long Island drivers had for them. These traumatized motorists found that the rush to the suburbs left them without an opportunity to rush anywhere. As demand continued to outpace supply, planners finally settled on adding twelve miles of lanes specifically for carpoolers—the state's first such highway lanes—known officially as HOV (for High

Occupancy Vehicle) corridors between Melville and Hauppauge. Using them during commuter hours (6 A.M. to 8 P.M. on weekdays) requires at least two people per car. Opened in 1994, the carpool lanes have been regarded as a qualified success, with the state claiming improvement and critics contending that the addition of normal lanes would have been more effective.

While many agencies and institutions ran into trouble because they failed to foresee the impact of the postwar migration, the Long Island Lighting Company was not one of them. Its problem was just the opposite: LILCO overestimated Long Islanders' electrical needs and their willingness to accept nuclear power as a solution. The price of this miscalculation is still being paid, not by LILCO executives or stockholders, but by Nassau and Suffolk homeowners and taxpayers, who pay the highest rates east of Hawaii.

The tale of nuclear energy on Long Island is a complex tragedy that began in the Sixties, with plans to build reactors in Shoreham and Jamesport. It ended in 1992 with the sale of the $5.5-billion Shoreham Nuclear Power Station to the Long Island Power Authority—for $1. The Shoreham plant never opened; the Jamesport plant was never even built. During the intervening decades, opposition to nuclear power mushroomed. The beginning of the end came in 1979 with a radiation leak at the Three Mile Island reactor in Pennsylvania. This precipitated the largest protest ever staged on Long Island, a 15,000-person demonstration against Shoreham, which at this point was well under construction. Governor Mario M. Cuomo needed no further incentive to spearhead the successful drive to prevent the plant from opening. The epilogue is still being written in tax litigation cases and governmental rulings. LILCO pulled the plug on itself in 1997 by merging with the Brooklyn Union Gas Company to become the New York Energy Company, a consolidation that promises as yet unspecified reductions for Long Island ratepayers.

Demonstrating that political shenanigans know no party, the farewell act of Democratic Nassau County Executive Eugene H. Nickerson, at the conclusion of his third term in 1970, was an attempt to push through an emergency no-bid contract for more than $2 million with a Democrat-friendly electrical firm to supply so-called "safe-patient centers," designed to protect patients from electrical hazards, at the Nassau County Medical Center. A *Newsday* investigation revealed the scheme, which did not go through. Nickerson went on to become a distinguished federal judge, as did his county attorney, Jack B. Weinstein.

But of all the population-boom problems that beset postwar Long Island, perhaps none was as symbolic and graphic as the garbage barge that was doomed to take a futile 187-day voyage in the spring of 1987 while three states and three countries refused to accept 3,186 tons of primarily Islip trash. Unequaled as a metaphor for excess and an example of poor planning, the episode was televised and T-shirted before becoming resolved through a state-city-town compromise. Commemorating the first anniversary of the sail, Islip Supervisor Frank Jones exulted: "If you had a public relations man trying to highlight what the problems were, I don't think he could have done it in a better way than to put the stuff on a barge and send it around the world."

Paradoxically, another Long Island town, Smithtown, had pioneered garbage disposal in the mid-Fifties by creating the first sanitary landfill, an important advance that buried garbage under dirt in order to avoid despoiling the environment. The most recent solution has been to truck Long Island's refuse to abandoned mine sites in West Virginia and Virginia, where garbage disposal is a profitable industry.

Another desperate need that arose in the frantic Fifties was the need for educational facilities at all levels. Between 1948 and 1954 elementary and high school enrollment on Long Island more than doubled, and by 1960 it had doubled again. One of the most extraordinary examples, as might be expected, was Levittown. In 1947 the Jerusalem School District consisted of a three-room schoolhouse and forty-seven pupils. Ten years later its successor, School District 5, was educating 16,300 students in fourteen buildings. Dramatizing the change is the Jonas F. Salk Middle School, a forty-room, $3 million struc-

The changing face of Long Island in 1996 is evident in this racially mixed primary classroom at the New Visions Elementary School in Freeport.

ture built opposite the original school on Jerusalem Road.

Concern about elementary and secondary education had been a Long Island tradition since colonial and Revolutionary times, but it took centuries for higher education to become available. Not until 1912, when the Legislature established a New York State School of Agriculture at Farmingdale, did the Island have its first public college. Students interested in careers other than farming had to wait until 1929, when Adelphi College, founded thirty-three years earlier as a women's institution in Brooklyn, moved to Garden City, where it became Long Island's first liberal arts school. In 1935, during the depth of the Depression, the Hempstead estate of a wealthy lumberman named William Hofstra was turned into a branch of New York University. Its name, Nassau College–Hofstra Memorial–New York University, hardly lent itself to a fight song. Two years later it separated from its parent institution to become Hofstra College.

The postwar crunch had its impact on higher education as well. Existing institutions expanded and new ones were born. Nassau's first college, the state agricultural school at Farmingdale, was absorbed into the state university system in 1948 and restructured as a two-year agricultural and technical college. Adelphi and Hofstra became universities, each initially educating more than 11,000 undergraduate and graduate students annually. In time, however, their fortunes varied significantly. Hofstra continued to grow, not only in the size of its student body, which by the late Nineties had reached 12,000, but in the quality of its faculty and the depth of its offerings. Conversely, Adelphi began to decline—in every respect. By the mid-Eighties, enrollment had dipped to about 7,000, financial collapse seemed possible, and desperation had led to the acceptance of 60 percent of its applicants. At this point, Adelphi's trustees took a step that not only failed to halt the slide but, a decade later, would plague the university.

The fateful decision occurred in 1985 when Dr. Peter Diamandopoulos, a

It was not until the twentieth century that Long Island's first college, the New York State School of Agriculture, opened at Farmingdale. But in the wake of the post-World War II exodus to the suburbs, higher education exploded, too. Adelphi (ABOVE) and Hofstra (MIDDLE) Colleges became universities; the Health Sciences Center gave a futuristic skyline to the State University of New York at Stony Brook (BELOW).

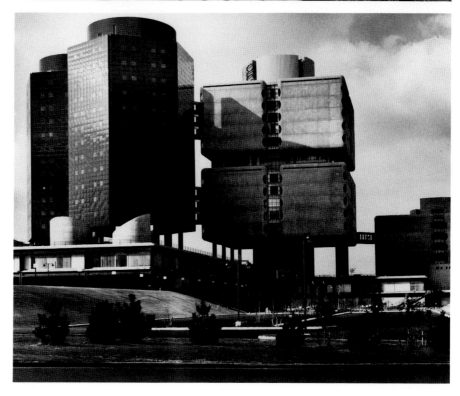

Harvard-educated philosophy professor at San Francisco State University, was hired as president. Armed with a daring plan to elevate the modest commuter school into a major liberal arts university, Diamandopoulos managed instead, in his fourteen-year tenure, to bring Adelphi to its knees. Running full-page advertisements that ranted "Harvard is the Adelphi of Massachusetts," he saw enrollment further dwindle to 4,600, the student-professor ratio balloon by one-third, and acceptances embrace 90 percent of applicants. But Diamandopoulos had a way with money. He increased Adelphi's endowment and reserves from $4 million to $48 million, while his 1994 salary of $523,000 made him the nation's second-highest-paid college president. (The highest paid, Dr. John Silber of Boston University, was on the three-member trustee panel that determined Diamandopoulos's pay.) When he was finally ousted in 1997—after his trustees had been removed by the New York State Board of Regents and replaced by a new board—Diamandopoulos was receiving more than $800,000 a year in salary and benefits.

The extraordinary demands of the postwar era could not be filled by Hofstra and Adelphi alone. New facilities arose, many on the luxurious estates adorning Nassau's Gold Coast. Long Island University opened its C. W. Post Center on the Brookville property of cereal heiress Marjorie Merriweather Post in 1955, where classes were first held in her stately fifty-nine-room Tudor mansion, and its Southampton College in 1963. New York Institute of Technology welcomed students to its Old Westbury campus on the onetime C. V. Whitney acreage in 1964; on the nearby fields of F. Ambrose Clark, the State University of New York College at Old Westbury began its program three years later.

In Suffolk, the fifty-two-acre former William K. Vanderbilt estate on the banks of the Connetquot River in Oakdale became the site of the county's first four-year college in 1955, when Adelphi established an extension and called it Dowling College. The institution became independent in 1968, and in 1993 acquired an additional 105 acres at Brookhaven Calabro Airport for the National Aviation and Transportation Center, which opened the next year.

Another Suffolk institution, the State University of New York at Stony Brook, is one of the Island's most prestigious centers of learning. Originally located in Oyster Bay in 1957 as the State University College to prepare high school mathematics and science teachers, it became a University Center in 1960, and moved to its present 1,000-acre campus in 1962. During the next thirty-five years its faculty grew from 175 to 1,600 and its student body from 1,000 to 17,000. The futuristic look of its Health Sciences Center, Long Island's tallest building when it was erected in 1976, has become a landmark, while the accomplishments of its faculty and graduates have gained international praise. An independent 1997 study ranked Stony Brook as the nation's third-best public research university, behind the University of California campuses at Berkeley and Santa Barbara.

The demand for local, low-cost education led to the creation of two-year community institutions in both counties. Nassau Community College opened in 1960 as part of the state university system and is now located at what had been Mitchel Air Force Base. Suffolk Community College, also founded in 1960, has campuses in Selden, Brentwood, and Riverhead.

Self-education on Long Island owes its origins to East Hampton's Reverend Samuel Buell, who, as early as 1753, organized the Philogrammatican Library. Six years later Huntington followed, as the Reverend Ebenezer Prime became custodian of a library society there. While many communities in both counties established public libraries before World War II, the population explosion of the Fifties triggered a corresponding demand for facilities. This was met in the two counties through formation of the Nassau Library System in 1959 and the Suffolk Cooperative Library System two years later. These provide consulting, processing, purchasing, and distribution services, and expedite the transfer of books from the shelves in one community to the readers in another. They also have benefited the public by helping various libraries to build collections in particular fields.

Although one might have suspected that the new Long Islanders would have resented the delayed arrival of the cultural venues that were readily available in the city, such was not the finding of an extensive study of suburban attitudes published by *Newsday* in 1973. Directed by two sociologists and entitled "The Real Suburbia," the survey debunked or, at least, challenged many of the characterizations of suburban life conveyed by films and novels. For example, the popular depiction of Long Island as a "cultural desert" was not endorsed by the Long Islanders interviewed. Almost two-thirds said that they were satisfied with Long Island's plays, concerts, and lectures. However, a similar proportion expressed disappointment with the number of museums and art galleries. But the significance of these responses is somewhat suspect, because the survey found that the more interest a respondent had in the arts, the more critical that person was of the adequacy of Long Island's facilities. Similarly, one interviewee, after admitting to never having visited a museum or art gallery anywhere, assumed that because plenty of shopping malls existed on Long Island the same must be true for galleries.

The study found that the major dissatisfactions with suburban living then—and probably now—were the cost of keeping up a house and the amount of time involved in traveling to work. These concrete concerns, Long Islanders indicated, were far more distressing than some of the frequently voiced complaints of social critics, such as the monotony of suburban life and the sameness of suburban residents. Residents told interviewers that far from being bored with the suburban scene, they liked what they had found.

More than nine out of ten respondents said that they would recommend their community to friends as a place in which to live. "It really bothers me," a Yaphank housewife said, "the way they call it 'suburbia' and make it sound so dreary. We think it's just fine."

The suburbanites said that they had encountered little difficulty in making friends or in coping with the relative isolation of their new environment.

Substantial majorities disagreed with the statement "I don't have as many friends here as I would like," saying that their neighbors were very friendly, and they reported visiting often with friends.

One mother in her late thirties remembered being quite concerned about moving to Dix Hills from her Queens apartment. "In the city neighborhood where I came from, everyone was very friendly," she recalled. "And I was very apprehensive, thinking that it would be very lonely out here, and that I would be stuck in the house all day with nothing to do. But when we settled in and I looked around, I found that many of the other women also came from a city environment and were just as anxious to make new friends. One thing I found was that in the city you never asked someone to go to the store with you, or pick something up, since it was very convenient to go by yourself. But now that you need a car to get to the store, neighbors will tell you when they're going—to see if you want a lift, or if there's anything they can get for you. That kind of cooperation makes for a very friendly atmosphere."

The overall contentment with suburban life found by the study was augmented by an absence of interest in the urban milieu. The Long Islanders told interviewers that they rarely went to New York City to shop, for entertainment or cultural events, or for any other reason. Only about 10 percent said that they visited at least once a month.

Such findings led to the conclusion that Nassau and Suffolk were emerging as a distinct suburban society with its own attitudes and values, one that no longer looked to New York for its needs. It also led to speculation that certain city dwellers had a clear propensity—socially, culturally, politically—for suburban living and that they eventually moved to the suburbs, leaving behind those with a more urban orientation.

As *Newsday* summed up: "It is a joke for Alan King, a vote for Richard Nixon, a sale for General Motors. It is a spawning ground for Big Mac and Little League, for professional buildings and amateur theatricals, for three-bedroom houses, two-car garages, one-stop shopping. It can be identified by an abundance of white collars and green lawns—and by a paucity of black faces. It is suburbia—the most populous, most desired, most debatable portion of America."

One of the 1973 survey's more intriguing findings dealt with the apparent political conversion that people underwent when moving from primarily Democratic New York City to primarily Republican Long Island. Many explanations have been given for this switch in party affiliation and voting behavior. Some observers attribute it to the desire to conform, some to the change that comes with acquiring property, and others to the persuasiveness of the Republican organizations in Nassau and Suffolk. However, the study found that New Yorkers who moved to Long Island were more likely to have always been Republicans than New Yorkers who remained.

Former Suffolk county executive and lifelong political observer John Klein articulated a more sophisticated and, probably, more accurate explanation. He attributed their political transformation to "enlightened self-interest." A

Former Suffolk County Executive John V. N. Klein describes his farm preservation program in 1977. The widely copied concept has kept thousands of acres out of developers' hands.

great many of the new Long Islanders, he said, were actually "New York City refugees." They had learned, he continued, that in New York City, "You enrolled in the Democratic Party, because if you didn't, you didn't get anything. Tammany Hall, like any efficient political machine, controlled everything that moved. So, if you were a Republican, you might as well forget about getting your kid a summer job, and so on, whereas if you were a Democratic committeeman, or a reliable Democratic voter, the situation was quite different. Understand, these were not philosophically rock-ribbed Democrats; they were Democrats because that was a pretty smart thing to do."

Klein said that these people loved where they had originally lived "as it originally was. But it underwent a great deal of change—none of which was for the better in the view of those who lived there, and so they decided to 'escape.' They came out here and discovered that the Republicans were in control, and they also found that it was a pretty nice way of life, and that whether actually, or only perceived, it was the Republicans who were 'keeping it that way.' And therefore maybe that's how I should be voting, and if I'm going to vote that way, maybe I should enroll that way. So, I think that had a lot to do with it: disenchantment with the city."

Disenchantment engendered by political corruption proved strong enough in 1959 to topple the traditional Republican hold. H. Lee Dennison, a Democrat who had never held political office, was elected the first Suffolk county executive and had a predominantly Democratic Board of Supervisors. The previous year, Suffolk voters had approved a charter providing for a county executive similar to the arrangement that had governed Nassau since 1938. Dennison won by only 559 votes, but he was twice reelected to four-year terms by substantially larger margins. There was little doubt that his success was based on personal popularity: Democrats lost control of the ten-member board and were in the minority on the eighteen-member county legislature that replaced it in 1970. (Nassau did not supplant its six-member board of supervisors with a nineteen-member legislature until 1996.) Republicans returned to power after Dennison and retained Suffolk's top executive office, except for one term, at least into the late Nineties.

In Nassau, the Republican grip was broken for the first time in 1961, when Democrat Eugene H. Nickerson was elected to the office of county executive; he was reelected in 1964 and again in 1967. Under the direction of dynamic county chairman John F. English, and under the spell of the Kennedy and Johnson administrations in Washington, the Nassau Democratic Party pulled one political upset after another and seemed to have the once omnipotent Republican machine in disarray. Misjudgment, internal power struggles, and evidence of corruption and conflicts of interest plagued the GOP in both counties during the chaotic postwar decades. It took years of grassroots effort, and the clever exploitation of demographic changes, before the party reestablished the dominance in local politics that had characterized it throughout most of the century.

One of the most significant political accomplishments of the postwar era in

Charisma and political sagacity were hallmarks of John F. English, the dynamic Nassau County Democratic chairman, seen bringing future president John F. Kennedy and his wife, Jacqueline, to the Party's annual dinner at the Garden City Hotel in 1959.

Nassau was the Republican organization's capture of traditionally Democratic Italian-Americans, who had become the county's largest ethnic group. Through the farsighted direction of GOP boss J. Russel Sprague, the once Anglo-Saxon Protestant hierarchy reached out to the newcomers by tapping Long Beach state senator Joseph Carlino for a leadership role. Control was sustained through party chairmen Joseph Margiotta and Joseph Mondello. (Margiotta, largely responsible for rebuilding the organization, later was imprisoned for taking part in a long-term kickback scheme.) Culminating these efforts was the upset victory in the 1980 U.S. Senate election of a little-known Hempstead presiding supervisor named Alfonse M. D'Amato.

Twice reelected to the Senate, by the late Nineties D'Amato had become the most potent politician in New York State. An extraordinary dealmaker and kingmaker (he handpicked George Pataki from virtual anonymity and helped him defeat incumbent governor Mario Cuomo in 1994), the legislator from obscure Island Park rose to head the influential Senate Banking Committee. And while even his devoted mother, a standard feature in his campaign commercials, doubtless does not seriously envisage his features on Mount Rushmore, D'Amato is arguably the most powerful Long Island Republican since Teddy Roosevelt.

If D'Amato fails to achieve historic stature it will not be due to any failure in his efforts on behalf of Long Island. Derided as "Senator Pothole" for his mundane values, he has converted that epithet into his trademark by assiduously bringing home the bacon and bagels to his constituents during a multi-term tenure. His accomplishments include enabling the Navy to convey 100 acres of the former Grumman Bethpage facility to Nassau County, getting more than $35 million for natural-gas buses and fueling facilities on Long

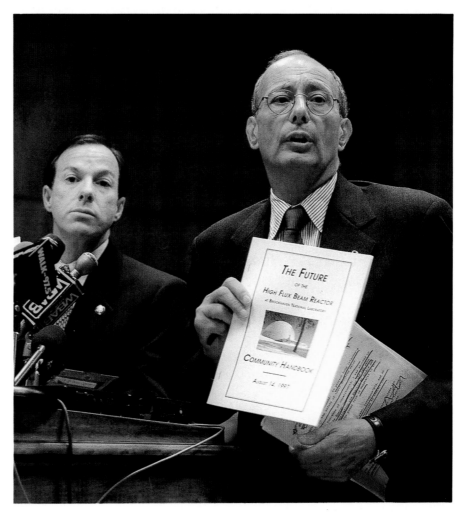

Island, obtaining more than $700 million from the Defense Department to fund breast cancer research and $47 million for a Long Beach restoration project. In addition to big money, the Senator shrewdly has focused on the little people, as when he convinced the Navy to pay fishing skipper Don Hand $220,000 as reimbursement for his eighty-two-foot trawler that was blown up when he caught an unexploded torpedo in his nets in December 1991.

However, D'Amato has been one of the nation's most controversial senators. Critics contend that his murky ethics, streetfighter style, transparent pandering to special interests, and lack of principles or convictions have made him more of an embarrassment than a boon to Long Island. This ambivalent reaction has been reflected repeatedly in statewide polls conducted by the Marist Institute for Public Opinion and by Quinnipiac College. While majorities of registered voters value D'Amato for his "leadership qualities" and for "getting things done," majorities also find him "not honest and trustworthy," "not someone you respect," nor "sympathetic to the problems of the poor."

Perhaps the most remarkable political story of the decade began with a tragedy. On December 7, 1993, as the Long Island Rail Road's 5:33 P.M. commuter train from Penn Station neared the Merillon Avenue stop in Garden

City, a thirty-five-year-old Jamaican immigrant named Colin Ferguson fired thirty rounds from a 9-mm semiautomatic pistol at fellow passengers, killing six and wounding nineteen. Among the dead was Dennis McCarthy; among the wounded, Kevin McCarthy, who was left partially paralyzed. Dennis was the husband, and Kevin the only child, of Carolyn McCarthy, a Mineola resident and enrolled Republican. No politician—she was a nurse who had never even run in a school board election—McCarthy, at fifty-two, decided to challenge her congressman, Representative Dan Frisa (R-Westbury), over his vote to repeal the assault-weapons ban. In a district where Republicans outnumber Democrats three to two, with a fervor born of the righteousness of her cause, she defeated the incumbent, a former assemblyman, in a 1996 election that deservedly drew national attention for its extraordinary drama.

Many of the revelations of wrongdoing that shocked voters and wounded politicians in the years following World War II resulted from investigations by *Newsday* reporters, especially Bob Greene, who, under the tough-minded leadership of managing editor Alan Hathway, turned up extensive evidence of collusion between political bosses, elected officials, union leaders, and private contractors. The first of the newspaper's sixteen Pulitzer Prizes for reporting, writing, photography, and cartooning was given in 1954 for an exposé of labor racketeering at Roosevelt Raceway. Others were awarded for investigations into political corruption (1970) and international heroin trafficking (1974), coverage of the debate over the proper medical treatment for "Baby Jane Doe" (1984), an examination of famine in Africa (1985), reporting on a New York City subway crash (1992), an investigation into "friendly fire" casualties during the Persian Gulf War (1992), disclosure of death camps in Bosnia (1993), probes into police disability claims (1995), insights into the Ebola virus in Zaire (1996), and a yearlong look at St. Brigid's Catholic parish in Westbury (1996).

Among the most valued Pulitzers was the 1997 prize in recognition of *Newsday*'s coverage of the crash of Trans World Airlines Flight 800 that killed all 230 passengers and crew members when it exploded and plunged into the Atlantic off Suffolk's South Shore on July 17, 1996. The strange circumstances of the disaster—flashes of light before the Boeing 747 burst into flame—initially triggered suspicions of terrorist sabotage and missile attack, in addition to malfunction, and made it an event of global significance that drew intense worldwide media competition.

The early awards gained *Newsday* national recognition, enabling its reputation to grow in tandem with its advertising and circulation, which by the late Nineties hovered around 560,000 daily and 650,000 Sunday, establishing it as the sixth-largest regional newspaper in the U.S., and one of the most profitable. Both of *Newsday*'s founders had already died: Alicia Patterson in 1963 and Harry Guggenheim in 1971. Two prominent journalistic figures—Mark Ethridge, Sr., and Bill Moyers—guided the paper until its purchase by the Times Mirror Company in 1970. David Laventhol became publisher in 1978, and the following year *Newsday* combined its Nassau and Suffolk operations

ABOVE

One of Newsday's *most recent Pulitzer Prizes involved a yearlong examination of life at St. Brigid's Catholic parish in Westbury by staffer Robert F. Keeler. St. Brigid's pastor, Father Frank Gaeta, shares his homily with parish children in 1995.*

OPPOSITE

In 1997, Newsday *won a Pulitzer for its coverage of the extraordinary crash and investigation of TWA Flight 800 that killed all 230 passengers and crew when it exploded mysteriously and sank off the South Shore of Long Island on July 17, 1996. The lengthy investigation finally concluded that the crash occurred due to mechanical error. The inexplicable circumstances intensified the suffering of victims' relatives, such as these participants in a Smith Point memorial service one year later.*

(and Garden City and Lake Ronkonkoma offices) when it moved to its present plant in Melville.

In 1985 Laventhol, a former *New York Herald Tribune* staffer, convinced the Los Angeles–based owners that New York City was ready for another tabloid and *New York Newsday* was born. It survived for a decade, largely on its readership in the boroughs, before succumbing to bottom-line economics on July 16, 1995. Its passing was mourned, even by its competitors, for the vitality, initiative, imagination, and understanding it had brought to a city of insatiable demands and insurmountable reading habits. Among its mementos were three Pulitzer Prizes and a loss estimated at tens of millions of dollars.

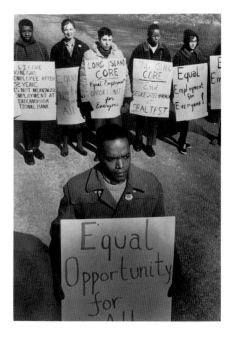

A significant focus of *New York Newsday* was on the impact and lifestyle of the city's minority enclaves, a story generally overlooked by the other newspapers. While the history of the metropolis, virtually from its colonial beginnings, has been the story of successive waves of immigrants and migrants, neighboring Long Island traditionally was seen as populated exclusively by upper–middle-class whites of European ancestry. Until the Sixties, when the civil rights movement in the South inspired minority groups to organize and seek equal opportunities, Long Island blacks, for example, were largely ignored as well as exploited.

The chronicle of blacks on Long Island goes back almost as far as that of whites. During the seventeenth century Dutch landowners put slaves to work primarily as laborers on farms in Brooklyn and Queens. Black slaves continued to be imported from Africa after the British seized control of Long Island in 1664. Among the earliest African-American settlements was one called Success, located near North Shore University Hospital in Manhasset, along what is now called Community Drive. Originally occupied by Matinecock Indians, it became a black and Indian slave camp in the eighteenth century and later attracted freed black slaves. Blacks and Indians joined together in 1832 to build the African Methodist Episcopal Zion Church that still stands across from the hospital amid older homes believed to have housed slaves.

At the Island's eastern end, slaves who bought their freedom from Shelter Island masters moved to the Amityville area, married Shinnecock Indians, and tried to form their own community in the early nineteenth century. Barred from membership in local churches, they established their own Bethel African Methodist Episcopal Church in 1815. Most slaves had been freed by the time slavery was ended in New York State in 1827, but vestiges of the institution lived on in education, housing, and employment.

On Long Island, African-Americans were compelled to attend separate, and clearly inferior, schools. But in 1895 one of the earliest desegregation victories was won in Amityville by a black laborer named Charles Brewster. When the school board constructed a new building for white pupils and Brewster's son was denied admission, he and other parents refused to send their children to the black school, charging that it did not provide equal education as required by state law. At a stormy meeting, the school board capitulated, closed the black school, and desegregated the white facility.

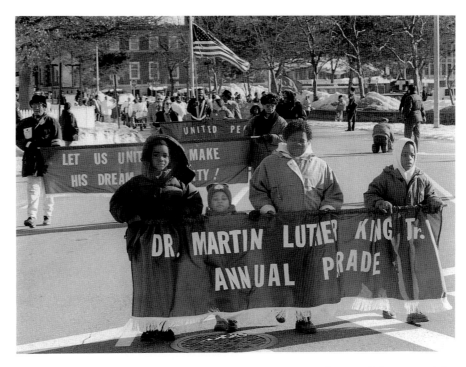

Similar challenges to school segregation were raised around the turn of the century in Hempstead and Roslyn with varying degrees of success. Although African-Americans had moved into many villages in both Nassau and Suffolk during the Twenties, they were confined by custom to specific neighborhoods, where they could easily be ignored. At the time, blacks constituted such a small proportion of the population—only about 2 percent—that even the revitalized Ku Klux Klan concentrated on other targets.

World War II brought many blacks to Long Island through service in the armed forces and jobs in defense plants. At the end of the war, some stayed on to live in communities with established black neighborhoods, such as Hempstead, Roosevelt, Glen Cove, New Cassel, Inwood, Amityville, Wyandanch, and Gordon Heights. The latter, situated near Yaphank, was created in the late Twenties by a Harlem real estate man who bought wooded property in that isolated area, subdivided it, and sold lots to his neighbors.

By the mid-Sixties the Island's African-American population had grown in number, strength, and dissatisfaction. Housing segregation, inexorably if not deliberately, had produced school segregation, particularly at the elementary level where the "neighborhood school" concept assured that children of similar backgrounds would attend the same schools. In Roosevelt, for example, when substantial numbers of middle-class blacks moved into the southeast area called "The Section" and began enrolling their children in the nearby Theodore Roosevelt Elementary School, many whites withdrew their youngsters and sent them to the Centennial Elementary School in the overwhelmingly white, northeast portion of the community. As a result, in 1963, 98 percent of the Theodore Roosevelt School population was black, and 98 percent of the pupils in the Centennial School were white.

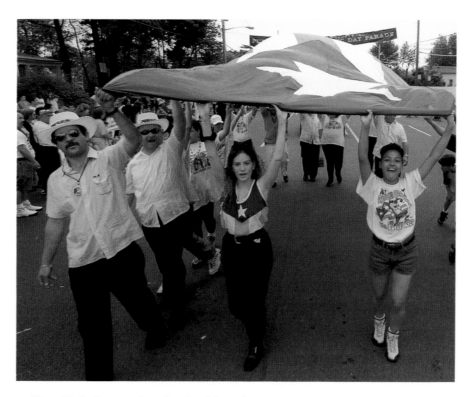

New York State ordered school boards to correct such patterns of *de facto* segregation, but opposition by white parents often resulted in lengthy court battles and the transfer of their children to private and parochial schools. Yet, led by tireless activists such as Long Island CORE (Congress of Racial Equality) chairman Lincoln Lynch and Glen Cove NAACP director James Davis, Long Island blacks marched, rallied, sat in, boycotted, picketed, and got arrested in largely unsuccessful efforts to gain better housing, employment, and education. By the Nineties, the black population had risen significantly—although the percentage of blacks in Long Island's population was still only half of the national percentage—but the steam had long since gone out of the protest movement, and conditions had not improved appreciably, if at all. Segregation was as much in evidence as ever. An extensive 1990 *Newsday* investigation found that the problem had worsened decade by decade. According to Douglas S. Massey, a University of Chicago professor and a leading researcher on racial housing patterns, Long Island was one of the most segregated suburbs in America. This characterization was hardly challenged by the 1990 Census, which found that 95 percent of Long Island blacks were concentrated in 5 percent of the census tracts. In economic terms, recessions and federal cutbacks in antipoverty programs no doubt had the harshest effect on African-Americans.

The most recent immigrants to arrive on Long Island in substantial numbers were Latinos, initially Puerto Ricans, but subsequently Spanish-speaking people from a wide variety of Central and South American countries, principally Salvadorans, Costa Ricans, Guatemalans, Hondurans, and Dominicans. Some estimates put the Latino population as high as one-quarter-million by the late Nineties. According to the 1990 Census, although Long Island's population was still overwhelmingly white (88.6 percent), Latinos constituted 7.5 percent, compared to 8.2 percent for African-Americans, and 3 percent for Asians. (Figures exceed 100 percent because some people describe themselves as belonging to more than one group.) Despite this preponderance of Caucasians, a new pattern seemed clear during the preceding decade: although the white population remained relatively static, the number of African-Americans had increased by 20 percent, Latinos by 62 percent, and the small Asian community by 150 percent. By the mid-Nineties, immigrants comprised more than a third of the annual influx, while the majority of residents moving away from Long Islanders were native born.

The first wave of Puerto Ricans came before World War II, when 1939 advertisements beckoned them to a place called "Victory Gardens," where property resembling their homeland could be purchased for $150 an acre. "Victory Gardens" turned out to be Brentwood in Suffolk, and its resemblance to lush Puerto Rico required a vivid imagination. But the immigrants were able to find jobs at Pilgrim State Hospital and put down their roots. They continued to come and Brentwood's Fifth Avenue business district took on the look and sound of their former island home, with bodegas and botanicas, Latin music and Spanish speech. Brentwood has long been the state's largest Puerto Rican community outside New York City. With more than a half century's experience on Long Island, Puerto Ricans seemed to be far ahead of other Latino groups in establishing an identity and making their voices heard. In the Town of Islip, for example, the 1977 Democratic candidate for supervisor was a Puerto Rican woman, Elizabeth Guanill, former head of the Suffolk County Human Rights Commission.

Cultural differences often led to misunderstanding and tension, particularly between Latinos and local police. When immigrants congregated on street corners on summer evenings, as was traditional in their native lands, the police, unfamiliar with such customs, broke up the gatherings of "loiterers" and occasionally made arrests. Such misinterpretations led to sensitivity training for law-enforcement officers, which helped to ease the problem. However, the influx of non-Puerto Rican Latinos has created conflicts within the Spanish-speaking community, engendering new frustrations for the more established groups. In one instance reported by *Newsday*, a Puerto Rican woman was offended when she applied for a job and was asked to show her green card; Puerto Ricans are United States citizens, yet they increasingly have been called upon to prove their nationality.

The majority of Long Island's Latino population reside in Suffolk; according to the 1990 Census, Latinos outnumber African-Americans in that county. Some of the first Latinos in Nassau took jobs in Glen Cove electronics plants or in menial positions at Long Beach hotels converted to homes for the elderly. In recent years, however, an increasing number of professionals and merchants have moved to Freeport and Rockville Centre, while sizable groups also live in the Hicksville, Hempstead, and Mineola areas.

Another minority that emerged on Long Island in the Nineties—although doubtless existing in Nassau and Suffolk for centuries—was the gay community. In 1991, chanting "We're here! We're queer! Get used to it," 800 people marched through Huntington village in the Island's first gay pride celebration to a generally receptive crowd of more than 3,000 spectators. At one time visible only at Fire Island's Cherry Grove, where they were periodically harassed by police, homosexuals made their presence known in ever-increasing numbers during the Nineties, demanding, but rarely obtaining, protection against discrimination in employment and housing. The gay liberation movement, slow to develop in the family-oriented suburbs, was accelerated by the growth of the AIDS plague, which claimed a greater number of victims from Long Island's homosexual and drug-abusing populations than from any other single suburb in the nation. In response, groups such as the Long Island Association for AIDS Care (LIAAC) and Parents, Families and Friends of Gays and Lesbians (P-FLAG) were organized to provide medical, financial, and emotional support to those in need.

Nonetheless, the Island seemed more traditional than ever. Census figures from 1990 reveal that more than 66 percent of Long Island households were headed by married couples—more than double the percentage in Manhattan and a far greater proportion than in such comparable suburban communities as Westchester, Fairfield County, Connecticut, and Prince Georges County, Maryland.

Despite its conventional veneer, Long Island has always appealed to creative people, who found in its beaches and ponds, farms and fields, the stimulation or serenity they required to produce their canvases and manuscripts. The Hamptons have proved to be one of the most enduring artists' colonies. Back in the spring of 1877, a dozen New York painters, including Winslow Homer, formed the Tile Club, thus named because they had spent the winter

Long Island was the inspiration for a group of eight artists, called the Ashcan School, who, after visiting Bellport in 1912, were affected by its quality of light and spent a productive period there. Their works, which attempted to give social meaning to commonplace scenes, include The Miner *(1925) by George Luks.*

OPPOSITE

Art flourished on Long Island during various periods and in various places, most notably in the Hamptons. One of the more striking figures on the art scene was William Merritt Chase, who painted and taught in the late nineteenth and early twentieth centuries. He built a house in eastern Long Island and in the 1890s founded the Shinnecock Summer School of Art, where he taught more than 1,000 pupils, many of them women. A proponent of plein air painting, as this photograph of one of his outdoor classes indicates (ABOVE), *he did not limit his subject matter, but portrayed indoor scenes as well, such as* A Friendly Call *(1895), painted at his Suffolk home* (BELOW). *Chase wore a monocle and boutonniere, kept a white wolfhound, and dressed his servant in a robe and fez.*

OPPOSITE ABOVE

Painters lived and worked on the North Shore, too. Arthur Dove, who lived in the Huntington and Centerport area during the Twenties, Thirties, and Forties, painted Indian Summer *during a brief period in November 1941, when the temperature soared to 60°. Dove frequently sailed in the Sound.*

Perhaps the best-known Long Island artists are some of the contemporary painters who burst on the scene in the postwar years and have made the Hamptons synonymous with modern art. Foremost among them are Willem de Kooning (OPPOSITE BELOW), *shown here in his East End studio; Alfonso Ossorio, seen here at his studio at the Creeks, his East Hampton estate, with* Rescue, *a combination of paint, plastic, and other materials* (ABOVE); *Lee Krasner, whose* Untitled (Red) *(1963)* (BELOW LEFT) *is in the collection of the Guild Hall, East Hampton; and Jackson Pollock, who pioneered the drip-painting technique seen here in* Number Five *(1948)* (BELOW RIGHT).

decorating Spanish tiles. Soon adding such notable members as Augustus Saint-Gaudens, William Merritt Chase, Stanford White, Thomas Moran, and Childe Hassam, the group decided to visit Long Island and capture its beauty with their sketches, watercolors, and oils. Traveling primarily by train, they covered the length of the Island and became enchanted by the village of East Hampton, returning to it repeatedly in subsequent summers for more than a decade.

Another eastern Long Island community, Bellport, was the attraction in 1912 for eight New York painters whose works had an extraordinary effect on American art and design for years to come. Known as the Ashcan School because of their focus on urban life, Arthur B. Davies, William J. Glackens, Robert Henri, Ernest Lawson, George Luks, Maurice Prendergast, Everett Shinn, and John Sloan made immeasurable contributions to the nation's culture while enjoying the breeze and spray of Great South Bay.

More recently, the area attracted such talents as Jackson Pollock, Lee Krasner, Willem de Kooning, Elaine de Kooning, Alfonso Ossorio, Saul Steinberg, Larry Rivers, Andy Warhol, Roy Lichtenstein, Robert Rauschenberg, and Chuck Close, who spent years living and painting amid the isolated splendor of the East End.

Writers, too, have drawn from Long Island's ambience. From James Fenimore Cooper, who lived in Sag Harbor in the early nineteenth century and used its milieu in his novels *The Spy* and *The Sea Lions*, to John Steinbeck, who lived there in the mid-twentieth and used it for *The Winter of Our Discontent*, the Island has provided grist for authors' typewriters. Others who followed Walt Whitman's literary footsteps on Long Island's sands include Truman Capote, Irwin Shaw, James Jones, Irvin S. Cobb, Mary Roberts Rinehart, Samuel Hopkins Adams, A. J. Liebling, Jack Kerouac, and P. G. Wodehouse.

The contemporary roster of writers who either were reared on the Island or reside there could fill several softball lineups—and in the summer, often does. It includes Norman Mailer, E. L. Doctorow, Joseph Heller, George Plimpton, Budd Schulberg, Wilfred Sheed, Tom Wolfe, Kurt Vonnegut, Avery Corman, Bruce Jay Friedman, Thomas Harris, Edward Albee, Lanford Wilson, Michael Thomas, Mario Puzo, Terrence McNally, William Gaddis, Peter Matthiessen, Betty Friedan, Susan Isaacs, Gail Sheehy, Rona Jaffe, Doris Kearns Goodwin, and Nelson DeMille.

While celebrities abound in the Hamptons, particularly in season, many major performers were born or reared or later lived in more prosaic surroundings. Jerry Seinfeld grew up in Long Beach, Billy Crystal in Massapequa, Howard Stern and Eddie Murphy in Roosevelt, Harry Chapin in Huntington, Billy Joel in Lloyd Neck, Michael Crichton in Roslyn, Alan King in Kings Point, and Guy Lombardo in Freeport. East Enders include Alan Alda, Alec Baldwin, Robert Benton, Jimmy Buffett, Dick Cavett, Chevy Chase, Betty Comden, Ron Delsener, Nora Ephron, Ben Gazzara, Adolph Green, Marvin Hamlisch, Anne Jackson, Sidney Lumet, Dina Merrill, Phyllis Newman, Alan

OPPOSITE ABOVE
With its proximity to the Big Apple, the media capital of the world, Long Island has produced a host of entertainers and celebrities. One who is either famous or notorious, depending on one's taste, is Howard Stern, radio broadcaster, author, and film personality. Reared in Roosevelt, he is here pictured with his parents, Ben and Rae, in 1997.

OPPOSITE BELOW LEFT
Singer-composer Billy Joel has identified himself with Long Island not only in his music but with his environmental activism. At this 1991 "Back at the Ranch" music festival at the Montauk Yacht Club benefitting the Nature Conservancy, Joel, second from left, performed with, left to right, Marc Cohn, noted musician Paul Simon, Mick Jones, and Jonathan Edwards.

OPPOSITE BELOW RIGHT
Harry Chapin, who gained international fame for his music and campaigns to fight hunger, entertained Northport High School students in 1974. His career ended tragically in 1981 when the thirty-eight-year-old personality was killed on the Long Island Expressway.

Pakula, Itzhak Perlman, Jerome Robbins, Gene Saks, Roy Scheider, Paul Simon, Barry Sonnenfeld, Steven Spielberg, Kathleen Turner, Eli Wallach, and Tony Walton.

However, in the century's final decades, Long Island found itself identified at least as much with notoriety as with celebrity. A succession of bizarre crimes and weird behavior became so associated with the Island that even the relatively staid *New York Times Magazine* ran a cover article on August 22, 1993 entitled "The Devil in Long Island," which asked, "What's possessed this once-somnolent suburban realm and turned it into a tabloid pandemonium of spouse-slayers, serial killers and demented dungeon-builders?"

Long Island's role as a prime supplier for trash radio, made-for-TV movies, and instant paperbacks probably began in midsummer 1984 with the discovery of the decomposing body of seventeen-year-old Gary Lauwers in Aztakea Woods near Northport Harbor and the initial description of the crime by the Suffolk homicide chief as "a sacrificial killing . . . . It's pure satanism." The arrest of two other teenagers, Richard Kasso, Jr., and James Troiano, linked the murder to witchcraft, devil worship, and heavy drug abuse, propelling it onto front pages and television screens around the globe. Two days after his arrest, Kasso hung himself in his cell, while Troiano ultimately was acquitted.

Less than two years later, in early 1986, Sean Pica, age sixteen, the son of a police officer and catechism teacher, hired himself out as a "hit kid" and gunned down James Pierson, Sr., the father of his classmate, sixteen-year-old Cheryl Pierson, who had been sexually abused by her father for five years. Cheryl, a student at Newfield High School in Selden, was sentenced to six months in the Riverhead jail. Sean, who collected only $400 of a promised $1,000 fee, got eight to twenty-four years in Great Meadow Correctional Facility.

Hypocrisy invariably makes satisfying news, and the more pious the hypocrite, the more satisfying the story. Consequently, the 1987 revelations of Jessica Hahn, a Massapequa church secretary, that she had a one-day stand seven years earlier in a Florida motel with married televangelist Jim Bakker became a big hit. So did her disclosure that the PTL founder paid her $287,000 to keep her mouth shut. Nonetheless, she quickly took to the talk-show circuit and posed for *Playboy*.

The same year brought more international attention to the Island when Walter Hudson slipped and became wedged in the doorway of his Hempstead home. It took a team of firefighters to free him—Hudson topped the scales at 1,400 pounds—and he then started a weight-reduction program, making him both a symbol and advocate for the overweight. After spending most of his life in his bedroom, Hudson died there on Christmas Eve, 1991, when his long-suffering heart finally gave up.

At about the time of Hudson's demise, General Motors discovered a disaster of major proportions: John McNamara, a Buick-Pontiac dealer in Port Jefferson Station, had bilked the world's largest automaker out of more than $6 billion in loans over eleven years on the pretext of exporting as many as

17,000 customized vans monthly to the Middle East. Seeking clemency from federal authorities, McNamara, who had used the money to build a vast real estate empire, testified against local officials he claimed to have bribed. They were acquitted of major charges; he was ultimately sentenced to five years in federal prison and ordered to repay $412 million to GM.

Probably the most infamous—and surely most publicized—of the crimes that stigmatized Long Island involved Amy Fisher, a seventeen-year-old senior at John F. Kennedy High School in Bellmore, her thirty-eight-year-old lover, Joey Buttafuoco, an auto body shop operator, and his thirty-seven-year-old wife, Mary Jo, whom Fisher shot in the head and wounded after Buttafuoco sought to end the affair in May 1992. The subject of three made-for-TV films and a $500,000 deal with the tabloid television show "A Current Affair," the tawdry tale brought Fisher, who previously had taken money in exchange for sex and had a pre-Buttafuoco abortion, recognition as the "Long Island Lolita," and earned her manfriend enduring fame when Vice President Al Gore jokingly contended that his Secret Service code name was "Buttafuoco." Amy was sentenced to five to fifteen years in the Albion Correctional Facility, Joey to six months in Nassau County Jail for statutory rape, and Mary Jo recovered.

There is little doubt that 1993 was a year Long Islanders will long remember, and wish they could forget. In addition to Colin Ferugson's Long Island Rail Road bloodbath and the windup of the Amy-Joey-Mary Jo scenario, that *annus horribilis* was the year of Katie Beers and John Esposito and Sal Inghilleri, of Sol Wachtler and Joy Silverman, and of Joel Rifkin and countless victims.

On December 28, 1993, two days before her tenth birthday, Katie Beers of Mastic Beach was reported missing by John Esposito of Bay Shore, a forty-three-year-old contractor and family friend. As Suffolk police searched for her, they uncovered a history of sex abuse and custody battles involving the adults closest to Katie, who never knew her father and lived most of her life with her godmother and her godmother's husband, Sal Inghilleri. Police further disclosed that three months earlier, Inghilleri had been charged with sexually abusing Katie. Sixteen days after reporting her disappearance, Esposito led police to a coffinlike box in an underground room beneath a garage adjacent to his office. There they found Katie alive. Esposito, whose motives were unclear, was sentenced to fifteen years to life after pleading guilty to kidnapping; Inghilleri, convicted of sexual abuse, was sentenced to four to twelve years.

Handsome, personable, intelligent, and highly successful, Sol Wachtler of Manhasset was the married and respected Chief Judge of the State Court of Appeals when the FBI stopped his car on the Long Island Expressway and arrested him. Wachtler was charged with harassing the mistress who had dumped him—Joy Silverman, a wealthy GOP fundraiser—and threatening to kidnap her fourteen-year-old daughter, to whom he had sent a raunchy note and a condom. His contention that medications were responsible for his behavior was rejected and the popular Republican, often mentioned as a gubernatorial candidate, resigned his post and was sentenced to fifteen months in a federal prison.

Joel Rifkin was not widely known at all before police stopped his truck for a traffic violation and found a decaying female corpse. The thirty-four-year-old landscape gardener, who lived with his mother in East Meadow, was reclusive, although hardly inactive. By the time he was sentenced to 200 years in prison, the victim count had risen to seventeen, although he insisted that the correct number was eighteen.

What was going on? Why did so much evil visit Long Island? Was it something in the air? The water? The high-tension lines? Or is it some as yet unexplained phenomenon, such as the Island's heavy incidence of breast cancer? It's anyone's guess. The theory most popular among Long Island boosters is that the *real* explanation lay not *in* or *on* Long Island but because of its unfortunate proximity to the epicenter of tabloid journalism, especially the broadcast media. Whatever.

If the reasons for the Island's spate of disreputable events are elusive, so too is its ethos. For if there is an identifiable Long Island culture, no one seems to have found it. In dress, in speech, in taste, in behavior, Long Islanders appear indistinguishable from those who live in other parts of the region or other suburbs in the nation. Even the phrase "Lon Guyland" is used chiefly by deriders from elsewhere.

Long Island's reputation, which presumably will outlive the fading rogues' gallery of infamy and depravity, rests in part on having provided more than its share of champions to various halls of fame. Football star Jim Brown played at Manhasset High School and Syracuse University before becoming one of the greatest running backs in professional history with the Cleveland Browns. In basketball, Roosevelt's Julius (Dr. J.) Erving was a superstar with the Long Island Nets and went on to even greater glory with the Philadelphia 76ers. Bridgehampton's Carl Yastrzemski was a standout Boston Red Sox slugger. Al Oerter of New Hyde Park, the incomparable discus hurler, won gold medals in four consecutive Olympiads. And despite its name, the National Hockey League's New York Islanders were the winners of four consecutive Stanley Cups from 1980 through 1983.

Prestige came to Long Island in science and technology as well. At the Grumman Aerospace Corporation plant in Bethpage during the Sixties, engineers designed a machine that would gain the envy of the most imaginative science-fiction writers. Called the LM (for Lunar Module), the spindly-legged, buglike craft was developed at a cost of more than $1 billion to ferry two astronauts from their orbiting command module to the moon's surface for a day-long exploration of the lunar landscape.

The LM's unqualified success on July 20, 1969, was the culmination of decades of struggle by Grumman to recapture the prominence it had enjoyed during World War II. Almost as soon as that conflict had ended, Grumman had laid off its entire 20,500-person workforce in the face of canceled military

In the Sixties, Seventies, and Eighties, Long Islanders excelled in a variety of sports. In basketball, Julius (Dr. J.) Erving, who grew up in Roosevelt and went on to star with the Nets before they left Long Island, soars up for a basket against Denver at the Nassau Coliseum in 1975 (BELOW RIGHT). In football, Jim Brown of the Cleveland Browns dominated the National Football League after starring at Syracuse University and, before that, at Manhasset High School, where he is shown at practice in 1951 (OPPOSITE BELOW). One of the nation's most accomplished athletes, discus hurler Al Oerter (BELOW) of New Hyde Park won gold medals in four consecutive Olympiads.

The Islanders (in white uniforms), shown here (ABOVE RIGHT) in action against the Detroit Red Wings at the Nassau Veterans Memorial Coliseum in 1980, became the toast of the National Hockey League after winning the Stanley Cup that year. Team members Dennis Potvin and Clark Gillies (OPPOSITE ABOVE) hoist the symbol of supremacy after the play-offs, a scene that was repeated in 1981, 1982, and 1983.

contracts, subsequently rehiring a fraction of that number as permanent personnel. Despite diversification and the sale of planes to the Navy during the Korean War, Grumman's substantial reliance on uncertain military needs made it vulnerable until the space program enabled it to beef up employment beyond its previous World War II peak.

But the end of the Cold War and cutbacks in the National Aeronautics and Space Administration (NASA) budget precipitated a nosedive from which Grumman never recovered. In 1994 the once fiercely independent industrial colossus was sold to Northrup, headquartered in Los Angeles, and became Northrup Grumman, with a Long Island payroll of just 3,500, which was slated to drop even further. In 1997, in a megadeal that shrunk the nation's military contractors to only three, the Lockheed Martin Corporation bought Northrup Grumman for $8.3 billion.

Thus, Grumman followed the misfortunes of Republic Aviation, which, despite development of its F-84 Thunderjet for the Korean War and the follow-up F-105 Thunderchief, was unable to survive on defense business. The Air Force grounded more than 500 F-105s in 1964 because of crashes, and, following a cutback in orders for the plane, Republic was taken over by the Fairchild Hiller Corporation the following year.

The experiences of Republic and Grumman brought home to Long Islanders the vicissitudes of dependence on defense contracts or, as Detroit learned, any single industry. It was a painful lesson. Gripped by a recession that lasted well into the Nineties, the Island saw its unemployment rate soar above 8 percent, driving out businesses and families, and driving down real estate prices. But the collapse of Grumman also opened the door to a spate of new enterprises: computer software, electronics, biotechnology, medical imaging, graphic communications, tourism, wine growing, and business-oriented services, such as law and accounting.

The growth of high-tech companies has been remarkable. Computer

Associates International, while lacking the public recognition of Microsoft or IBM, is the world's third-largest software manufacturer. Moreover, based on annual revenue, it ranks significantly behind two other Long Island giants, Arrow Electronics Inc. of Melville, and Avnet Inc. of Great Neck, the largest distributors of electronic components in the world. Other major public corporations in Long Island include Pall Corporation, Symbol Technologies, Olsten, and Cablevision Systems.

Fueled in part by Wall Street's raging bull market, Long Island's economy, which had suffered the most of any in the New York metropolitan region, made a remarkable comeback. By the middle of 1997 its rate of unemployment fell to a mere 3.5 percent, one of the region's lowest.

Ranking among the highest per-capita income areas in the nation, Nassau and Suffolk continued to attract major retailers eager to satisfy the desires of free-spending consumers. Attesting to the Island's appeal, Nordstrom, internationally regarded for its upscale offerings, made its Long Island debut at Roosevelt Field, while other well-known names flocked to a nearby mall, Roosevelt Centre, built on the Roosevelt Raceway site.

While production of traditional Long Island staples—potatoes, ducks, and clams—dropped to a fraction of their former output, the development of vineyards in the East End, as well as a switch to trendy vegetables, nurseries, and organic farming helped keep Suffolk the state's top agricultural county. The wine industry, pioneered by Alec and Louisa Hargrave in Cutchogue in 1973, has steadily grown in size, profits, and reputation, and its chardonnay, merlot, pinot blanc, and sauvignon blanc have gained kudos from connoisseurs worldwide.

Recognition of a more profound nature has come to Long Island as a result of two world-renowned research institutions: the Cold Spring Harbor Laboratory and the Brookhaven National Laboratory. Begun in 1890, the Cold Spring Harbor Laboratory is a unique facility that combines high-level biological research and top-drawer education. Directed by Nobel laureate James D. Watson, who with Francis Crick discovered the structure of the DNA molecule, and numbering among its scientists Dr. Barbara McClintock, who won the 1983 Nobel Prize for Medicine for determining that genes could move around on plant chromosomes and cause changes in heredity, the laboratory is dedicated to basic research. One of its long-term goals is the discovery of a cure for cancer. In 1981, together with research teams from two other institutions, Cold Spring Harbor scientists made what was described as a potential breakthrough by isolating a gene that transforms a healthy cell into one that is cancerous.

Ironically, the laboratory maintains such a low profile that it is far less recognized than the state fish hatchery located across from it on Route 25A. "I am constantly astounded," said a visiting British scientist, "that this lab is one of the best known worldwide, and yet Long Islanders are, by and large, unaware of its existence."

Brookhaven rose phoenixlike from the remains of Camp Upton following

The development of the wine industry, pioneered in 1973 by Alec and Louisa Hargrave in Cutchogue, helped Long Island compensate for Suffolk's declining potato, duck, and clam markets. Processing grapes during the 1996 harvest at the Pugliesi Vineyard, are, from left to right, Ralph, Peter, and Larry Pugliesi.

Directed by Dr. James D. Watson (BELOW), *the Cold Spring Harbor Laboratory* (OPPOSITE BELOW) *attracts scientists from around the world to its summer symposiums.*

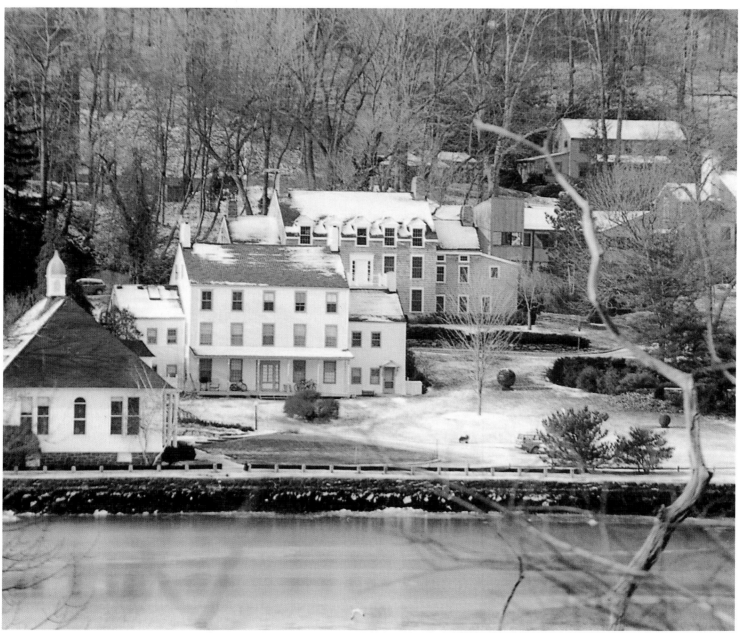

World War II. Medical specialists at Brookhaven sought noninvasive techniques to diagnose disease, measured the impact on health of various energy sources, and continued the laboratory's pioneering research into the biological effects of ionizing radiations. More specifically, they sought the cause of Lyme disease and the treatment of bone cancer, and have carried out studies of AIDS and influenza. Physicists inquired into new ways to produce and store energy, while laboratory scientists tried to design the ideal oil burner and build the most efficient solar house. Nuclear chemists developed ways to date ancient artifacts and expose art forgeries. Scientists sought to create materials for a cable two feet in diameter capable of transmitting enough power to light New York City. Biologists studied the mechanics of acid rain and monitored the persistence of viruses in treated sewage effluents.

However, the outcome of these and other experiments was severely jeopardized in 1997 following the discovery of a storage tank radiation leak that imperiled the safety of drinking water in the vicinity. The federal government first dismissed the lab's contractor for putting research ahead of protection of the public, then shut down the facility after a construction worker was killed in an industrial accident. Uncertainty about Brookhaven's fate temporarily halted much of the research in progress, threatening, in the words of one chemist, "a disaster to American science."

To some, the destiny of Long Island itself is in doubt. Notwithstanding the economic imagination and vitality, the renewed perception of the region's high quality of life, and the general revival of optimism, the area faces, according to preeminent planner Dr. Lee E. Koppelman, "serious problems." Executive director of the Long Island Regional Planning Board for more than thirty years and director of the Center for Regional Policy Studies at the State University at Stony Brook, Koppelman points to a basic flaw in the Island's development that casts a shadow over its future: "Viable communities have to replicate the life cycle, from birth all the way through. Long Island didn't develop that way. At the end of World War II, there was one set of cohorts—namely those from, say, twenty-one to forty, the childbearing age group—and that's who settled Long Island." This demographic group, he says, came predominantly in search of single-family homes, largely disdaining any other form of housing. As they aged and became "empty nesters," retirees, widows, and widowers, they no longer needed such large houses. The property continued to appreciate in value, and often the owners became unable to afford the taxes. Nor could their children.

"The consequence has been," Koppelman says, "that it's hard to hold onto the young people. If you don't have housing, how are you going to hold them? And if you don't hold them, where are you going to get the labor market for the high-tech industries and the diversification of employment that you want to have? We have not replicated the life cycle. And this is a most serious problem."

Besides a shortage of both appropriate housing and an adequate workforce with the skills vital to survival in the next century, Nassau and Suffolk are still

ABOVE

In the aftermath of World War II, Brookhaven National Laboratory became distinguished for its research into medicine, physics, nuclear chemistry, and biology. But in 1997 its work was jeopardized by the discovery of a storage tank radiation leak. Shown here is the storage area for spent nuclear fuel within Brookhaven's nuclear reactor.

OPPOSITE ABOVE

Long Island's survival as a viable and desirable place to live, work, and play depends on its ability to strike a balance between the aims of developers and environmentalists. Density, exemplified by this view of Nassau's South Shore, has dramatically altered the landscape of Long Island from its natural state.

The distinctive and fragile ecosystem of the Pine Barrens (ABOVE), *found along Suffolk's South Shore, is especially vulnerable. The spectacular fires that periodically renew them, most recently in the late summer of 1995* (BELOW), *are reminders that nature has its own processes that are not necessarily in step with human needs.*

plagued with too much traffic, too much garbage, and ever more uncomfortably crowded recreational facilities. Long Island is a victim of its own appeal.

Once a region of surpassing natural loveliness and ecological harmony, the Island was beset by exploitation and betrayed by indifference. Each generation of Long Islanders bears, along with the power for destruction, the responsibility for protection. Those parts of the Island that remain unspoiled are not only its most precious heritage, they are its most vital resource. But, as history constantly reminds us, a glorious past is no guarantor of a viable future.

Yet Koppelman and other experts say they are optimistic, confident that plans and programs will provide solutions. In the past this has been true. But as the twenty-first century beckons, one certainty exists: Long Island will have a new look. The newest Long Islanders are from Latin America, the Caribbean, Asia, and they are displacing the traditional European-oriented stock, bringing different languages, different styles, different cultures. How they are received, what opportunities are afforded or denied, whether they are integrated or isolated will markedly affect the region's direction. For once again, Long Island is in for a change. And it won't only be at Jamaica.

Selected Bibliography

Adams, James Truslow. *History of the Town of Southampton*. Southampton: Hampton Press, 1917.

Adkins, Edwin. *Setauket: The First Three Hundred Years, 1655–1955*. New York: Three Village Historical Society, 1980 reprint.

Bailey, Paul. *A History of Two Great Counties, Nassau and Suffolk*. New York: Lewis Historical Publishing Co., 1949, 3 Vols.

Bailey, Paul. *Colonial Long Island*. Amityville: The Long Island Forum, 1958.

Bayles, Richard M. *History of Suffolk County, New York*. New York: W. W. Munsell & Co., 1882.

Braff, Phyllis. *Thomas Moran, a Search for the Scenic: His Landscape Paintings of the American West, East Hampton, and Venice*. East Hampton: Guild Hall, 1981.

Braunlein, John. *Colonial Long Island Folklife*. Stony Brook: Museums at Stony Brook, 1976.

Bunce, James and Harmond, Richard. *Long Island as America—A Documentary History to 1896*. Port Washington: Kennikat Press, 1977.

Caro, Robert A. *The Power Broker: Robert Moses and the Fall of New York*. New York: Alfred A. Knopf, 1974.

Carse, Robert. *Rum Row*. New York: Rinehart and Co., 1959.

Cavaioli, Frank J. "The Ku Klux Klan on Long Island." Amityville: *Long Island Forum*, May 1979.

Denton, Daniel. *A Brief Description of New York, Formerly Called the New Netherlands, With the Places Thereunto Adjoining, etc.* London, 1670.

DiScala, Raymond V. *Development of the Aerospace Industry on Long Island, A Chronology: 1833–1965*. Vol. III. Hempstead: Hofstra University Yearbook of Business, 1968.

Doggett, Marguerite. *Long Island Printing, 1791–1830*. Brooklyn: Long Island Historical Society, 1979.

Dyson, Verne. *Anecdotes and Events in Long Island History*. Port Washington: Ira Friedman, 1969.

————. *A Century of Brentwood*. Brentwood: Brentwood Village Press, 1950.

————. *The Human Story of Long Island*. Port Washington: Ira Friedman, 1962 reprint.

————. *Modern Times: the Founding of Brentwood, L.I.* Smithtown: Rambler Publishing Co., 1964.

Epstein, Jason and Elizabeth Barlow. *East Hampton: A History and Guide*. Wainscott, Medway Press, 1975.

Failey, Dean. *Long Island is My Nation: The Decorative Arts & Craftsmen, 1640–1830*. Setauket: Society for the Preservation of Long Island Antiquities, 1976.

Flint, M. B. *Long Island Before the Revolution*. Port Washington: Ira Friedman, 1967 reprint.

Frankenstein, Alfred. *William Sidney Mount*. New York: Harry N. Abrams, 1975.

Furman, Gabriel. *Antiquities of Long Island*. Port Washington, Ira Friedman, 1968 reprint.

Gabriel, Ralph. *The Evolution of Long Island*. New Haven: Yale University Press, 1921.

Gardiner, David. *Chronicles of the Town of East Hampton*. Sag Harbor: private printing, 1973.

Gass, Margaret. *History of Miller's Place*. Port Jefferson Station: St. Gerard Printing, 1971.

Gonzalez, Ellice B. *Storms, Ships and Surfmen: the Life Savers of Fire Island*. New York: Eastern Acorn Research Series, Fire Island National Seashore, 1982.

Hall, Warren. *Pagans, Puritans and Patriots: Yesterday's Southold*. Cutchogue: Cutchogue-New Suffolk Historical Council, 1975.

Hazelton, Henry. *The Boroughs of Brooklyn and Queens Counties of Nassau and Suffolk, N.Y., 1609–1924*. New York: Lewis Historical Publishing, 1925. 7 Vols.

History of Suffolk County. New York: W. W. Munsell, 1882.

Howell, George P. *The Early History of Southampton, Long Island, New York, with Genealogies*. 2nd ed. Southampton: Yankee Peddlar Book Co., 1970 reprint.

Huntington Vignettes. Huntington: The Huntington Historical Society, 1976.

Ireland, Ralph R. "Slavery on Long Island: A Study of Economic Motivation." *The Journal of Long Island History*, 1966.

Jaray, Cornell, ed. *Historic Chronicles of New Amsterdam, Colonial New York and Early Long Island*. Port Washington: Ira J. Friedman, Empire State Historical Publications Series No. 35, 1968.

Kaiser, William K., ed. *Development of the Aerospace Industry on Long Island; 1904–1964*. Vol. I. Hempstead: Hofstra University Yearbook of Business, 1968.

Kammen, Michael. *Colonial New York: a History*. New York: Scribner, 1975.

Klein, Howard and Patricia Windrow. *Three Village Guidebook*. Port Jefferson Station: Three Village Historical Society, 1976.

LaGumina, Salvatore J., ed. *Ethnicity in Suburbia: The Long Island Experience*. Private printing: 1980.

Levine, Gaynell Stone, ed. *Readings in Long Island Archaeology and Ethnohistory*. Stony Brook: Suffolk County Archaeological Association. 1977–83. Vols. I–VII.

Lewis, Cyril A. *Historical Long Island, Paintings and Sketches*. Westhampton Beach: The Long Island Forum, 1964.

Luke, Myron and Robert Venables. *Long Island in the American Revolution*. Albany: N.Y.S. Bicentennial Commission, 1976.

Mabee, Carleton. "Long Island's Black 'School War' and the Decline of Segregation in New York State." *New York History*. October 1978.

Manley, Seon. *Long Island Discovery—An Adventure into the History, Manners, and Mores of America's Front Porch*. New York: Doubleday & Co., 1966.

Martin, Linda and Bette Weidman. *Nassau County, Long Island, in Early Photographs, 1869–1940*. New York, Dover, 1981.

Mather, Frederic. *The Refugees of 1776 from Long Island to Connecticut*. Albany: J. B. Lyon Co., 1913.

McDermott, Charles. *Suffolk County, New York*. New York: James Heineman, Inc., 1965.

Ment, David. *The Shaping of a City: A Brief History of Brooklyn*. Brooklyn: The Brooklyn Educational & Cultural Alliance, 1979.

Monner, Fred and Linda. *Where to Go on Long Island*. Smithtown: SCOPE, 1979.

———. *Museums on Long Island*. Syosset: Long Island Museums Assn., 1983.

———. *Guide to New York City Landmarks*. New York: New York City Landmarks Preservation Commission, 1982.

Onderdonk, Henry. *Revolutionary Incidents of Suffolk and Kings Counties*. New York: Ira Friedman, 1970 reprint.

Overton, Jacqueline. *Long Island's Story*. Garden City: Doubleday & Co., 1929.

———. *The Rest of the Story, 1929–1961*. Bernice Marshall, ed. Port Washington: Ira Friedman, 1961.

Pisano, Ronald. *The Long Island Landscape, 1865–1914: the Halcyon Years*. Southampton: Parrish Art Museum, 1981.

Prime, N. S. *A History of Long Island from Its First Settlement by the Europeans to the Year 1845*. New York and Pittsburgh: R. Carter, 1845.

Prince, Helen Wright, ed. *Civil War Letters & Diary of Henry W. Prince: 1862–1865*. Private printing: 1979.

Randall, Monica. *The Mansions of Long Island's Gold Coast*. New York: Hastings House, 1979.

Rattray, Everett. *The South Fork: The Land and the People of Eastern Long Island*. New York: Random House, 1979.

Rattray, Jeannette. *East Hampton History*. Garden City: Country Life Press, 1953.

Rattray, Jeanette. *Ship Ashore!* New York: Coward McCann, 1955.

Rockwell, Verne. *Colonel Rockwell's Scrapbook*. Smithtown: Smithtown Historical Society, 1968.

Ross, Peter. *A History of Long Island*. Philadelphia: The Lewis Historical Publishing Co., 1902. 3 Vols.

Sclare, Liisa and Donald. *Beaux-Arts Estates: A Guide to the Architecture of Long Island*. New York, Viking Press, 1980.

Scott, Kenneth and Susan E. Klaffky, *A History of the Joseph Lloyd Manor House*. Setauket: Society for the Preservation of Long Island Antiquities, 1976.

Seyfried, V. F. *The Long Island Railroad*. New York: Garden City, 1961.

Smith, M. H. *History of Garden City*. Manhasset: Channel Press, 1963.

Smits, E. V. *Nassau—Suburbia U. S. A.* New York: Doubleday, 1974.

Stevens, William O. *Discovering Long Island*. New York: Dodd, Mead, & Co., 1939.

Strong, Kate. *True Tales from the Early Days of Long Island*. Amityville: The Long Island Forum, 1939.

Thompson, Benjamin. *History of Long Island*. 3rd ed. New York: Dodd & Mead, 1918. 3 Vols.

Tomlinson, R. G. *Witchcraft Trials of Connecticut*. Hartford: The Bond Press, 1978.

Tooker, William Wallace. *The Indian Place-Names on Long Island and Islands Adjacent*. Port Washington: Ira Friedman, 1962 reprint.

Tuckerman, Bayard, ed. *Diary of Philip Hone, 1828–1857*. New York: Dodd, Mead & Co., 1889.

Vagts, Christopher. *Huntington at the Turn of the Century*. Huntington: Huntington Historical Society, 1974.

———. *Huntington in Our Time*. Huntington: Huntington Historical Society, 1975.

Van Liew, Barbara F. *Long Island Domestic Architecture of the Colonial and Federal Periods: An Introductory Study*. Setauket: Society for the Preservation of Long Island Antiquities, 1974.

Waller, Henry D. *History of the Town of Flushing*. Harrison: Harbor Hill Books, 1975 reprint.

Weigold, Marilyn. *The American Mediterranean—An Environmental, Economic and Social History of Long Island Sound*. Port Washington: Kennikat Press, 1974.

Weisburg, Henry and Lisa Donneson. *Guide to Sag Harbor*. Sag Harbor: The John Street Press, 1975.

Williamson, W. M. *Adriaen Block: 1611–14*. New York: Marine Museum of the City of New York, 1959.

Williamson, W. M. *Henry Hudson, Discoverer of the Hudson River, 1609*. New York: Marine Museum of the City of New York, 1959.

Wines, Roger. "Vanderbilt's Motor Parkway: America's First Auto Road." *Journal of Long Island History*, Fall 1962.

Wood, Silas, *A Sketch of the First Settlement of the Several Towns of Long Island*. New York: A. Spooner, 1828.

Wood, Simeon. *A History of Hauppauge*, 2nd ed. revised by Jack Marr. Hauppauge: Exposition Press, 1981.

Ziel, Ron and George Foster. *Steel Rails to the Sunrise*. New York: Hawthorn Books, 1965.

Acknowledgments

The planning, preparation, writing, and editing of this book have constituted a rich learning experience about the subject, about myself, and about others. Among those at *Newsday* to whom I am particularly grateful are Stan Asimov, who involved me in this project, was an enthusiastic and considerate resource throughout, and a keen critic, too; Mary Ann Skinner, who cheerfully and speedily lent expert assistance in obtaining information and authenticating facts; Leo Seligsohn, who was unfailingly responsive to my excessive requests for advice and support; Dave Kahn, who gave confidence based on experience; Andy Ippolito, who was cooperative beyond expectation; and Dave Laventhol and Tony Insolia, who generously provided the opportunity and permitted total independence.

Of those I met through this experience, I am especially appreciative of the extensive help and expertise afforded by Steve Englebright; of the depth of commitment, unremitting energy, broad knowledge, and vital insights offered by my researcher, Gaynell Stone; and of the deep understanding, solid judgment, and thoughtful restraint furnished by my editor, Nora Beeson. In addition, I wish to acknowledge the immeasurable contributions of Marilyn Frucht, of which I alone am aware.

Many colleagues and strangers responded to requests for historical materials, and I would like to thank them for their spirit and their trust, although it was not always possible to utilize what they offered. They include: Audrey Clinton, Dick Zander, Cyril A. Lewis, Rhoda C. Milligan, Dan Russell, Mary Ann Mrozinsky, George Bailey, Frank Cavaioli, Mark Moro, Arthur L. Pollinger, Mrs. Mary Dougherty, D. W. Houghton, Prof. Ronald Lipp, Robert Winowitch, Anthony Marino, Steve Gonsalez, George Lobner, Ralph W. Bastedo, Mary Miller, Sister Frances Maureen Carlin, Fred Monner, William Cahill, Francis McGee, Jean Kadlic, Mary Jane Lippert, Loraine Erickson, Mrs. Thomas P. Duggan, Hank Boerner, Dr. Sidney Canarick, Helen Tylenda, Teresa Roberts, Barbara Randall, Morris Silverman, Charles F. Krauss, Ruth Winkler, Gladys Grimm, Tristram Walker Metcalfe II, R. Surprenant, Patricia Vars Nance, Edward Ferrea, William J. Ferguson, Jr., Carolyn K. Creed, Ward Ackerson, Mrs. George Mack, D. E. Edcris, William Benham, Mrs. Ardell Beckhans, Marilyn Mello, Dorothy Kappenberg, Harry Huson, Sister Anne F. Pulling, Carol Goldstein, Mary Klem, and Cliff Weinberg.

I am also indebted to many historians, librarians, educators, and other professionals who extended cooperation far beyond the requirements of their positions or responsibilities. They include: Rufus Langhans, Richard Winsche, Dan Kaplan, William Kaiser, Gary Hammond, Phyllis Braff, Mrs. Irwin Smith, Louis Harson, Robert Farwell, George A. Finckenor, Sr., Christopher Vagts, Preston R. Bassett, Beverly Tyler, Ron Ziel, Carl Starace, Vincent Seyfried, Frank Turano, Ronald Pisano, Dr. Betsy Kornheiser, Kenneth Newman, James Abbe, Valdemar Peterson, William Golder, Dr. and Mrs. Roger Gerry, Jean Lauer, Frank Braynard, John Drennan, Dr. Ralph Solecki, Donna Ottusch-Kianka, Mrs. Orme Wilson, and Mrs. Louise Hall.

For significant assistance in the preparation of this second edition, I am indebted to former Suffolk County Executive John V. N. Klein; to Lee E. Koppelman, director of the Center for Regional Policy Studies at the State University at Stony Brook; to my editor, Eric Himmel, and to Rachel Tsutsumi and Nicole Columbus, also from Abrams; and to those at *Newsday*, particularly Theresa Kiely, library director; Bob Keane, executive editor; Peter Bengelsdorf, director of electronic publishing; Jim Toedtman, Washington Bureau chief, and to David Kahn.

Index

Photo Credits

Adelphi University, Garden City: 233 above; Adams, Joseph, Brookhaven: 46, 53, 61 center left and below, 65, 77 below, 209 above; American Museum of Natural History, New York: 31; Argeroplos, George, Newsday: 231 below; Ballweg, Brian M., Hofstra University: 233 middle; Bereswill, Paul J., Newsday: 255 top; Bokress, David L., Newsday: 255 below right; Bowne House Historical Society, Flushing, 49; Brookhaven National Laboratory, Camp Upton History Collection, Upton: 173 center left and right, below left and right, 175; Brooklyn Museum: 118 above (*Winter Scene in Brooklyn*, c. 1817–20, by Francis Guy); Carpenter, Ralph, East Hampton: 92; Cavanagh, Jim, Newsday, 238; Cold Spring Harbor Laboratory Research Library Archives: 258; Cornell, John, Newsday: 231 above; Cradle of Aviation Museum, Mitchel Field, Garden City: 164 above; Davis, Bill, Newsday: 239 left, 245, 255 left; DeBear, Cliff, Newsday: 224 above, 237; Dombroski, J. Michael, Newsday: 257 right; Fairchild Republic Company, Farmingdale: 219; Ferrara, Thomas A., Newsday: 239 right; Garden City Archives: 173 above left and right; Grumman Aerospace Corporation, Bethpage: 218; Gerry, Collection of Dr. and Mrs. Roger G.: 53; Glen Cove Public Library, Long Island History Collection: 126; Guild Hall Museum, East Hampton: 156, 249 below left; The Heckscher Museum Huntington: 136 below right, 139 (artist, James Long Scudder), 248 above: Held, Mrs. John, Jr., original painting for *Life:* 180 above; Hofstra University, Hempstead: 233 middle; Honda, Stan, Newsday: 251 below left; Hoops, Jay, Southampton: 156; Huntington Historical Society: 96 above (engraving from drawing by Edward Lange, c. 1882), 99 center, 114 below, 150 below (Thanksgiving Day Hunt, Estate of Henry L. Stimson, c. 1915), 159 (Ben Conklin negative); Jacobsen, Collection of Mr. and Mrs. Valdemar F.: 138; Jerome, Tony, Newsday: 259 above; Kaywood, Flushing: 49; Keating, John, Newsday: 241, 261; Kmonicek, Kathy, Newsday: 262 above; Kraus, Dick, Newsday: 243, 251; Library of Congress, Washington, D.C.: 169, 170 above, 174, 190, 198: Litchfield Historical Society, Conn.: 78 left and right; Long Island Historical Society, Brooklyn: 51 below right, 70, 99 above, 216; Long Island State Park and Recreation Commission, Babylon: 203, 204; Los Angeles County Museum: 43 below; Meurer, Ross, Cold Spring Harbor: 258; Luckey, Newsday: 214 above; Maguire, Tom, Newsday: 168 above; Memorial Library of Setauket: 112; Metropolitan Museum of Art, New York: 113 above, 120 above left; Mintz, Ari, Newsday: 251 above; Morris Studio, Southampton: 247 above; Murray, Edna, Newsday: 225; Museum of the City of New York: 25; The Museums at Stony Brook, Long Island: 34 below, 113 below, 133; Namuth, Hans, New York: 248 below; NASA, Washington, D.C.: 256; Nassau County Historical Museum, East Meadow: 84 below; Nassau County Museum, Port Washington: 139 below right; National Gallery of Art, Washington, D.C., Gift of Chester Dale: 246, 247 below; Neville, Dan, Newsday: 224 below; Newsday: 168 above, 179 above and below left, 200, 214 above, 215, 222, 224, 225, 231, 232, 237, 238, 239, 240, 241, 242, 243, 244, 245, 251, 252, 253, 254 , 255, 257 right, 259, 260, 261, 262; The New York Historical Society: 61 center right; New York Institute of Technology at Old Westbury: 187 below; The New York Public Library Prints Division: 39, 43 above; Ossorio and Dragon, formerly collection of: 249 below right; Oyster Ponds Historical Society, Long Island, L. Vinton Richards Collection: 96 below, 154/other: 85, 94, 121 right; Paraskevas, John, Newsday: 262 below; Park Department, Salem, Mass.: 44; Pokress, David, Newsday: 244, 252; Private Collections: 46, 53 above, 61 center left and below; The Queens Borough Public Library, Jamaica: 64, 150 below right, 159 below (Fred Weber negative, Long Island History Collection); Raynham Hall, Oyster Bay, Property of the Town of Oyster Bay: 77 below; Rhode Island Historical Society, Providence: 79 above; Roosevelt Field Merchants Association, Long Island: 227; Sagamore Hill National Historic Site, National Park Service, Oyster Bay: 168 below, 170 below; Seyfried, Vincent F., Garden City: 136 above left; Shelter Island Historical Society: 134 center and below, 135; Smithsonian Institution, Washington, D.C.: 199 above; Society for the Preservation of Long Island Antiquities, Setauket: 57, 58, 72; Southampton Colonial Society, Inc.: 247 below; Spencer, Ken, Newsday: 222, 240; Stabile, K. Wiles, Newsday: 232; The State University College at Old Westbury: 187 center; State University of New York at Stony Brook: 233 below; Suffolk County Historical Society, Fullerton Collection: 153 above, 155 above, 158; Suffolk County Whaling Museum, Sag Harbor: 91 center and below, 98 above; Sussman, Newsday: 200, 242; Tiernan, Audrey C., Newsday: 260; Toledo Museum of Art, Ohio, Gift of Florence Scott Libbey: 79 below; Vanderbilt Museum, Centerport: 161; Washington and Lee University, Lexington, Virginia: 82; Weber, Harvey A.: 1, 2-3, 4, 5, 6-7, 8, 10, 12, 15, 16, 19, 20, 21, 22, 24, 26, 28, 29, 33, 34 above, 37, 41, 45, 48, 51, 54, 55, 56, 57, 58, 61 above, 66, 67, 73, 75, 76, 77 above, 83, 84 above, 85, 91, 93, 94, 96 below, 97, 98, 101 above, 102-103, 104, 107, 108, 109, 111, 114 above, 116, 121, 125, 127, 128, 129, 130-131, 132, 137, 139 above, 140, 142, 143 below, 144 above, 145, 146, 147, 148, 149, 150 above, 152, 153 above, 154, 155, 157, 158, 159 below, 161 163, 166, 173 above left and right, 176, 181, 184, 185, 187 above, 189, 195, 197, 205, 206-207, 214 below; Wide World Photos, New York, AP: 208, 209 below, 212, 213, 220, 221/other: 179 below right, 188, 191 above and below, 257 right; Yarwood, Dick, Newsday: 253, 259 below; Ziel, Ron, Bridgehampton: 99 below, 101 below, 134 above (J. Burt negative), 193 (Burt Photo Collection, Williston).